Simplified Small Business Accounting

1st Edition

by Daniel Sitarz
Attorney-at-Law

Nova Publishing Company
Small Business and Legal Publications
Carbondale, Illinois

...net Harris Sitarz.

...Spectrum Graphics, Murphysboro, IL.

ISBN 0-935755-152

Library of Congress Catalog Card Number 95-16478

Library of Congress Cataloging-in-Publication Data
        Sitarz, Dan, 1948-
        Simplified Small Business Accounting / by Daniel Sitarz - 1st ed.
        256 p. cm. -- (Small Business Library Series)
        includes index;
        ISBN 0-935755-152 : $17.95
        1. Small business-- Accounting I. Title. II. Series
        HF5657.S528   1995   95-16478
        657' .9042--dc20   CIP

Nova Publishing Company is dedicated to providing up-to-date and accurate legal information to the public.
All Nova publications are periodically revised to contain the latest available legal information.

1st Edition; 1st Printing: October, 1995

This publication is designed to provide accurate and authoritative information in regard to the subject matter
covered. It is sold with the understanding that the publisher and author are not engaged in rendering legal,
accounting, or other professional services. If legal advice or other expert assistance is required, the services
of a competent professional person should be sought.

*From a Declaration of Principles jointly adopted by a Committee of
the American Bar Association and a Committee of Publishers*

DISCLAIMER

Because of possible unanticipated changes in governing statutes and case law relating to the application of
any information contained in this book, the author, publisher, and any and all persons or entities involved in
any way in the preparation, publication, sale, or distribution of this book disclaim all responsibility for the
effects or consequences of any document prepared or action taken in reliance upon information contained
in this book. No representations, either express or implied, are made or given regarding the consequences
of the use of any information contained in this book. Purchasers and persons intending to use this book for
the preparation of any documents are advised to check specifically on the current applicable laws in any
jurisdiction in which they intend the documents to be effective. This book is not printed, published, sold,
circulated, or distributed with the intention that it be used to procure or aid in the procurement of an effect
or consequence in any jurisdiction in which such procurement or aid may be restricted by statute.

Nova Publishing Company
Small Business and Legal Publications
1103 West College Street
Carbondale IL 62901
1(800)748-1175

Distributed to the trade by:
National Book Network
4720 Boon Way
Lanham MD 20706
1(800)52-6420

Table of Contents

8

Preface

This book is part of Nova Publishing Company's continuing Small Business Library series. The various business guides in this series are designed to provide concrete information to small business owners to assist them in understanding and operating their own businesses with a minimum of outside assistance.

With the proper information, the average person in today's world can easily understand and operate a small business. However, each year many thousands of small businesses fail because the owners have been unable to manage their financial, legal, or management affairs properly. This book and others in Nova's Small Business Library series are intended to provide the necessary information to those members of the public who wish to understand and operate their own businesses.

However, in an area as complex as business accounting, it is not always prudent to attempt to handle every situation which arises without the aid of a competent professional. Although the information presented in this book will give readers a basic understanding of the areas of accounting and bookkeeping covered, it is not intended that this text entirely substitute for experienced professional assistance in all situations. Throughout this book there are references to those particular situations in which the aid of an accountant or other professional is strongly recommended.

Regardless of whether or not an accountant or other professional is ultimately retained in certain situations, the information in this handbook will enable the reader to understand the framework of accounting and bookkeeping and effectively use this knowledge in the operation of their business. To try and make that task as easy as possible, technical accounting jargon has been eliminated whenever possible and plain English used instead. When it is necessary in this book to use an accounting term which may be unfamiliar to most people, the word will be shown in *italics* and defined when first used. A glossary of accounting terms most often encountered is included at the end of this book.

Introduction

Keeping accurate and clear business financial records can, for many business owners, be the most difficult part of running a business. For most business owners, understanding those records is, at best, a struggle. And yet maintaining a set of clear and understandable financial records is perhaps the single most important factor which separates successful businesses from those that fail. The purpose of this book is to provide the small business owner with a clear, concise, and easily-understood system for setting up a financial record-keeping system, keeping the books for a business, and, perhaps most importantly, actually understanding those records.

Modern business practices have tended to complicate many areas of business when, in many cases, simplification is what most business owners need. In law, in management, and in accounting, many important business functions have been obscured from their owners by intricate systems and complex terminology. Business owners must then turn the handling of these affairs over to specialized professionals in a particular field. The result, in many cases, is that business owners lose crucial understanding of those portions of their business. With this loss of understanding comes the eventual and almost inevitable loss of control.

This is particularly true for small business owners and their financial records. It is absolutely vital that small emerging business owners intimately understand their financial position. Daily decisions must be made which can make or break a fledgling business. If the financial records of a small business are delegated to an outside accountant or bookkeeper, it is often difficult, if not impossible, for a novice business owner to understand the current financial position of the business on a day-to-day basis. Critical business decisions are then made on the basis of incomplete or often unknown financial information.

The financial record-keeping system presented in this book seeks to remedy this situation. The basic aspects of the accounting system outlined in this book have been used successfully by millions of businesses in the past. The record-keeping forms in this book have been developed to make accuracy, clarity, and ease-of-use the primary objectives. The system presented in this book is designed to be set up and initially used by the business owners themselves. This will insure that the system is both thoroughly understood by the owner and provides the type of information which the owner actually wants. As a business grows and becomes more complex, and as a business owner becomes more comfortable with financial record-keeping, other more sophisticated and complex accounting systems may become appropriate.

The first chapter outlines the basic fundamentals of business financial record-keeping and presents some basic terminology. The second chapter outlines how the financial record-keeping system in this book operates. Chapter 3 discusses setting up a chart of accounts for your business. Setting up the business bank account and petty cash fund is the topic of the fourth chapter. Chapter 5 shows how to track business assets. Chapter 6 does the same for business debts. The seventh chapter explains business expense records in detail. Chapter 8 does the same for income records. In the ninth chapter, the details of payroll are explained and clarified. Chapter 10 shows how to prepare profit and loss statements with the information relating to income and expenses. The eleventh chapter explains how to prepare a balance sheet for your business. Chapter 12 explains how to analyze these two basic financial statements. Chapter 13 presents schedules of financial record-keeping and the mechanics of how to actually use the forms and records in practice. Finally, Chapter 14 explains which tax forms are necessary for businesses, presents tax filing schedules, and provides a sample of each appropriate form. Throughout each chapter, the actual record-keeping forms are presented, along with clear instructions on how to fill them in. A Glossary of Accounting Terms is provided at the end of this book to explain any unfamiliar accounting terms you might encounter.

Although there are dozens of financial record forms provided, not all of them are appropriate for all businesses. As each chapter is read, the reader is prompted to assess the needs of their individual business and decide which of the forms would be most appropriate for their needs. Checklists are provided for most chapters for quick review of the essential elements. Finally, if, after reading through this book, you are unable to understand how to set up the books for your company, you are urged to seek the assistance of a competent accounting professional. Although the majority of small businesses can successfully use the system which is outlined in this book, some few types of business finances are not susceptible to being handled by this system. Other types of more complex accounting systems may be more appropriate if the proposed business is extremely complex, is involved at all in securities or other interstate financial transactions, or expects to handle very large amounts of daily transactions. If there is any question that the system outlined will not be appropriate, please consult an accounting professional. Please note that the forms in this book are not designed to be torn out of this book (particularly if you are reading a library copy of this book!) Please photo-copy the necessary forms to use as master copies.

The purpose of this book is to allow small business owners to have the tools they will need to set up a clear record-keeping system and understand their financial situation. As with any tools, there are dangers if they are misused. Please read all of the instructions carefully and be certain that you understand the concepts before using the financial record-keeping system which is presented.

Chapter 1

Understanding Business Financial Record-Keeping

Each year, thousands of small businesses fail because their owners have lost control of their finances. Many of these failures are brought on by the inability of the business owners to understand the complex accounting processes and systems which have become relatively standard in modern business. Accounting and bookkeeping have, in most businesses, been removed from the direct control and, therefore, understanding of the business owners themselves. If business owners can not understand the financial situation of their own businesses, they have little chance of succeeding. The purpose of this book is to present a simplified system of business record-keeping that small business owners themselves can use to track their company's financial situation.

The purpose of any business financial record-keeping system is to provide a clear vision of the relative health of the business, both on a day-to-day basis and periodically. Business owners themselves need to know whether they are making a profit, why they are making a profit, which parts of the business are profitable and which are not. This information is only available if the business owner has a clear and straight-forward record-keeping system. Business owners also need to be able to produce accurate financial statements for income tax purposes, for loan proposals, and for the purpose of selling the business. Clear, understandable, and accurate business records are vital to the success of any small business. In order to design a good record-keeping system for a particular business, an understanding of certain fundamental ideas of accounting is necessary. For those unfamiliar with the terms and concepts of accounting, grasping these basic ideas may be the most difficult part of accounting, even simplified accounting.

Record-Keeping Terminology

First, let's get some of the terminology clarified. *Accounting* is the design of the record-keeping system which a business uses and the preparation and interpretation of reports based on the information which is gathered and put into the system. *Bookkeeping* is the actual input of the financial information into the record-keeping system. In this book, these two activities will be combined to allow the small business owner to understand how the records are organized, how to keep the records, and how to prepare and interpret summarized reports of the records.

The purpose of any business record-keeping system is to allow the business owner to easily understand and use the information gathered. Certain accounting principles and terms have been adopted as standard over the years to make it easier to understand a wide range of business transactions. In order to understand what a record-keeping system is trying to accomplish, it is necessary to define some of the standard ways of looking at a business. There are two standard reports which are the main sources of business financial information and which will be the focus of this book: the **balance sheet** and the **profit and loss statement**.

The Balance Sheet

The purpose of the balance sheet is to look at what the business owns and owes on a specific date. By seeing what a business owns and owes, anyone looking at a balance sheet can tell the relative financial position of the business at that point in time. If the business owns more than it owes, it is in good shape financially. On the other hand, if it owes more than it owns, the business may be in trouble. The balance sheet is the universal financial document used to view this aspect of a business. It provides this information by laying out the value of the assets and the liabilities of a business. One of the most critical financial tasks which a small business owner must confront is keeping track of what the business owns and owes. Before the business buys or sells anything or makes a profit or loss, the business must have some assets.

The *assets* of a business are anything that the business owns. These can be cash, on hand or in a bank account; they can be personal property, like office equipment, vehicles, tools, or supplies; they can be inventory, or material which will be sold to customers; they can be real estate, buildings and land; and they can be money which is owed to the business. Money which is owed to a business is called its *accounts receivable*, basically the money which the business hopes to eventually receive. The total of all of these things which a business owns are the business assets.

The *liabilities* of a business are anything that the business owes to others. These consist of long-term debts, such as a mortgage on real estate or a long-term loan. It also consists of any short-term debts, such as money owed for supplies or taxes. Money which a business owes to others is called its *accounts payable*, basically the money which the business hopes to eventually pay. In addition to money owed to others, the *equity* of a business is also considered a liability. The equity of a business is the value of the ownership of the business. It is the value which would be left over if all of the debts of the business were paid off. If it is a partnership or a sole proprietorship, the business equity is referred to a the *net worth* of the business. If the business is a corporation, the owner's equity is called the *capital surplus* or *retained capital*. All of the debts of a business and its equity are together referred to as the business' liabilities.

The basic relationship between the assets and liabilities can be shown in a simple equation:

$$\text{Assets} = \text{Liabilities}$$

This simple equation is the basis of business accounting. When the books of a business are said to *balance*, it is this equation which is in balance: the assets of a business must equal the liabilities of a business. Since the liabilities of a business consists of both equity and debts, the equation can be expanded to read:

$$\text{Assets} = \text{Debts} + \text{Equity}$$

Rearranging the equation can provide a simple explanation of how to arrive at the value of a business to the owner, or its equity:

$$\boxed{\text{Equity} = \text{Assets} - \text{Debts}}$$

A basic tenet of record-keeping is that both sides of this financial equation must always be equal. The formal statement of the assets and liabilities of a specific business on a specific date is called a *balance sheet*. A balance sheet is usually prepared on the last day of a month, quarter, or year. A balance sheet simply lists the amounts of the business assets and liabilities in a standardized format.

On a balance sheet, the assets of a business are generally broken down into two groups: *current assets* and *fixed assets*. Current assets consist of cash, accounts receivable (remember, money which the business intends to receive; basically, bills owed to the business); and inventory. Current assets are generally considered anything that could be converted into cash within one year. Fixed assets are more permanent-type assets and include vehicles, equipment, machinery, land, and buildings owned by the business.

The liabilities of a business are broken down into three groups: *current liabilities*, *long-term liabilities*, and *owner's equity*. Current liabilities are short-term debts, generally those which a business must pay off within one year. This includes accounts payable (remember, money which the business intends to pay; basically, bills the business owes), and taxes which are due. Long-term liabilities are long-term debts such as mortgages or long-term business loans. Owner's equity is whatever is left after debts are deducted from assets. Thus the owner's equity is what the owner would have left after all of the debts of the business are paid off. Owner's equity is the figure which is adjusted to make the equation of assets and liabilities balance.

Let's look at a simple example. Later on in the following chapters, we'll look at a more complicated example. But for now let's look at a basic sales business.

Smith's Gourmet Foods has the following assets: Smith has $500.00 in a bank account, is owed $70.00 by customers who pay for their food monthly, has $200.00 worth of food supplies, and owns food preparation equipment worth $1,300.00.

These are the assets of Smith's Gourmet Foods and they are shown on a balance sheet as follows:

Cash	$ 500.00
+ Accounts owed to it	$ 70.00
+ Inventory	$ 200.00
+ Equipment	$1,300.00
= Total Assets	$2,070.00

Smith also has owes the following debts: $100.00 owed to the supplier of the food, $200.00 owed to the person from whom she bought the food equipment, and $100.00 owed to the state for sales taxes which have been collected on food sales. Thus, the debts of Smith's Gourmet Foods are shown as follows:

Accounts it owes	$ 100.00
+ Loans it owes	200.00
+ Taxes it owes	$ 100.00
= Total Debts	$ 400.00

To find what Smith's equity in this business is, we need to subtract the amount of the debts from the amount of the assets. Remember: Assets - debts = equity. Thus, the owner's equity in Smith's Gourmet Foods is as follows:

Total Assets	$2,070.00
- Total Debts	$ 400.00
= Owner's Equity	$1,670.00

That's it. The business of Smith's Gourmet Foods has a net worth of $1,670.00. If Smith paid off all of the debts of the business, there would be $1,670.00 left. This basic method is used to determine the net worth of businesses world-wide, from the smallest to the largest. Assets = debts + equity or Assets - debts = equity. Remember, both sides of the equation always have to be equal. We'll get into more detail regarding balance sheets in Chapter 11.

The Profit and Loss Statement

The other main business report is called the *profit and loss statement*. This report is a summary of the income and expenses of the business during a certain period. Profit and loss statements are generally prepared monthly, quarterly, or annually, depending on the type of business. Profit and loss statements are sometimes referred to as *income statements* or as *operating statements*.

Generally, income for a business is any money which it has received or will receive during a certain period. Expenses are any money which it has paid or will pay out during a certain period. Simply put, if the business has more income than expenses during a certain period, it has made a profit. If it has more expenses than income, then the business has a loss for that period of time.

Income can be broken down into two basic types: service income and sales income. The difference between the two types of income lies in the need to consider inventory costs. Service income is income derived from performing a service for someone (cutting hair, for example). Sales income is revenue derived from selling a product of some type. With service income, the profit can be determined simply by deducting the expenses which are associated with making the income. With sales income, however, in addition to deducting the expenses of making the income, the cost of the product which was sold must also be taken into account. This is done through inventory costs. Thus, for sales income, the actual income from selling a product is actually the sales income minus the cost of the product to the seller. This inventory cost is referred to as the *cost of goods sold*.

A profit and loss statement begins with a sale. Back to the food business. Smith had the following transactions during the month of July: $250.00 worth of food was sold, the wholesale cost of the food which was sold was $50.00, the cost of napkins, condiments, other supplies, and rent amounted to $100.00, and interest payments on the equipment loan were $50.00. Thus, Smith's profit and loss statement would be prepared as follows:

Gross sales income	$250.00
- Cost of food	$ 50.00
= Net sales income	$200.00

Operating Expenses	$100.00
+ Interest payments	$ 50.00
= Net expenses	$150.00

Thus, for the month of July, Smith's business performed as follows:

Net sales income	$200.00
- Net expenses	$150.00
= Net profit	$ 50.00

Again, this simple set-up reflects the basics of profit and loss statements for all types of businesses, no matter their size. For a pure service business, with no inventory of any type sold to customers: Income - expenses = net profit. For a sales-type business or a sales/service combined business: income - cost of goods sold - expenses = profit.

These two types of summary reports, the balance sheet and the profit and loss statement are the basic tools for understanding the financial health of any business. The figures on them can be used for many purposes to understand the operations of a business. The balance sheet shows what proportion of a business assets are actually owned by the business owner and what proportion is owned or owed to someone else.

Looking at Smith's balance sheet, we can see that the owner's equity is $1,670.00 of assets of $2,070.00. Thus, we can see that the owner has over 80% ownership of the business, a very healthy situation. There are numerous ways to analyze the figures on these two financial statements. Understanding what these figures mean and how they represent the health of a business are keys to keeping control of a businesses finances. Chapter 12 explains how to analyze these statements in further detail.

Accounting Methods

There are a few more items which must be understood regarding financial record-keeping. First is the method for recording the records. There are two basic methods for measuring transactions: the *cash method* and the *accrual method*. Cash method accounting is a system which records income when it is received and records expenses when they are paid. With cash accounting, there is no effective method to accurately reflect inventory costs. Thus, Internal Revenue Service regulations require that the cash method of accounting may only be used by those few businesses which are solely service businesses and do not sell any materials to their customers at all, even a few spare parts. If a business sells any type of product or material whatsoever, it must use the accrual method of accounting.

The accrual method of accounting counts income and expenses when they are due to the business. Income is recorded when the business has a right to receive the income. In other words, accounts receivable (bills owed to the business) are considered as income which has already been received by the business. Expenses are considered and recorded when they are due, even if they are not yet paid. In other words, accounts payable (bills owed by the business) are considered expenses to the business when they are received, not when they are actually paid. The record-keeping system in this book provides a simplified method of keeping accrual-method books. There is, however, a clear explanation provided in Chapter 10 on how to easily convert the records to the cash method. The vast majority of businesses will wish to use the accrual method of accounting. A business must choose to keep its records either on the accrual basis or on the cash basis. Once this decision is made, approval from the Internal Revenue Service must be obtained before the method can be changed. After you select the type of accounting you will use, please consult a tax professional if a change in the system must be made.

Accounting Systems

In addition, there are two basic types of record-keeping systems: *single-entry* or *double-entry*. Both types are able to be used to keep accurate records, although the double entry system has more ways available to double-check calculations. Double-entry record-keeping is, however, much more difficult to master, in that each and every transaction must be entered in two separate places in the records. The system which is used in this book is a modified form of single-entry accounting. The benefits of ease of use of a single-entry system far outweigh the disadvantages of this system. The Internal Revenue Service recommends single-entry records for beginning small businesses, and states that this type of system can be "relatively simple ... used effectively ... and is adequate for income tax purposes." Many accountants will disagree with this and insist that only double-entry accounting is acceptable. For the small business owner who wishes to understand his or her own company's finances, the advantages of single-entry accounting far outweigh the disadvantages.

Accounting Periods

A final item to consider is the accounting period for your business. A business is allowed to choose between a *fiscal year* accounting period and a *calendar* year period. A fiscal year consists of 12 consecutive months that do not end on December 31st. A calendar year consists of 12 consecutive months that do end on December 31st. There are complex rules relating to the choice of fiscal year accounting. If a sole-proprietorship reports income on a fiscal year, then all non-business income must also be reported on the same fiscal year. This most often unnecessarily complicates tax reporting and should generally be avoided. Partnerships and S corporations may generally only choose to report on a fiscal year basis if there is a valid business purpose which supports the use of a fiscal year. This, again, generally, complicates the reporting of income and should be avoided unless there is an important reason to choose a fiscal year accounting period. If a fiscal year period is considered necessary, please consult a tax or accounting professional as there are complicated rules to comply with.

For the majority of small businesses, the choice of a calendar year period is perfectly adequate and, in most cases, will simplify the tax reporting and accounting record-keeping. In the year in which a business is either started or ended, the business year for reporting may not be a full year. Thus, even for those who choose to use a calendar year, the first year may actually start on a date other than January 1st.

Record-Keeping Review

The purpose of a business financial record-keeping system is to provide a method for the owner to keep track of the on-going health of the business. This is done primarily by providing the owner with information on two basic financial statements. The balance sheet provides the business owner with a quick look at the assets and debts of the business and at the equity or ownership value of the business. The profit and loss statement furnishes the owner with an immediate view of the current flow of income and expenses of the business.

The business record-keeping system that is provided in this book will detail how to set up the books for a small business. The method of reporting for this system is the accrual method. The type of system used is a single-entry system of accounting. The time period used for the system is a calendar year.

Chapter 2

Simplified Accounting System

The simplified small business accounting system which is provided in this book is a modified single-entry accounting system. It is presented as a system for accrual-basis accounting for small businesses. The records are designed to be used on a calendar-year basis. Within these basic parameters, the system can be individually tailored to meet the needs of most small businesses.

The backbone of the record-keeping system is the *chart of accounts* for your business. A chart of accounts will list each of the income, expense, asset, or debt categories that you wish to keep track of. Every business transaction that you make and every financial record that you create will fit into one of these four main categories. Your transactions will either be money coming in (income) or money going out (expenses). Your records will also track either things the business owns (assets) or things the business owes (debts). The chart of accounts which you create in the next chapter will allow you to itemize and track each of these four broad categories in detail.

After you have set up a basic chart of accounts for your business, you will proceed with your first financial transaction: setting up a business bank account and a petty cash fund. Every business must have at least one business checking account to be used to keep a record of payments for expenses and to record income deposits. How to use a check register and the reconciliation of bank accounts will be explained. Additionally, every business should set up a petty cash fund in order to simplify the recording of cash transactions. Some businesses will have few and some may have many such cash transactions. Regardless of the number of transactions, a clear and understandable system to keep track of such transactions is necessary. The use of petty cash reports will be explained.

After the bank account and petty cash fund are set up, the first of the record-keeping accounts that you set up will be the asset accounts. Each of the assets of a business within a single category will be assigned a separate asset account. Any real estate owned by the business will have an account; any vehicles will have an account; any inventory will have an account. Using these asset accounts, you will be able to track the ongoing value of your business possessions. Double-entry accounting provides that every income and expense transaction also alters various asset and liability account balances. While this is true, for most business purposes it is unnecessary and overburdening to keep a day-to-day balance in most asset and liability accounts. Thus, these accounts will be updated only periodically; either monthly, quarterly, or annually, depending on your particular business needs.

When you set up asset accounts, you will also set up inventory accounts. This particular form of asset has its own rules which govern how the accounts should be arranged in order to provide you with a clear picture of your inventory and to comply with tax regulations. You will be shown how to record additions and reductions to your inventory.

You will also be setting up debt accounts for any debts of your business. Each debt will be assigned a separate account so that the principal and interest of each debt can be clearly recorded and tracked. As with the asset accounts, you will be updating these accounts only on a periodic basic, depending on your business needs.

Expense accounts will most likely be the most complex and numerous of the type of accounts which you will set up. You will be setting up an account for each type of expense that you may encounter in your business. Most of these accounts will be arranged to correspond to the information that you will need to supply for tax purposes. The various expense accounts that you set up will allow you to substantiate all of the business deductions that you take at tax time. Expense accounts may also, of course, need to be set up to allow you to track expenses for particular projects, particular properties, or particular portions of your business. The purpose of setting up your expense accounts is to allow you to categorize and itemize the amounts which you spend on each particular aspect of your business. This will then allow you to see what your costs are per category at a glance. In order to do this you will be shown how to keep daily or weekly track of your expenses and how to total your expenses periodically to summarize your spending. The use and tracking of purchase orders will also be explained.

As you set up expense accounts, you will also be setting up a system of record-keeping to keep track of certain expenses for which the Internal Revenue Service requires more detailed records. Automobile expenses and expenses associated with travel, entertainment, meals, and lodging are some of these types of expenses.

Income accounts will be set up for each type and category of income that you will be dealing with. This will allow you to track the sources and amounts of revenue that your business takes in. The use of invoices and statements as well as the details of credit sales will be coordinated with the record-keeping requirements of income accounts.

Payroll is a subset of business expenses that is one of the most difficult for most business owners to understand. How to set up a simple system to deal with payroll will be clearly explained. The payment and record-keeping necessary for payroll taxes will also be explained.

You will be shown how to summarize the information from your income and expense account records and prepare periodic profit and loss statements. Depending on your type of business, these statements may be prepared monthly, quarterly, or only annually. Clear forms for their easy preparation will be presented and explained. The analysis of the information on your profit and loss statement will also be detailed.

Summaries of the information from your asset and liability accounts will be used to prepare balance sheets on a periodic basis. This will allow you to monitor the relative health of your business. Numerous methods for analyzing the figures on your balance sheet will be explained.

How to actually set up and operate the financial record-keeping system will be explained. Clear schedules of tasks will be outlined for your use as you work with the forms.

The preparation of your tax returns will be covered in the final chapter. We'll take a look at federal tax forms for sole proprietorships, partnerships, and corporations and see which forms will be necessary for each. Note, however, that this book is in no way a substitute for detailed information on taxes or for competent tax preparation assistance if needed.

Following is a checklist for setting up your business financial record-keeping using this book:

Financial Record-Keeping Checklist

☐ Read through the entire book before you begin.

☐ Set up your business chart of accounts.

☐ Open a business checking account.

> ☐ Prepare a check register.

☐ Set up a business petty cash fund.

> ☐ Prepare a petty cash register.

☐ Set up asset accounts.

> ☐ Prepare current asset account records.

> ☐ Prepare fixed asset account records.

☐ Set up expense account records.

> ☐ Prepare auto expense records.

> ☐ Prepare meals, entertainment, and travel expense records.

> ☐ Set up purchase order system.

- ☐ Set up income account record.

    - ☐ Prepare income records.

    - ☐ Prepare credit sales records.

    - ☐ Set up invoicing and statement system.

- ☐ Set up payroll system.

    - ☐ Prepare payroll time sheets.

    - ☐ Prepare payroll depository records.

- ☐ Prepare profit and loss statement.

- ☐ Prepare balance sheet.

- ☐ Analyze profit and loss statements and balance sheets.

- ☐ Determine proper tax forms for use in business.

Chapter 3

Business Chart of Accounts

The financial record-keeping system that you will set up using this book is designed to be adaptable to any type of business. Whether your business is a service business, a manufacturing business, a retail business, a wholesale distributorship, or combination of any of these, you will be able to easily adapt this simplified system to work with your particular situation. A key to designing the most useful record-keeping system for your particular needs is to examine your type of business in depth. After a close examination of the particular needs and operations of your type of business, you will need to set up an array of specific accounts to handle your financial records. This set of general accounts is called a *chart of accounts*.

A chart of accounts will list all of the various categories of financial transactions which you will need to track. There will be an account for each general type of expense which you want to keep track of. You will also have separate accounts for each type of income your business will receive. Accounts will also be set up for your business assets and liabilities. Setting up an account for each of these categories consists of the simple task of deciding which items you will need to categorize, selecting a name for the account, and assigning a number for the account.

Before you can set up your accounts, you need to understand the reason for setting up these separate accounts. It is possible, although definitely not recommended, to run a business and merely keep track of your income and expenses without any itemization at all. However, you would be unable to analyze how the business is performing beyond a simple check to see if you have any money left after paying the expenses. You would also be unable to properly fill in the necessary information for business income tax returns. A major reason for setting up separate accounts for many businesses expense and income transactions is to separate and itemize the amounts spent in each category so that this information is available at tax time. This insures that a business is taking all of its allowable business deductions. The main reason, however, to set up individual accounts is to allow the business owner to have a clear view of the financial health of the business. With separate accounts for each type of transaction, a business owner can analyze the proportional costs and revenues of each aspect of the business. Is advertising costing more than labor expenses? Is the income derived from sales items worth the discounts of the sale? Only by using the figures obtained from separate itemized accounts can these questions be answered.

In the following sections, you will select and number the various accounts for use in your business chart of accounts. You will select various income accounts, expense accounts, asset accounts, and liability accounts. For each account, you will also assign it a number. For ease of use, you should assign a particular number value to all accounts of one type. For example, all income accounts may be assigned numbers 10-29. Sales income may be Account #11; service income may be assigned Account #12, interest income may be Account #13. Similarly, expenses may be assigned #30-79. Balance sheet accounts for assets and liabilities may be #80-99. Be sure to leave enough numbers for future expansion of your list of accounts. There will normally be far more expense accounts than any other type of account.

If you have income or expenses from many sources, you may wish to use 3-digit numbers to identify each separate category. For example, if your business consists of renting out residential houses and you have 10 properties, you may wish to set up a separate income and expense account for each property. You may wish to assign accounts #110-119 to income from all properties. Thus, for example, you could then assign rental income from property #1 to account #111, rental income from property #2 to account #112, rental income from property #3 to account

#113 and so on. Similarly, expenses can be broken down into separate accounts for individual properties. Advertising expenses might all be accounts #510-519, thus advertising expenses for property #1 might then be assigned #511, advertising expenses for property #2 would be assigned account #512, etc.

How your individual chart of accounts will be organized will be specific to your particular business. If you have a simple business with all income coming from one source, you will probably desire a two-digit number from, perhaps, 10-29 assigned to that income account. On the other hand a more complex business with many sources of income and many different types of expenses may wish to use a system of 3-digit numbers. Take some time to analyze your specific business to decide how you wish to set up your accounts. Ask yourself what type of information will you want to extract from your financial records. Do you need more details of your income sources? Then you should set up several income accounts for each type and possibly even each source of your income. Would you like more specific information on your expenses? Then you would most likely wish to set up clear and detailed expense accounts for each type of expense that you must pay.

Be aware that you may wish to alter your chart of accounts as your business grows. You may find that you have set up too many accounts and unnecessarily complicated your record-keeping tasks. You may wish to set up more accounts once you see how your balance sheets and profit and loss statements look. You may change, add, or delete accounts at any time. Remember, however, that any transactions that have been recorded in an account must be transferred to any new account or accounts that take the place of the old account.

Income Accounts

These are accounts that are used to track the various sources of your company's income. There may be only a few sources of income for your business, or you may wish to track your income in more detail. The information which you collect in your income accounts will be used to prepare your profit and loss statements periodically. Recall that a profit and loss statement is also referred to as an income and expense statement.

On the chart of accounts that is used in this book, income is separated into several categories. You can choose the income account categories which best suit your type of business. If your business is a service business, you may wish to set up accounts for labor income and for materials income. Or you may wish to set up income accounts in more detail, for example: sales income, markup income, income from separate properties, or income from separate sources in your business, etc. Non-sales income such as bank account interest income or income on the sale of business equipment should be placed in separate individual income accounts. You may also wish to set up separate income accounts for income from different on-going projects or income from separate portions of your business.

Following is a list of various general income accounts. Decide how much detail you will want in your financial records regarding income and then choose the appropriate accounts. You may wish to name and create different accounts than are listed here. After you have chosen your income accounts, assign a number to each account.

INCOME CHART OF ACCOUNTS

Account #	Account Name and Description
	Income from sale of goods
	Income from services
	Income from labor charges
	Income from sales discounts
	Income from interest revenue
	Income from consulting
	Miscellaneous income

Expense Accounts

These are the accounts that you will use to keep track of your expenses. Each separate category of expense should have its own account. Many of the types of accounts are dictated by the types of expenses which should be itemized for tax purposes. You will generally have separate accounts for advertising costs, utility expenses, rent, phone costs, etc. One or more separate accounts should also be set up to keep track of inventory expenses. These should be kept separate from other expense accounts as they must be itemized for tax purposes.

Following is a list of various general expense accounts. Please analyze your business and determine which accounts would be best suited to select for your particular situation. You will then number these accounts, as you did the income accounts. The categories presented are general categories which match most IRS forms. You may, of course, set up separate accounts which are not listed to suit your particular needs. Try not to set up too many accounts or you will have a hard time trying to remember all of them. Also note that you may add or delete accounts as you need them. If you delete an account, however, you must shift any transactions that you have recorded in that account to the new account.

EXPENSE CHART OF ACCOUNTS

Account #	Account Name and Description
	Advertising expenses
	Auto expenses
	Cleaning and maintenance expenses
	Charitable contributions
	Dues and publications
	Office equipment expenses
	Freight and shipping expenses
	Business insurance expenses
	Business interest expenses
	Legal expenses
	Business meals and lodging
	Miscellaneous expenses
	Postage expenses
	Office rent expenses
	Repair expenses
	Office supplies
	Sales taxes paid
	Federal unemployment taxes paid
	State unemployment taxes paid
	Telephone expenses
	Utility expenses
	Wages and commissions

Asset and Liability Accounts

Asset and liability accounts are collectively referred to as *balance sheet accounts*. This is because the information collected on them is used to prepare your business balance sheets. You will set up current and fixed asset accounts and current and long-term liability accounts. Types of current asset accounts are cash, short-term notes receivable, accounts receivable, inventory, and pre-paid expenses. Fixed assets may include equipment, vehicles, buildings, land, long-term notes receivable, and long-term loans receivable.

Types of current liability accounts are short-term notes payable (money due within one year), short-term loans payable (money due on loan within one year), unpaid taxes, and unpaid wages. Long-term liability accounts may be long-term notes payable (money due over one year); long-term loans payable (money due over one year). Finally, you will need an owner's equity account to tally the ownership value of your business.

Choose the asset and liability accounts which best suit your business and assign appropriate numbers to each account.

BALANCE SHEET CHART OF ACCOUNTS

Account #	Account Name and Description
	Accounts receivable (current asset)
	Bank checking account (current asset)
	Bank savings account (current asset)
	Cash on hand (current asset)
	Notes Receivable (current asset - if short-term)
	Loans Receivable (current asset - if short-term)
	Inventory (current asset)
	Land (fixed asset)
	Buildings (fixed asset)
	Vehicles (fixed asset)
	Equipment (fixed asset)
	Machinery (fixed asset)
	Accounts payable (current debt)
	Notes payable (current - if due within 1 year)
	Loans payable (current - if due within 1 year)
	Notes payable (long-term debt - if over 1 year)
	Loans payable (long-term debt - if over 1 year)
	Mortgage payable (long-term debt - if over 1 year)
	Owner's equity (if sole-proprietorship)
	Partner's equity (if partnership)
	Retained capital (if corporation)

Sample Chart of Accounts

After you have selected and numbered each of your accounts, you should prepare your chart of accounts. Simply type the number and name of each account in a numerical list. You will refer to this chart often as you prepare your financial records. Following is a sample completed chart of accounts.

This sample chart is set up to reflect the business operations of our sample company: Smith's Gourmet Foods. This is a sole proprietorship company which prepares and packages food products and delivers the products directly to consumers in their homes.

The chart reflects that the income will primarily come from one source: direct customer payments for the products which are sold. The expense accounts are chosen to cover most of the standard types of business expenses which a small business will encounter. The balance sheet accounts reflect that the business will only have as assets a bank account, some accounts receivable, inventory, and some equipment. The only liabilities that this business will have, at least initially, will be a loan for equipment and accounts payable.

Although this sample chart of accounts is fairly brief, it covers all of the basic accounts which the business will need as it begins. There is sufficient room in the numbering system chosen to add additional accounts as the business expands.

SAMPLE CHART OF ACCOUNTS

Account #	Account Name and Description
11	Income from sale of goods
12	Miscellaneous income
31	Advertising expenses
32	Auto expenses
33	Cleaning and maintenance expenses
34	Equipment expenses
35	Business insurance expenses
36	Business meals and lodging
37	Miscellaneous expenses
38	Postage expenses
39	Repair expenses
40	Supplies
41	Sales taxes paid
42	Telephone expenses
43	Rent
51	Cash on hand (current asset)
52	Accounts receivable (current asset)
53	Bank checking account (current asset)
54	Inventory (current asset)
61	Equipment (fixed asset)
71	Accounts payable (current debt)
81	Loans payable (long-term debt)
91	Owner's equity

Chapter 4

Business Bank Accounts and Petty Cash Fund

The first financial action which a new small business should take is to set up a business bank account. A bank account is necessary to provide the business owner with a clear written record of all initial transactions. There are numerous types of business bank accounts available; some pay interest, some charge for each check written or deposited, some return your cancelled checks each month, and some provide other benefits. Check with various local banking institutions to see which types are available and then choose the bank account which is best suited to your needs.

The business bank account will be the first record of many of your businesses financial transactions. All of the income received by a business and all of the expenses which a business pays should be recorded in the check register for the business banking account. Your business bank account should always be a separate checking account. However, there may be instances when certain items will need to be paid for with cash. For this purpose, a *petty cash fund* will need to be set up. This is explained at the end of this chapter.

Bank Account Procedures

There are certain guidelines which should be adhered to regarding the use of the business bank account.

① Every transaction should be recorded in the check register. The details of each transaction will be important as you prepare your financial records. What you need to record is explained later in this chapter.

② All of your business expenses and bills should be paid by check. If it is necessary to pay by cash, carefully record the payment in the Petty Cash Register which follows. Don't write checks to "Cash".

③ Balance your checking account every month. This is vital in keeping close track of your finances. If the bank's statement does not match your records, contact the bank to determine where the discrepancy is. Bouncing a check because you have insufficient funds in the bank will leave a blemish on the reputation of your business.

④ Never use your business bank account to pay for personal expenses. Keep all of your business finances scrupulously separate from your personal affairs. If some expenses are part personal and part business, make a careful record of the amount of each portion of the expense.

⑤ Retain your cancelled checks and bank statements for at least three years. If your business is ever audited by the Internal Revenue Service, you will need to produce these records to substantiate your business income and deductions.

In many respects, your business bank account is the main financial corridor for your business. In dealings with banks, suppliers, employees, and other businesses, your business account is the primary conduit for conducting your financial transactions. It is vital to your success that you are able to keep the records for this main financial account straight. On the next few pages, the following forms are provided to help you in this task: Check Register, Monthly Bank Statement Reconciliation Sheet, and a Petty Cash Register.

For each of these forms, instructions for their use are provided, as well as a filled-in sample check register based on information provided for our fictitious company, Smith's Gourmet Foods.

Check Register Instructions

Although most people have handled money in a bank account by the time they open a business, many people have difficulty with the method by which transactions are recorded in a bank account. By following a specific set of recording rules, a business bank account can provide a detailed and clear record of the financial flow of a business.

① The first transaction in the account will be the initial deposit. Put this on the first line in the register. Fill in the amount in the Deposit column. Carry this amount over into the Balance column.

② If you desire, each transaction may take up two lines in the Register. The first line may be used to record the details of the transaction. The second line may be used to figure the balance. By using two lines, you will leave yourself enough room to allow for easy reading of the transactions.

③ For each check that is written, record the following information:
   - The date the check was written.
   - The number of the check.
   - The name of person or company that the check was written to.
   - A description of the reason for the check (ie. what was purchased, what was paid for, etc.).
   - What expense account the check should be listed under. In the previous chapter, you set up Expense Account numbers for each type of expense. The appropriate account number should be entered in this column.
   - The amount of the check

④ For each deposit, record the following information:
   - The date of the deposit.
   - A description of the deposit. This should include information regarding what specific checks were deposited or if the deposit was cash.
   - What Income Account number the deposit should be credited to.
   - The amount of the deposit.

⑤ For each transaction, the current balance of the check book should be calculated. This should be done at the time that you write the check or make the deposit. Don't let the balance go uncalculated for any length of time. Errors are more likely if you do not keep an accurate running balance.

CHECK REGISTER

Date	CK #	Description	Acct #	Clear	Payment	Deposit	Balance

Sample Check Register

Lets look at the finances of our fictitious company: Smith's Gourmet Foods. Sandy Smith has decided to open a business which delivers gourmet food directly to the consumer. She will start the business with $10,000.00, which she has managed to save over a period of several years and an additional $10,000.00 which she has borrowed from her local bank. Her very first financial transaction as a business is to open a business bank account and deposit the $20,000.00 into the account. Ms. Smith has decided to operate as a sole proprietorship.

Once the bank account is open, Ms. Smith's first transaction is to buy inventory for $5,000.00. The next day, she makes her first sale for $150.00. She then withdraws $50.00 to set up a petty cash fund. The procedures for this are detailed later in this chapter. Ms. Smith's next transaction is the rental of an office for the cost of $300.00 per month. She writes a separate check for a security deposit for the office, amounting to another $300.00.

Her next transactions are the purchase of various supplies and services. She purchases the following items:

- $2,200.00 worth of office supplies from the Office Mart.
- $3,000.00 worth of cooking equipment from Restaurant Supply Company.
- $500.00 worth of office furniture from the Furniture Mart.
- $300.00 worth of advertising from the Local Newspaper Company.
- She also hires a free-lance artist to design a logo for the company and brochure for the company. This costs her $400.00.
- She has the flyers printed for $200.00 by Printing is Us Company.

On the following page, all of these transactions are recorded on the sample Check Register. Note that the account's numbers are listed for each transaction. Also note that there are two account numbers for the equipment purchases. This is because the transactions will be listed as both an equipment purchase (expense) and as a fixed asset. Please see Chapter 5 for more details about fixed assets.

SAMPLE CHECK REGISTER

Date	CK #	Description	Acct #	Clear	Payment		Deposit		Balance
2/13		Initial Deposit					10,000	00	10,000.00
2/13		Deposit loan proceeds	81				10,000	00	20,000.00
2/13		Food Wholesalers	54		5,000	00			15,000.00
2/14		Joanne Wheeling (first sale!)	11				150.00		15,150.00
2/14		Petty cash fund	51		50	00			15,100.00
2/15		Harry Jones (office rent)	43		300	00			14,800.00
2/15		Harry Jones (security deposit)	43		300	00			14,500.00
2/16		Office Mart	40		2,200	00			12,300.00
2/17		Restaurant Supply Company	34/61		3,000	00			9,300.00
2/20		Furniture Mart	34/61		500	00			8,800.00
2/21		Local Newspaper Company	31		300	00			8,500.00
2/22		Freddy Harris (logo design)	31		400	00			8,100.00
2/23		Printing is US	31		200	00			7,900.00

Reconciling Your Monthly Bank Statement

Perhaps the most difficult part of handling money through a bank account is getting the account to balance each month. Every month you will get a statement from the bank which will detail all of the transactions which occurred during the previous month. The bank statement will normally list all of the checks by number and amount. It will also list all of the deposits by date and amount. Any service charges or charges for bank checks will be shown. Finally, any returned checks, other charges, or interest paid will be listed.

The bank statement will normally also state your balance at the beginning of the month and your balance at the end of the month. Neither of these balances will generally ever match the balance shown in your check register. This is because the bank only records the transactions when the checks you write are actually paid by the bank. This may be weeks or even months after you write the check. The following procedure should help you to reconcile your bank statement with your check register each month.

① Carefully review the bank statement when you receive it each month. Make a note of any extra items such as service charges or interest paid. Sort all of the cancelled checks into numerical order. Some banks no longer supply cancelled checks back to the account holder. In this case, refer to your bank statement for cancelled check details.

② Using either the sorted cancelled checks or the statement, match the checks which the bank has processed with your own check register. Put a checkmark in the "Clear" column of the check register for each check that has cleared the bank and been returned to you (or been noted on the statement). There will be some checks which you have written which have not cleared. We will deal with these later.

③ Do the same for your deposits. If the bank has supplied your deposit slips, sort them by date. If not, use your bank statement. Match each deposit slip or statement entry against your record in your check register. For each match, check it off in the "Clear" column of the register.

④ If there are additional items such as service charges or interest paid to you, enter an appropriate entry in your register and then check it off as "Clear".

⑤ Finally, take one of the Monthly Bank Statement Reconciliation Sheets out and follow the directions on the next page to fully complete your monthly reconciliation.

Monthly Bank Statement Reconciliation sheet

On the next page you will find a Monthly Bank Statement Reconciliation. Every month, on this form, you will compare your bank statement with the balance in your Check Register. Using the method outlined will give you a clear picture of any discrepancies between the bank's records and your own. To fill in this form, follow these instructions:

① Fill in the month and year on the form. Fill in your account balance from your *bank statement* where shown. Fill in your account balance from your *check register* on the last line where shown.

② Using your check register, under Outstanding Checks on this form, fill in the amounts for each check that you have written that has not be checked off as "Clear". Total this amount and **add** it to the Bank Statement Balance where shown.

③ Again using your check register, under Outstanding Deposits on this form, fill in the amounts for any deposits which you have made that have not been checked off as "Clear". Total these deposits and **subtract** this amount from your Bank Statement Balance where shown.

④ If there are any service charges or other fees on your Bank Statement, total these and **subtract** them from the Bank Statement Balance where shown. If your account has earned any interest, **add** this to your Bank Statement Balance where shown.

⑤ Finish all of the calculations. The Final Balance shown on this sheet should match the balance shown on your Check Register. If it doesn't, go back over all of your calculations and try again. If it still doesn't match, carefully check your cancelled checks and deposits to make certain that you have checked off as "Clear" all of the appropriate items. If this does not rectify the error, you will need to check all of the amounts on all of the checks and deposits. This is often where the error was made. Check and recheck all of your calculations and entries. If you still can not find the discrepancy, take your bank statement, check register, cancelled checks and deposit slips to your bank and ask them to check the balances. Most banks are more than willing to help their customers.

⑥ When you have finally reconciled your monthly statement with your check register, file the cancelled checks and bank statement. You will need to keep these bank records for at least three years.

MONTHLY BANK STATEMENT RECONCILIATION

Checks Outstanding		
Number	Amount	
TOTAL		

Deposits Outstanding		
Date	Amount	
TOTAL		

BANK STATEMENT BALANCE	
ADD Outstanding Deposits	
ADD Interest Earned	
SUBTOTAL	
SUBTRACT Outstanding Checks	
SUBTRACT Service Charges/Fees	
TOTAL This should agree with your CHECK REGISTER BALANCE	

Petty Cash Fund

The handling of cash often poses problems for small businesses. Unless you have a simple system to keep track of your petty cash in place, it is often difficult to keep accurate and current records of the use of cash in your business. The use of a petty cash fund is to provide you with a clear record of the payment of expenses with small amounts of cash; amounts which are too small to be handled by the use of a check. Petty cash is different from the cash which you might use in a cash register to take in payments for merchandise or services. That use of cash is discussed in Chapter 8. For a petty cash fund, you generally will not need to set aside more than $50.00. Following is how to handle your petty cash:

① Get a small cash box or something similar, with a lock and key.

② Write a check from your business bank account made out to "Petty Cash" for the amount that you will begin your fund with. In your check register, record the account # as the account listed for your current asset account for cash on hand. Put the cash in the cash box.

③ Using the Petty Cash Register on the next page, record the starting amount as "Cash in", just like you would record a deposit in a checkbook register. Record cash which you pay out as "Cash out", similar to how you would record a payment in a check register.

④ Record each transaction that you make using your petty cash fund just as you would in a check register. Record the date, description of the use of the money or of money taken in, the account which it should be listed under, and the amount of the transaction.

⑤ When your petty cash fund gets low, note what the balance is and write another check to "Petty Cash" which will cause your balance to equal the amount which you have chosen as a total for your petty cash fund. For example, you have decided to have a $50.00 petty cash fund. In two months, you have used up $46.00 of the cash (and recorded each transaction). You should have $4.00 in cash left in your box and as a written balance on your Petty Cash Register. Simply write a check to "Petty Cash" for $46.00, cash the check, and put the cash in the box to replenish the petty cash fund.

⑥ At the time that you replenish your petty cash fund, you will need to record all of your transactions on your main income and expense record sheets. You will simply transfer all of the amounts to the main sheets and check the box on the petty cash ledger marking them as cleared transactions. The use of your main income and expense record sheets will be explained in Chapters 7 and 8.

PETTY CASH REGISTER

Date	Description	Acct #	Clear	Cash out	Cash in	Balance

Bank Account Checklist

❑ Obtain business checking account.

❑ Prepare Check Register sheet.

❑ On a daily or weekly basis, record all checks and deposits on the Check Register.

❑ On a monthly basis, reconcile your Check Register balance with your bank statement.

❑ On a monthly basis transfer information from Check Register to the appropriate Expense Record (See Chapter 7).

❑ File your bank statements, cancelled checks, and Check Registers and retain for 3 years.

Petty Cash Fund Checklist

❑ Buy petty cash fund cashbox or equivalent.

❑ Prepare Petty Cash Register.

❑ Write check to "Petty Cash" to begin petty cash fund.

❑ Record all petty cash transactions in Petty Cash Register.

❑ On a monthly basis, replenish petty cash fund with check for "Petty Cash".

❑ On a monthly basis transfer information from Petty Cash Register to the appropriate Expense Record (See Chapter 7).

❑ Retain your Petty Cash Registers and cash receipts for 3 years.

Chapter 5

Tracking Business Assets

After setting up a chart of accounts, a bank account, and a petty cash fund, the next financial record-keeping task for a business will consist of preparing a method to keep track of the assets of the business. Recall that the assets of a business are everything that is owned by the business. They are either current assets that can be converted to cash within a year or fixed assets that are more long-term in nature. Each of these 2 main categories of assets will be discussed separately.

Current Assets

Following is a list of typical current assets for a business:

* Business bank checking account,
* Business bank savings account,
* Cash (petty cash fund and cash on hand),
* Accounts receivable (money owed to the company),
* Inventory.

A company may have other types of current assets such as notes or loans receivable, but the five listed are the basic ones for most small businesses. In complex double-entry accounting systems, the current asset account balances are constantly being changed. In a double-entry system, each time an item of inventory is sold, for example, the account balance for the inventory account must be adjusted to reflect the sale. In the type of single-entry system that is presented in this book, all asset and liability accounts are only updated when the business owner wishes to prepare a balance sheet. This may be done monthly, quarterly, or annually. At a minimum, this updating must take place at the end of the year in order to have the necessary figures available for tax purposes. The forms and instructions in this book provide a simple method for tracking and updating the required information for business assets and liabilities.

The main form for tracking your current business assets will be a Current Asset Account sheet. A copy of this form follows this discussion. On this form, you will periodically track of the value of the current asset that you are following, except for your inventory. (For inventory, you will use specialized inventory records.) You should prepare a separate Current Asset Account sheet for each asset. For example, if your current assets consist of a business checking account, cash on hand, and accounts receivable, you will have three separate Current Asset Accounts, one for each category of asset. These forms are very simple to use. Follow the instructions below:

① Simply fill in the Account # for the Current Asset Account for which you are setting up the form. You will get this number from your Chart of Accounts. Fill in also a description of the Account. For example: Account #53 - Business Banking Account.

② You must then decide how often you will be preparing a balance sheet and updating your balance sheet account balances. If you wish to keep close track of your finances, you may wish to do this on a monthly basis. For many businesses, a quarterly balance sheet may be sufficient. All businesses, no matter how small, must prepare a balance sheet at least annually, at the end of the year. Decide how often you wish to update the balances and enter the period in the space provided.

③ Next enter the date that you open the account. Under description, enter "Opening Balance". Under the "Balance" column, enter the opening value. The amount to enter for an opening balance will be as follows:

+ For a bank account this will be the opening balance of the account.

* For cash on hand, this will be the opening balance of the petty cash fund and cash on hand for sales, such as the cash used in a cash register. (See Chapters 4 and 8).

+ For accounts receivable, this will be the total amount due from all accounts (See Chapter 8).

④ Periodically, you will enter a date and new balance. You will enter these new balances from the following sources:

+ For bank accounts, this figure will come from your Check Register balance column on a particular date (Chapter 4).

+ For cash, this new figure will come from your Petty Cash Register balance (Chapter 4) and your Monthly Cash Report Summary (see Chapter 8) on a certain date.

+ For accounts receivable, the balance will come from your monthly Credit Sales Aging Report (see Chapter 8).

⑤ After you have entered the balances on the appropriate Current Asset Account sheet, you will transfer the balances to your Balance Sheet. This will be explained in Chapter 11.

CURRENT ASSET ACCOUNT

Account #	Account Name:		Period:
Date	Description of Asset	Balance	

Inventory

Any business which sells an item of merchandise to a customer must have a system in place to keep track of inventory. *Inventory* is considered any merchandise or materials which are held for sale during the normal course of your business. Inventory costs include the costs of the merchandise or products themselves and the costs of the materials and paid labor which goes into creating a finished product. Inventory does not include the costs of the equipment or machinery that you need to create the finished product.

There are several reasons you will need a system of inventory control. First, if you are stocking parts or supplies to sell, you will need to keep track of what you have ordered, what is in stock, and when you will need to reorder. You will also need to keep track of the cost of your inventory for tax purposes. The amount of money which you spend on your inventory is not immediately deductible in the year spent as a business deduction. The only portion of your inventory costs which will reduce your gross profit for tax purposes is the actual cost of the goods which you have sold during the tax year.

The basic method for keeping track of inventory costs for tax purposes is to determine the cost of goods sold. First, you will need to know how much inventory is on hand at the beginning of the year. To this amount, you add the cost of any additional inventory you purchased during the year. Finally, you determine how much inventory is left at the end of the year. The difference is essentially the cost (to you) of the inventory which you sold during the year. This amount is referred to as the *Cost of Goods Sold*. Every year at tax time, you will need to figure the Cost of Goods Sold. Additionally, you may need to determine your Cost of Goods Sold monthly or quarterly for various business purposes.

Four inventory control sheets are provided for use in tracking inventory costs: Physical Inventory Report, Periodic Inventory, Perpetual Inventory, and Cost of Goods Sold sheet.

Using our sample company, Smith Gourmet Foods, we will start her first year in business with an inventory of $0. When her business begins, there is no inventory. During the first year, she purchases $17,500.00 worth of products which are for selling to customers. At the end of the year, she counts all of the items which are left in her possession and determines her cost for these items. The cost of the items left unsold at the end of the year is $3,700.00.

The calculation of the Cost of Goods Sold for the first year in business is as follows:

Inventory at beginning of first year	$00.00
+ Cost of inventory added during year	$17,500.00
= Cost of inventory	$17,500.00
- Inventory at end of first year	$3,700.00
= Cost of goods sold for first year	$13,800.00

For the second year in business, the figure for the inventory at the beginning of the year is the value of the inventory at the end of the previous year. Thus, if Smith Gourmet Foods added $25,000.00 additional inventory during the second year of operation and the value of the inventory at the end of the second year was $4,800.00, the cost-of-goods-sold calculations for the second year would be as follows:

Inventory at beginning of second year	$3,700.00
+ Cost of inventory added during year	$25,000.00
= Cost of inventory	$28,700.00
- Inventory at end of second year	$4,800.00
= Cost of goods sold for second year	$19,900.00

Thus for the second year in operation the cost of goods sold would be $19,900.00 This amount would be deducted from the gross revenues that Smith's Gourmet Foods took in for the year to determine the gross profit for the second year in business.

Physical Inventory Report

This form should be used to record the results of an actual physical counting of the inventory at the end of the year and at whatever other times during the year you decide to take a physical inventory. If you decide that you will need to track your inventory monthly or quarterly, you may need to prepare this form for those time periods. To prepare this form, take the following steps:

① The form should be dated and signed by the person doing the inventory.

② The quantity and description of each item of inventory should be listed, along with an item number if applicable.

③ The cost (to you) of each item should be then listed under "Unit price". A total per item cost is then calculated by multiplying the quantity of units X the unit price. This total per item cost should be listed in the far right hand column. You will need to extract this per item unit price from your Periodic or Perpetual Inventory forms (explained next).

④ The total inventory cost should be figured by adding all of the figures in the far right hand column.

PHYSICAL INVENTORY REPORT

Date:		Taken by:			
Quantity	Description	Item #	Unit Price	Total	
		TOTAL			

Periodic Inventory

This is the form which you will use to keep continual track of your inventory if you have a relatively small inventory. If you have an extensive inventory, you will need to use the Perpetual Inventory form which is supplied next. You will use the Periodic Inventory form for the purposes of keeping track of the costs of your inventory and of any orders of additional inventory. You will refer to this report when you need to order additional inventory, when you need to determine when an order should be received, and when you need to determine the cost of your inventory items at the end of the year, or other times if desired.

① Prepare a separate Periodic Inventory sheet for each item of inventory. Identify the type of item which is being tracked by description and by item number, if applicable. You may also wish to list the supplier of the item.

② The first entry on the Periodic Inventory sheet should be the initial purchase of inventory. On the right hand side of the sheet list the following items:
   * Date purchased,
   * Quantity purchased,
   * Price per item,
   * Total price paid,
   * Shipping charges should not be included in the prices entered. Only the actual costs of the goods should be listed.

③ When you are running low on a particular item and place an order, on the left hand side of the sheet enter the following information:
   * Date of the order,
   * The order number,
   * The quantity ordered,
   * The date the order is due to arrive.

④ When the order arrives, enter the actual details about the order on the right hand side of the page. This will allow you to keep track of your order of inventory items and also allow you to keep track of the cost of your items of inventory.

PERIODIC INVENTORY

Item:				Item #:

Supplier:				

Inventory Ordered				Inventory Received			
Date	Order #	Quantity	Due	Date	Quantity	Price	Total

Perpetual Inventory

This is the form which you will use to keep continual track of your inventory if you have a relatively extensive inventory. You will refer to this report when you need to order additional inventory, when you need to determine when an order should be received, and when you need to determine the cost of your inventory items at the end of the year. Additionally, on this form you will keep track of the number of items of each type of inventory which have been sold.

① Prepare a separate Perpetual Inventory sheet for each item of inventory. Identify the type of item which is being tracked by description and by item number, if applicable. You may also wish to list the supplier for the item.

② The first entry on the Perpetual Inventory sheet should be the initial purchase of inventory. On the lower left hand side of the sheet, under Inventory Received, list the following information:
   * Date purchased,
   * Quantity purchased,
   * Price per item,
   * Total price paid,
   * Shipping charges should not be included in the amounts entered.

③ When you are running low on a particular item and place an order, on the upper left hand side of the sheet enter the following information:
   * Date of the order,
   * Order number,
   * Quantity ordered,
   * The date the ordered inventory is due.

④ When the order arrives, enter the actual details on the lower left hand side of the page, under Inventory Received.

⑤ On the right hand side of the sheet, keep a running total of the number of items of inventory sold. Decide how often you will be checking your stocks to update your inventory counts and stick to the schedule: weekly, monthly, or quarterly. Enter the number of items sold at each count and figure the totals. This will give you a running total of the amount of inventory you have in stock at any given time. You will, however, still need to take a physical inventory count at the end of the year (or more often) to check for lost, stolen, miscounted, or missing items and as a check against your calculations.

PERPETUAL INVENTORY

Item: _____   Item #: _____

Supplier: _____

	Inventory Ordered		
Date	Order #	Quantity	Due

	Inventory in Stock		
Date	Quantity	Price	Total

	Inventory Received		
Date	Quantity	Price	Total

Cost of Goods Sold

The final sheet for inventory control is the Cost of Goods Sold Report. It is on this sheet that you will determine the actual cost to your business of the goods which were sold during a particular time period. There are numerous methods to determine the value of your inventory at the end of a time period. The three most important are the Specific Identification method, the first-in first-out method (called FIFO) and the last-in first-out method (called LIFO).

Specific Identification is the easiest to use if you have only a few items of inventory, or one-of-a-kind types of merchandise. With this method, you actually keep track of each specific item of inventory. You keep track of when you obtained the item, its cost, and when you sold the specific item.

With the FIFO method, you keep track only of general quantities of your inventory. Your inventory costs are calculated as though the oldest inventory merchandise was sold first: The first items which you purchased are the first items which you sell.

With the LIFO method, the cost values are calculated as though you sell your most-recently purchased inventory first. It is important to note that you do not necessarily have to actually sell your first item first to use the FIFO method and you do not have to actually sell your last item first to use the LIFO method of calculation.

Although there may be significant advantages in some cases to using the LIFO method, it is also a far more complicated system than the FIFO. The Specific Identification allows you to simply track each item of inventory and deduct the actual cost of the goods which you sold during the year. The FIFO method allows you to value your inventory on hand at the end of a time period based on the cost of your most recent purchases. Using either your Periodic or Perpetual Inventory sheets, valuing your inventory is a simple matter.

① At the end of your chosen time period (monthly, quarterly, or annually), take an actual physical inventory count on your Physical Inventory Report.

② Using the most recent purchases as listed on your Periodic or Perpetual Inventory sheet, determine the unit price of the items left in your inventory and enter this under the Unit Price column on your Physical Inventory Report.

③ Once all of your items of inventory have been checked, counted, and a unit price determined, simply total each item and then total the value of the entire inventory. If you are conducting your final annual inventory, this final figure is your Inventory value at year end.

④ On the Cost of Goods Sold sheet, enter this number on the line titled: Inventory Value at End of Period. If this is your first year in business, enter zero as the Inventory Value at Beginning of Period. For later periods, the Inventory Value at Beginning of Period will be the Inventory Value at End of Period for the previous period.

⑤ Using either your Periodic Inventory or your Perpetual Inventory sheets, total the amounts of orders during the period which are listed under the Inventory Received column. This total will be entered on the Inventory Added During Period line. Now simply perform the calculations. You will use the figures on this sheet at tax time to prepare your taxes.

NOTE: This type of inventory calculation is not intended for manufacturing companies which manufacture finished goods from raw materials or for those with gross annual receipts over $10 million. For those type of companies, an additional calculation is necessary because of uniform capitalization rules. This tax rule requires that manufacturing inventory values include the overhead associated with the manufacturing process. Please consult an accounting professional if you fall into this category of business.

COST OF GOODS SOLD

Period Ending:

Inventory Value at Beginning of Period

Plus Inventory Added During Period

Equals Total Inventory Value

Less Inventory Value at End of Period

Equals Cost of Goods Sold

Beginning Inventory Value for next Period:
[Take from Inventory Value at end of this period]

Fixed Assets

The final category of assets which you will need to track are your fixed assets. Fixed assets are the more permanent assets of your business: generally the assets which are not for sale to customers. The main categories of these fixed assets are:

- Buildings,
- Land,
- Machinery,
- Tools,
- Furniture and Equipment,
- Vehicles.

There are many more types of fixed assets such as patents, copyrights, and goodwill. However, the six listed are the basic ones for most small businesses. If your business includes other types of fixed assets, please consult an accounting professional. For those with basic fixed assets, you will need to keep track of the actual total costs to you to acquire them. These costs include sales taxes, transportation charges, installation costs, etc. The total cost of a fixed asset to you is referred to as the asset's *cost basis*. With a major exception explained below, the cost of fixed assets are, generally, not immediately deductible as a business expense. Rather, except for the cost of land, their costs are deductible proportionately over a period of time. This proportionate deduction is referred to as *depreciation*. Since these assets generally wear out over time (except for land), each year you are allowed to deduct a portion of the initial cost as a legitimate business expense. Each type of fixed asset is given a specific time period for dividing up the cost into proportional amounts. This time period is called the *recovery period* of the asset. Depreciation is a very complex subject and one whose rules change nearly every year. The full details of depreciation are beyond the scope of this book. What follows is a general outline of depreciation rules only. It will allow you to begin to set up your fixed asset sheets. However, you will either need to consult an accounting or tax professional or consult specific tax preparation manuals for details on how your specific assets should be depreciated.

The major exception to depreciation rules is that, under the rules of IRS Code Section 179, every year a total of $17,500.00 of your fixed asset costs can be immediately used as a business deduction. This means that if your total purchases of equipment, tools, vehicles, etc. during a year amounted to less than $17,500.00, you can deduct all of the costs as current expenses. If your total fixed asset costs are over $17,500.00, you can still deduct the first $17,500.00 in costs and then depreciate the remaining costs over time. Here are some basic rules relating to depreciation:

① The depreciation rules which were in effect at the time of the purchase of the asset will be the rules which apply to that particular asset.

② The actual cost to you of the asset is the cost basis which you use to compute your depreciation amount each year.

③ Used assets which you purchase for use in your business can be depreciated in the same manner as new assets.

④ Assets which you owned prior to going into business and which you will use in your business can be depreciated. The cost basis will be the lower of their actual market value when you begin to use them in your business or their actual cost to you. For example, you start a carpentry business and use your personal power saw in the business. It cost $150.00 new, but is now worth about $90.00. You can depreciate $90.00 (or deduct this amount as an expense if the total of your fixed asset deductions is under $17,500.00).

⑤ You may depreciate proportionately those assets which you use partially for business and partially for personal use. In the above example, if you use your saw 70% of the time in your business and 30% for personal use, you may deduct or depreciate 70% of $90.00 or $63.00.

The tax depreciation rules set up several categories of asset types for the purpose of deciding how long a period you must use to depreciate the asset. Cars, trucks, computer equipment, copiers, and similar equipment are referred to as 5-year property. Most machinery, equipment, and office furniture is referred to as 7-year property. This means that for these types of property the actual costs are spread out and depreciated over 5 or 7 years; that is, the costs are deducted over a period of 5 or 7 years.

There are also several different ways to compute how much of the cost can be depreciated each year. There are three basic methods: straight line, MACRS, and ACRS. Straight line depreciation spreads the deductible amount equally over the recovery period. Thus for the power saw which is worth $90.00 and is used 70% of the time in a business, the cost basis which can be depreciated is $63.00. This asset has a recovery period of 7 years. Spreading the $63.00 over the 7 year-period allows you to deduct a total of $9.00 per year as depreciation of the saw. After the first year, the saw will be valued on your books at $54.00. Thus, after 7 years, the value of the saw on your books will be zero. It will have been fully depreciated. You will have finally been allowed to fully deduct its cost as a business expense. Of course, if you have fixed asset costs of less than $17,500.00 for the year you put the saw in service, you will be allowed to claim the entire $63.00 deduction that first year.

Other methods of depreciation have more complicated rules which must be applied. For full details, please refer to a tax preparation manual or consult a tax or accounting professional.

On the next page are listed various types of property which are depreciable or deductible. Consult this list to determine which of your business purchases may be depreciated and which of them may be written off as an immediately deductible expense. Recall that up to $17,500.00 of depreciable assets may be immediately deductible as a special Section 179 deduction.

Deductible Expenses

Advertising
Bad debts
Bank charges
Books and periodicals
Car and truck expenses
 Gas, repairs, licenses, insurance, maintenance
Commissions to sales persons
Independent contractor costs
Donations
Dues to professional groups
Educational expenses
Entertainment of clients
Freight costs
Improvements under $100.00
Insurance
Interest costs
Laundry and cleaning
Licenses for business
Legal and Professional fees
Maintenance
Office equipment under $100.00
Office furniture under $100.00
Office supplies
Pension plans
Postage
Printing costs
Property taxes
Rent
Repairs
Refunds, returns, allowances
Sales taxes collected
Sales taxes paid on purchases
Telephone
Tools under $100.00
Uniforms
Utilities
Wages paid

Depreciable Property

Business buildings (not land)
Office furniture over $100.00
Office equipment over $100.00
Business machinery
Tools over $100.00
Vehicles used in business

Fixed Asset Account

Recall that fixed assets are business purchases which are depreciable, unless you elect to deduct fixed asset expenses up to $17,500.00 per year. For record-keeping purposes, you will prepare a Fixed Asset Account sheet for each fixed asset which you have if you have acquired over $17,500.00 in a calendar year. If you have acquired less than $17,500.00 worth in a year, you may put all of your fixed asset records on one Fixed Asset Account sheet.

To prepare your Fixed Asset Account sheet, follow the following instructions:

① List the date on which you acquired the property. If the property was formerly personal property, list the date on which you converted it to business property.

② Then list the property by description. Enter the actual cost of the property. If the property is used, enter the lower of the cost of the property or the actual market value of the property. If the property is part business and part personal, enter the value of the business portion of the property.

③ If you will have over $17,500.00 worth of depreciable business property during the year, you will additionally need to enter information in the last 3 columns on the sheet. First, you will need to enter the recovery period for each asset. For most property other than buildings, this will be either 5 or 7 years. Please consult a tax manual or tax professional.

④ You will need to enter the method of depreciation. Again, check a tax manual or tax professional.

⑤ Finally, you will need to determine the amount of the deduction for the first year (Hint: tax manual or tax professional).

⑥ Once you have set up a method for each fixed asset, each year you will determine the additional deduction and update the balance. You will then use that figure on your business tax return and in the preparation of your balance sheet (explained in Chapter 11).

FIXED ASSET ACCOUNT

Date	Item	Cost		Years	Method	Annual		Balance	

Business Assets Checklist

☐ Prepare a Current Asset Account sheet for the following business assets:

> ☐ Business checking account,

> ☐ Petty cash fund,

> ☐ Accounts receivable.

> ☐ Periodically update the information on your Current Asset Accounts for use in preparing a Balance Sheet. Use the following records to update your Current Asset Accounts:

>> ☐ Business checking account: Check Register,

>> ☐ Petty cash fund: Petty Cash Register,

>> ☐ Accounts receivable: Credit Sale Aging Report

☐ If you will have inventory, choose to track it on either a periodic or perpetual basis. Prepare the appropriate Inventory forms.

> ☐ Track your inventory orders and receipts on your Perpetual or Periodic Inventory sheets.

> ☐ Periodically, make a Physical Inventory Report.

> ☐ Periodically, determine your Cost of Goods Sold for use on your Profit and Loss Statements.

☐ Prepare a Fixed Asset Account sheet for each permanent asset.

> ☐ Determine the Cost basis for each asset,

> ☐ Determine the method of depreciation for each asset,

> ☐ Periodically, determine your annual depreciation deduction for each asset and update each Fixed Asset Account balance.

Chapter 6

Tracking Business Debts

Business debts are also referred to as business liabilities. However, technically, business liabilities also includes the value of the owner's equity in the business. We will deal with owner's equity more fully in Chapter 11 when we discuss balance sheets.

Business debts can be divided into two general categories. First are current debts, those which will normally be paid within 1 year. The second general category is long-term debts. These are generally more long-term debts or those that will not be paid off within 1 year.

Current debts for most small businesses consist primarily of accounts payable and taxes which are due during the year. For small businesses, the taxes which are due during a year fall into three main categories: estimated income tax payments, payment of collected sales taxes, and payroll taxes. Estimated income tax payments will be discussed in Chapter 14 when we look more closely at taxes. Payroll tax record-keeping will be explained in Chapter 9 when we discuss payroll in depth. Since the collection and payment of sales taxes are handled differently in virtually every state, you will need to contact your state's department of revenue or similar body to determine the specific necessary record-keeping requirements for that business debt. In Chapter 8, when we discuss the records you will need to track your income, you will be shown how to handle the record-keeping to keep track of your sales taxes.

That leaves us only with accounts payable to track as a current debt. You will have only one simple form to use to keep track of this important category. Accounts payable are the current bills which your business owes. They may be for equipment or supplies which you have purchased on credit or they may be for items which you have ordered on account. Regardless of the source of the debt, you will need a clear system to record the debt and keep track of how much you still owe on the debt.

Long-term debts of a business are those debts which will not be paid off within one year. These can either be debts based on business loans for equipment, inventory, business-owned vehicles, or business property. In the accounting system outlined in this book, you will only keep track of the current principal and interest for these debts. For long-term debts of your business, you will fill in the Long-Term Debt Record, which is explained later in this chapter.

Combined Accounts Payable Recording

On the following page, you will find an Accounts Payable Record sheet. If you have only a few accounts which you do not pay off immediately, you can use this form. If you have many accounts payable, you will need to complete an Individual Account Payable sheet for each separate account. That form and its instructions immediately follow the Accounts Payable Record sheet.

Accounts Payable Record

On the following form, you will enter any bills or short-term debts which you do not pay immediately. If you pay the bill off upon receipt of the bill, you need not enter the amount on this sheet. Your records for expenses will take care of the necessary documentation for those particular debts. Follow these instructions to prepare and fill in this particular form:

① For those debts which you do not pay off immediately, in the left hand column of the sheet, you will need to record the following information:
  ♦ The date the debt was incurred,
  ♦ To whom you owe the money,
  ♦ Payment terms (for instance: due within 30, 60 or 90 days),
  ♦ The amount of the debt.

② In the right hand column of the Accounts Payable record sheet, you will record the following information:
  ♦ The date of any payments,
  ♦ To whom the payments were made,
  ♦ The amount of any payments made.

③ By periodically totalling the left and right hand columns, you will be able to take a look at the total amount of your unpaid accounts payable. You may wish to do this weekly, monthly, or quarterly. You will also need the figure for your total unpaid accounts payable for the preparation of your balance sheet.

④ When you have totaled your accounts payable at the end of your chosen periodic interval, you should start a new sheet and carry the unpaid accounts over to it. Using this simple record, you will be able check your accounts payable at a glance and also have enough information available to use to prepare a balance sheet for your business, as explained later in Chapter 11.

ACCOUNTS PAYABLE RECORD

Period from: _____ to: _____

Unpaid Accounts				
Date	Due to	Terms	Amount	
		TOTAL		

Payments			
Date	Paid to	Amount	
	TOTAL		

Total Unpaid Accounts

Less Total Payments

Equals Total Accounts Payable

Individual Accounts Payable Recording

If your business has many accounts payable which must be tracked, it may be a good idea to prepare an individual account payable sheet for each account. On the following page, you will find an Individual Account Payable sheet to be used for this purpose. In order to fill in this sheet, follow these directions:

① You will need to enter the following information for each account to whom a bill is owed:
- Name,
- Address,
- Contact person,
- Phone number,
- An account number, if applicable.

② As you receive a bill or invoice, enter the following information off the bill or invoice:
- Date,
- Invoice number,
- Any terms,
- Amount due.

③ When an amount is paid, enter this information:
- Check number,
- Date paid,
- Amount paid.

④ Total the balance due after each transaction. Using this method of tracking accounts payable will allow you to always have a running total of your individual accounts payable available.

⑤ To prepare a balance sheet entry for accounts payable, you will simply need to total all of the various account balances for all of your accounts payable.

INDIVIDUAL ACCOUNT PAYABLE RECORD

Company:

Address:

Contact Person: Phone:

Account #:

Date	Invoice/Check	Terms	Amount		Balance	

Long-Term Debts

If your business has any outstanding loans which will not be paid off within one year, you will prepare a Long-Term Debt Record for each loan. You will track the principal and interest paid on each long-term debt of your businesss. This information will enable you to have long-term debt figures for use in preparing your Balance Sheet and interest paid figures for use in preparing your Profit and Loss Statements. On the following page, you will find a sheet to be used for this purpose. In order to fill in this sheet, follow these directions:

① You will need to enter the following information for each company to whom a loan is outstanding:
- Name,
- Address,
- Contact person,
- Phone number,
- Loan account number,
- The loan interest rate,
- The original principal amount of the loan,
- The term of the loan.

② You will need a loan payment book or amortization schedule in order to obtain the necessary information regarding the amounts of each of your payments which are principal and interest. As you make a payment, enter the following information :
- Date of payment,
- Amount of principal paid,
- Amount of interest paid,
- Balance due (previous balance - payment).

④ Total the balance due after each payment. Using this method of tracking accounts payable will allow you to always have a running total of your long-term liability for each long-term debt.

⑤ To prepare a balance sheet entry for long-term debts, you will simply need to total all of the various account balances for all of your long-term debts.

⑤ You should also periodically total all of the columns of on your Long-term Debt record. You will need the totals for Interest paid for your Quarterly and Annual Expense Summaries (see Chapter 7).

LONG-TERM DEBT RECORD

Company:

Address:

Contact Person: Phone:

Account #:   Interest Rate:

Original Loan Amount: Term:

Date	Payment		Principal		Interest		Balance	
TOTALS								

Business Debts Checklist

❑ Track current debts.

> ❑ Track business estimated tax liability (individual or corporate) by using quarterly Profit and Loss Statements.

> ❑ Track sales tax liability on periodic Income Records.

> ❑ Track payroll tax liability on Payroll Depository Record.

> ❑ Track total accounts payable with Accounts Payable sheet.

>> ❑ Update separate accounts on Individual Account Payable sheets when payments are made.

> ❑ Transfer current debt information to Balance Sheet periodically.

❑ Track long-term debts.

> ❑ Update business loan balances on Long-term Debt sheet when payments are made.

> ❑ Update mortgage balances on Long-term Debt sheet when payments are made.

> ❑ Transfer long-term debt balances to Balance Sheet periodically.

Chapter 7

Tracking Business Expenses

The expenses of a business are all of the transactions of the business in which money is paid out of the business, with two general exceptions. Money paid out of the business to the owner (as a draw rather than as a salary) and money paid out of the business to pay off the principal of a loan are not considered expenses of a business. Very often, the bulk of a small businesses record-keeping will consist of tracking its expenses. Because of the tax deductibility of the cost of most business expenses, it is crucial for a business to keep careful records of what has been spent to operate the business. But even beyond the need for detailed expense records for tax purposes, a small business needs a clear system which will allow for a quick examination of where business money is being spent. The tracking of business expenses will allow you to see at a glance where your money is flowing. With detailed records, it will also be an easy task to apply various financial formulas to analyze and understand your expense/income ratios in greater depth. This will allow you to see if certain costs are out-of-line, if certain expenses are increasing or decreasing, and if your business expenses make clear business sense.

In order to track your business expenses, you will use two main forms, either a Daily or a Weekly Expense Record (depending on the volume of your business expenses) and a Monthly Expense Record Summary. You may also need to use a number of additional specialized forms if your business needs dictate their use. The specialized forms which are included will cover the additional record-keeping which is necessary to document travel expenses, meals and entertainment expenses, and vehicle expenses. There is also a Quarterly and Annual Expense Record Summary for totaling your expense payments.

Tracking Expenses

All of your expenses will initially be recorded on either the Daily or Weekly Expense Record sheet. You will have to choose if you desire to track your expenses on a daily form or a weekly form. If you anticipate having a great number of entries, choose a daily sheet for recording the expenses. If your expense transactions will generally number under 30 per week, you can use the weekly record. Regardless of which time period you choose to have on each sheet, you should record the expenditures at least weekly so that you do not fall too far behind in keeping it up-to-date. You may switch between recording periods if your level of expenses changes.

On your expense record sheet, you will record all of your business expenses in chronological order. The expense transactions will generally come from 2 main sources: your business bank account check register and your petty cash register. You will transfer all of the expenses from these two sources to the main expense record sheets. This will provide you with a central listing of all of the expenditures for your business.

From this record sheet (whether it is a daily or weekly record), you will transfer your expenses to a Monthly Expense Summary sheet. On the Monthly Expense Summary sheet, you will enter a line for each expense type which you have listed on your business Chart of Accounts (see Chapter 3). You will then go through your Daily or Weekly Expense Record sheets for each month and total the expenses for each account. You will enter this total in the column for the specific type of expense.

Finally, on a monthly basis, you will transfer the totals for your various expense categories to the Annual Expense Summary sheet. On this sheet, you collect and record the total monthly expenses. With these figures, you will be able to easily total your expense amounts to ascertain your quarterly and annual expenses.

By recording your business expenses in this manner, you should have little difficulty being able to keep track of the money flowing out of your business on a daily, weekly, monthly, quarterly, and annual basis. You will have all of the information which you will need to easily provide the necessary expenditure figures for preparing a Profit and Loss Statement (which will be explained in Chapter 10).

On the next few pages you will be given a detailed explanation of how to fill in these various simplified forms. Remember that you must tailor the forms to fit your particular business.

Daily and Weekly Expense Records

On the following pages are both the Daily Expense Record and Weekly Expense Record forms. These forms are identical except for the period which they are intended to cover. To use these forms, follow these steps:

① Decide which time period you wish to use for completing the forms. If you anticipate over 30 expense transactions a week, you should probably choose the Daily Expense Record. Otherwise, the Weekly Expense Record should be sufficient.

② Fill in the date or dates which the form will cover at the top where indicated.

③ Beginning with your Bank Account Check Register, transfer the following information from the register to the Expense Record:
   ♦ The date of the transaction,
   ♦ The check number,
   ♦ To whom the amount was paid,
   ♦ The expense account number (off your Chart of Accounts),
   ♦ The amount of the transaction.

④ Next, using your Petty Cash Register, transfer the following information from your Petty Cash Register to the Expense Record:
   ♦ The date of the transaction,
   ♦ In the column for Check Number, put PC to indicate that the expense was a petty cash expense.
   ♦ To whom the amount was paid,
   ♦ The expense account number (off your Chart of Accounts),
   ♦ The amount of the transaction,
   ♦ Do not list the checks that you make out to "Petty Cash" as an expense.

⑤ For credit cards transactions, follow these rules:
- Do not list the payment to a credit card company as an expense.
- List the monthly amount on the credit card bill for interest as an interest expense.
- Individually, list each of the business purchases on the credit card as a separate expense item, assigning an account number to each separate business charge. Make a notation for the date, to whom the expense was paid, and the amount. In the column for Check #, provide the type of credit card (for example: V for Visa).
- Do not list any personal charge items as business expenses.
- If a charged item is used partially for business and partially for personal reasons, list only that portion which is used for business reasons as a business expense.

⑥ At the end of the period (daily or weekly), total the Amount column. You will use this daily or weekly total expense amount to cross check your later calculations.

⑦ It is a good idea to keep all of your various business expense receipts for at least 3 years after the tax period to which they relate. You may wish to buy envelopes for each weekly period, label each appropriately, and file your weekly business expense receipts in them. This will make it easy to find each specific receipt, if necessary.

DAILY EXPENSE RECORD

Date:

Date	Check #	To Whom Paid	Account	Amount	
			Daily Totals		

WEEKLY EXPENSE RECORD

Week of

Date	Check #	To Whom Paid	Account	Amount	
			Weekly Totals		

Monthly Expense Summary

Using this record sheet, you will compile and transfer the total expense amount for each expense category. In this way, you will be able to keep a monthly total of all of the expenses, broken down by category of expense.

To fill in this form, do the following:

① Indicate the month which the Summary will cover where shown at the top.

② In the first column on the left hand side, list all of your expense account numbers from your business Chart of Accounts.

③ In the next column, using your daily or weekly Expense Records, transfer the amounts for each expense. If you have more than four expense amounts for any account, use a second Monthly Expense Summary sheet to record additional amounts.

④ In the total column, list the total expenses in each category for the month.

⑤ At the bottom of the page, total the amount for all of the categories for the month. Don't forget to include any amounts from any additional sheets in your totals.

⑥ To double check your transfers and your calculations, total all of your Daily or Weekly Expense Record sheet Total amounts. This figure should equal your Monthly Expense Summary sheet total for that month. If there is a discrepancy, check each of your figures until you discover the error.

MONTHLY EXPENSE SUMMARY

Account Name	Amount		Amount		Amount		Amount		Total	
TOTALS										

Annual Expense Summary

① Fill in the year. Fill in your Account numbers from your Chart of Accounts across the top row. If you have more than 9 expense accounts, use a second and third page, if necessary.

② On a monthly basis, carry the totals from all of the rows on your Monthly Expense Record forms to the appropriate column of the Annual Expense Summary form.

③ At the end of each quarter, total all of the monthly entries to arrive at your quarterly totals for each category.

④ To double check your monthly calculations, total your categories across each month and put this total in the final column. Compare this total with the total on your Monthly Expense Record sheets. If there is a discrepancy, check each of your figures until you discover the error. Don't forget to include your extra sheets if you have more than 9 expense accounts to list.

⑤ To double check your quarterly calculations, total your monthly totals in the final quarterly column. This figure should equal the total of the quarterly category totals across the quarterly row. If there is a discrepancy, check each of your figures until you discover the error.

⑥ Finally, total each of your quarterly amounts to arrive at the annual totals. To cross check your calculations, total the quarterly totals in the final column. This figure should equal the total for all of the annual totals in each category across the Annual Total row. If there is a discrepancy, check each of your figures until you discover the error.

ANNUAL EXPENSE SUMMARY

Year of:

Account # →											Total
January											
February											
March											
1st Quarter											
April											
May											
June											
2nd Quarter											
July											
August											
September											
3rd Quarter											
October											
November											
December											
4th Quarter											
Annual Total											

Travel, Auto, and Entertainment Expenses

Travel, auto, and entertainment expenses are treated slightly differently than other business expenses because you are required by the Internal Revenue Service to support your expenses with adequate additional records or evidence. These records can be in the form of trip diaries, account books, or similar items. Weekly, Monthly, and Annual Travel Expense Account Record sheets are provided to assist in keeping accurate records for IRS and your own accounting purposes. In addition, Weekly, Monthly, and Annual Auto Expense Record sheets are included to track your business auto expenses.

The following list is a general guide to those travel, auto, meal, and entertainment expenses which can be deducted as legitimate business expenses:

• Transportation: the cost of plane, train, or bus travel to the business destination. Also the cost of taxi, bus, or limousine between airports, stations, hotels, and business locations. This includes any costs for baggage transfers.

• Car: The cost of operating your car when away from home on business. You can deduct your actual expenses or you may use the standard mileage rate. If you use the standard rate, you can also deduct tolls and parking expenses. As of 1995, the standard mileage rate was 29 cents per mile.

• Lodging: If your business trip is overnight, you can deduct the cost of your lodging.

• Meals: If your business trip is overnight, you can deduct the cost of meals, beverages, and tips. You may also choose instead to use a standard meal allowance. As of 1995, the standard meal allowance was between $26-$38 per day for meals, depending where your business trip is located. For complete information on this, please refer to IRS Publication 463: *Travel, Entertainment, and Gift Expenses*. Whether you choose to deduct the actual cost or the standard allowance, your deduction is limited to 50% of your expenses.

• Entertainment: You can deduct the cost of business-related entertainment if you entertain a client, customer, or employee and it is directly related to your business. As with meals, entertainment expense deductions are limited to 50% of your actual expenses.

For travel, car, and entertainment expenses, you should also keep additional records which indicate the dates the expenses were incurred, the location of the expenses, and the business reason for the expenses. These can be noted on any receipts for the expenses.

Weekly or Monthly Travel Expense Records

① Decide whether you will need to track your travel expenses on a weekly or monthly basis. For most businesses a monthly record will be adequate.

② Fill in the time period and the employee name.

③ For each separate expense, fill in the date and a description of the item. Place the amount for the item in the appropriate column (Travel, Lodging, Meals, or Other). Carry the amount over to the Total column.

④ At the end of the month (or week if you are keeping records on a weekly basis), total each column in the final Total row. To check for accuracy, the totals of the Travel, Lodging, Meals, and Other columns should equal the total for the Total column.

WEEKLY TRAVEL EXPENSE RECORD

Week of: _____   Employee Name: _____

Date	Item	Travel	Lodging	Meals	Other	Total
Weekly Total						

MONTHLY TRAVEL EXPENSE RECORD

Month of: _____   Employee Name: _____

Date	Item	Travel	Lodging	Meals	Other	Total
Monthly Total						

Annual Travel Expense Summary

① Fill in the year and employee name.

② On a monthly basis, carry the totals from all of the columns on your Weekly or Monthly Travel Expense Record forms to the appropriate column of the Annual Travel Expense Summary form.

③ At the end of each quarter, total all of the monthly entries to arrive at your quarterly totals for each category.

④ To double check your monthly calculations, total your categories across each month and put this total in the final column. Compare this total with the total on your Weekly or Monthly Travel Expense Record sheets. If there is a discrepancy, check each of your figures until you discover the error.

⑤ To double check your quarterly calculations, total your monthly totals in the final quarterly column. This figure should equal the total of the quarterly category totals across the quarterly row. If there is a discrepancy, check each of your figures until you discover the error.

⑥ Finally, total each of your quarterly amounts to arrive at the annual totals. To cross check your calculations, total the quarterly totals in the final column. This figure should equal the total for all of the annual totals in each category across the Annual Totals row. If there is a discrepancy, check each of your figures until you discover the error.

⑧ When you use the information on this form, remember that duplicate expenses may be recorded on this form and on the Annual Expense Record Summary. The purpose of this form is to keep track of your annual travel expenses as required by the IRS.

ANNUAL TRAVEL EXPENSE SUMMARY

Year of: Employee Name:

Date	Item	Travel		Lodging		Meals		Other		Total	
January											
February											
March											
1st Quarter											
April											
May											
June											
2nd Quarter											
July											
August											
September											
3rd Quarter											
October											
November											
December											
4th Quarter											
Annual Totals											

Weekly or Monthly Auto Expense Records

① Decide whether you will need to track your auto expenses on a weekly or monthly basis. For most businesses a monthly record will be adequate.

② Fill in the time period , the employee name, car make and model, and license number.

③ For each separate expense, fill in the date and a description of the item. Place the amount for the item in the appropriate column (Gas/Oil or Other). Carry the amount over to the Total column. List the mileage driven for the period.

④ At the end of the month (or week if you are keeping records on a weekly basis), total each column in the final Weekly or Monthly Totals row. To check for accuracy, the totals of the Gas/Oil and Other columns should equal the total for the Total column.

WEEKLY AUTO EXPENSE RECORD

Week of:		Employee Name:	
Car Make/Model:		License #:	

Date	Description	Mileage	Gas/Oil		Other		Total	
Weekly Total								

MONTHLY AUTO EXPENSE RECORD

Month of:		Employee Name:
Car Make/Model:		License #:

Date	Description	Mileage	Gas/Oil		Other		Total	
Monthly Total								

100

Annual Auto Expense Summary

① Fill in the year, employee name, car make and model, and license number.

② On a monthly basis, carry the totals from all of the columns on your Weekly or Monthly Auto Expense Record forms to the appropriate column of the Annual Auto Expense Summary form.

③ At the end of each quarter, total all of the monthly entries to arrive at your quarterly totals for each category.

④ To double check your monthly calculations, total your categories across each month and put this total in the final column. Compare this total with the total on your Weekly or Monthly Auto Expense Record sheets. If there is a discrepancy, check each of your figures until you discover the error.

⑤ To double check your quarterly calculations, total your monthly totals in the final quarterly column. This figure should equal the total of the quarterly category totals across the quarterly row. If there is a discrepancy, check each of your figures until you discover the error.

⑥ Finally, total each of your quarterly amounts to arrive at the annual totals. To cross check your calculations, total the quarterly totals in the final column. This figure should equal the total for all of the annual totals in each category across the Annual Totals row. If there is a discrepancy, check each of your figures until you discover the error.

⑧ When you use the information on this form, remember that duplicate expenses may be recorded on this form and on the Annual Expense Record Summary. The purpose of this form is to keep track of your annual auto expenses as required by the IRS.

ANNUAL AUTO EXPENSE SUMMARY

Year of:			Employee Name:		
Car Make/Model:			License #:		

Month	Description	Mileage	Gas/Oil	Other	Total
January					
February					
March					
1st Quarter					
April					
May					
June					
2nd Quarter					
July					
August					
September					
3rd Quarter					
October					
November					
December					
4th Quarter					
Annual Totals					

Purchase Orders

Two final forms which may be used for business expenses are the Purchase Order and the Purchase Order Record. A Purchase Order is used for placing orders for business merchandise when a credit account has been established with a company in advance. You should use the following Purchase Order in conjunction with the Purchase Order Record which follows. Your Purchase Order Record provides you with a simple record of what you have ordered using your Purchase Orders.

① Place your business card in the upper left hand corner of the blank Purchase Order form from this book and make a master copy on a copier machine. Make a number of copies of the master copy of your Purchase Order. Number your Purchase Orders consecutively.

② Using your first numbered Purchase Order, enter the date. Under Ship Via: enter how you wish the order to be shipped to you (ie. UPS ground, US Mail, Freight Carrier, etc.).

③ If you have a delivery deadline date, enter under Deliver By:.

④ Enter the appropriate information under Bill To: and Ship To: .

⑤ For each item ordered enter the following:
  ♦ Item #,
  ♦ Quantity,
  ♦ Description,
  ♦ Price and Amount.

⑥ Subtotal and add tax and shipping if you know the correct amounts. Check the appropriate box under Terms.

⑦ Upon completing each Purchase Order, enter the following information on your Purchase Order Record:
  ♦ Purchase Order #,
  ♦ Date,
  ♦ Vendor name,
  ♦ Brief description of what was ordered,
  ♦ Date when due,
  ♦ Amount of the purchase order.

PURCHASE ORDER

Date:
Purchase Order #:
Ship Via:
Deliver By:

Bill To:

Ship To:

Item #	Quantity	Description	Price		Amount	

Terms

☐ Cash
☐ COD
☐ On Account
☐ MC/Visa

Sub-total

Tax

Shipping

TOTAL

PURCHASE ORDER RECORD

PO #	Date	Issued to	For	Due	Amount

Business Expenses Checklist

❐ On a daily or weekly basis, transfer the details of your business expenses from your Check Register and Petty Cash Register to your Expense Record sheets.

❐ On a monthly basis, transfer the totals for your expenses to your Monthly Expense Summary sheet.

❐ On a monthly basis, transfer the totals for your expenses to your Annual Expense Summary sheet.

❐ Periodically, record your travel expenses on your Travel Expense Record sheet.

❐ On a monthly basis, transfer the totals for your travel expenses to your Annual Travel Expense Summary sheet.

❐ Periodically, record your auto expenses on your Auto Expense Record sheet.

❐ On a monthly basis, transfer the totals for your auto expenses to your Annual Auto Expense Summary sheet.

❐ As needed, prepare Purchase Orders.

❐ Each time you prepare a Purchase Order, enter the information from the Purchase Order on your Purchase Order Record.

Chapter 8

Tracking Business Income

The careful tracking of your businesses income is one of the most important accounting activities you will perform. It is essential for your business that you know intimately where your income comes from. Failure to accurately track income and cash are one of the most frequent causes of business failure. You must have in place a clear and easily-understood system to track your business income. There are 3 separate features of tracking business income that must be incorporated into your accounting system. You will need a system in place to handle cash, a system to track all of your sales and service income, and a system to handle credit sales.

The first system you will need is a clear method for handling cash on a daily or weekly basis. This is true no matter how large or small your business may be and regardless of how much or how little cash is actually handled. You must have a clear record of how much cash is on hand and of how much cash is taken in during a particular time period. You will also need to have a method to tally this cash flow on a monthly basis. For these purposes, three forms are provided: a Daily or Weekly Cash Report and a Monthly Cash Report Summary.

The second feature of your business income tracking system should be a method to track your actual income from sales or services. This differs from your cash tracking. With these records you will track taxable and non-taxable income whether the income is in the form of cash, check, credit card payment, or on account. Please note that when *non-taxable income* is referred to, it means only income which is not subject to any state or local sales tax (generally, this will be income from the performance of a service). These records will also track your intake of sales taxes, if applicable. For this segment of your income tracking, you will have either a Daily, or Weekly Income Record, depending on your level of income activity. You will also track your income on Monthly and Annual Income Summaries, which will provide you with a monthly, quarterly, and annual report of your taxable income, non-taxable income, and sales taxes collection.

The third feature of your business income tracking consists of a method to track and bill credit sales. With this portion of income tracking, you will list and track all of your sales to customers which are made on account or on credit. The accounts which owe you money are referred to as your *accounts receivable*. They are the accounts from whom you hope to receive payment. The tracking of these credit sales will take place on either a Daily, Weekly, or Monthly Credit Sales Record. You will also use a Credit Sales Aging Report to see how your customers are doing over time. The actual billing of these credit sales will incorporate an Invoice, Statement, and Past Due Statement. Finally, a Credit Memo will be used to track those instances when a customer is given credit for any returned items.

Tracking Your Cash

Most businesses will have to handle cash in some form. Here we are not talking about the use of petty cash. Petty cash is the cash that a business has on hand for the payment of minor expenses which may crop up and for which the use of a business check is not convenient. The cash handling discussed in this section is the daily handling of cash used to take money in from customers or clients and the use of a cash drawer or some equivalent. You must have some method to accurately account for the cash used in your business in this regard. Three forms are provided: a Daily or Weekly Cash Report and a Monthly Cash Report Summary. The use of these forms is explained on the next pages.

Daily or Weekly Cash Report

This form is used each day or week to track the cash received in the business from customer payments to the business, not petty cash. The cash may be in a cash box, or some type of cash register. Regardless of how your cash is held, you need a method to account for the cash. Please follow these instructions:

① First, you will need to decide if you wish to track your cash transactions on a daily or weekly basis. Depending on the level of your business, choose to use either a Daily or Weekly Cash Report.

② You will need to decide how much cash you will need to begin each period with sufficient cash to meet your needs and make change for cash sales. Usually $100 should be sufficient for most needs. Choose a figure and begin each period with that amount in your cash drawer. Excess cash which has been collected should be deposited in your business bank account. Each period, fill in the date and the cash on hand on your Cash Report.

③ As you take in cash and checks throughout the period, record each item of cash taken in, checks taken in, and any instances of cash paid out. Cash out does not mean change which has been made, but rather cash paid out for business purposes (for example: for a refund).

④ Your business may have so much daily cash flow that it will be burdensome to record each item of cash flow on your sheet. In that case, you will need a cash register of some type. Simply total the cash register at the end of the day and record the total cash in, checks in, and cash out in the appropriate place on the Daily Cash Report.

⑤ At the end of each period, total your Cash in and Checks in. Add these two amounts to your Cash on Hand at the beginning of the period. This equals your Total Receipts for the day. Subtract any Cash paid out from this amount. This figure should equal your actual cash on hand at the end of the period. Make a bank deposit for all of the checks and for all of the cash in excess of the amount which you will need to begin the next period.

⑥ In the space for deposits, note a deposit number, if applicable; the date of the deposit; the deposit amount; and the name and signature of who made the deposit. Don't forget to also record your deposit in your business Bank Account Check Register.

DAILY CASH REPORT

Date: _____   Cash on Hand Beginning: _____

#	CASH OUT Name	Amount	CHECKS IN Name	Amount	CASH IN Name	Amount
1						
2						
3						
4						
5						
6						
7						
8						
9						
10						
11						
12						
Total						

Deposit #:	
Deposit Date:	
Deposit Amount:	
Deposited by:	
Signed:	

Total Cash In	
+ Total Checks In	
+ Cash on Hand Beginning	
= Total Receipts	
- Total Cash Out	
= Balance on Hand	
- Bank Deposit	
= Cash on Hand Ending	

110

WEEKLY CASH REPORT

Week of: Cash on Hand Beginning:

#	CASH OUT Name	Amount	CHECKS IN Name	Amount	CASH IN Name	Amount
1						
2						
3						
4						
5						
6						
7						
8						
9						
10						
11						
12						
Total						

Deposit #:	
Deposit Date:	
Deposit Amount:	
Deposited by:	
Signed:	

Total Cash In	
+ Total Checks In	
+ Cash on Hand Beginning	
= Total Receipts	
- Total Cash Out	
= Balance on Hand	
- Bank Deposit	
= Cash on Hand Ending	

Monthly Cash Report Summary

This form will be used to keep a monthly record of your Daily or Weekly Cash Reports. It serves as a monthly listing of your cash flow and of your business bank account deposits. You will, of course, also record your bank deposits in your business Bank Account Check Register. To use this form, follow these instructions:

① On a daily or weekly basis, collect your Daily or Weekly Cash Reports. From each Report, record the following information:
   - Cash on hand at the beginning of the period,
   - Cash taken in,
   - Checks taken in,
   - Cash paid out,
   - The amount of the daily bank deposit,
   - Cash on hand at the end of the period and after the bank deposit.

② You can total the deposit column as a cross check against your bank account Check Register record of deposits.

MONTHLY CASH REPORT SUMMARY

Date	On Hand		Cash In		Checks In		Cash Out		Deposit		On Hand	
1												
2												
3												
4												
5												
6												
7												
8												
9												
10												
11												
12												
13												
14												
15												
16												
17												
18												
19												
20												
21												
22												
23												
24												
25												
26												
27												
28												
29												
30												
31												

Tracking Income

The second feature of your business income tracking system should be a method to keep track of your actual income. This portion of the system will provide you with a list of all taxable and non-taxable income and of any sales taxes collected, if applicable. For sales tax information, please contact your state's sales tax revenue collection agency. If your state has a sales tax on the product or service which you provide, you will need accurate records to determine your total taxable and non-taxable income and the amount of sales tax which is due. For this purpose and for the purpose of tracking all of your income for your own business analysis, you should prepare a Daily or Weekly Income Record. The information from these reports will then be used to prepare Monthly and Annual Income Summaries.

Daily or Weekly Income Records

To use this form, do the following:

① Depending on the level of your business, decide which time period you would like to track on each form: daily or weekly. Fill in the appropriate date or time period.

② You will need to contact your state taxing agency for information on how to determine if a sale or the provision of a service is taxable or non-taxable. You will also need to determine the appropriate rates for sales tax collection.

③ For each item, record the following information:
  • Invoice number,
  • Taxable income amount,
  • Sales tax amount,
  • Non-taxable income amount,
  • Total income (Taxable, sales tax, non-taxable amounts combined).

④ On a daily or weekly basis, total the amounts in each column to determine the totals for the particular time period. These figures will be carried over to the Monthly and Annual Income Summary sheets, which will be explained next.

DAILY INCOME RECORD

Date of

INVOICE #	Taxable Income		Sales Tax		Non-Taxable Income		Total Income	
Daily Total								

WEEKLY INCOME RECORD

Week of

INVOICE #	Taxable Income		Sales Tax		Non-Taxable Income		Total Income	
Weekly Total								

Monthly Income Summary

To use this form, do the following:

① Fill in the appropriate month.

② Using your Daily or Weekly Income Records, record the following information for each day or week:
- Total taxable income amount,
- Total sales tax amount,
- Total non-taxable income amount,
- Total income (Taxable, sales tax, non-taxable amounts combined).

③ On a monthly basis, total the amounts in each column to determine the totals for the particular month. These figures will be carried over to the Annual Income Summary sheet, which will be explained next.

MONTHLY INCOME SUMMARY

Month of

Date	Taxable Income		Sales Tax		Non-Taxable Income		Total Income	
1								
2								
3								
4								
5								
6								
7								
8								
9								
10								
11								
12								
13								
14								
15								
16								
17								
18								
19								
20								
21								
22								
23								
24								
25								
26								
27								
28								
29								
30								
31								
Monthly Total								

Annual Income Summary

① Fill in the year.

② On a monthly basis, carry the totals from all of the columns on your Monthly Income Summary form to the appropriate column of the Annual Income Summary form.

③ At the end of each quarter, total all of the monthly entries to arrive at your quarterly totals for each category.

④ To double check your monthly calculations, total your categories across each month and put this total in the final column. Compare this total with the total on your Monthly Income Summary sheets. If there is a discrepancy, check each of your figures until you discover the error.

⑤ To double check your quarterly calculations, total your monthly totals in the final quarterly column. This figure should equal the total of the quarterly category totals across the quarterly row. If there is a discrepancy, check each of your figures until you discover the error.

⑥ Finally, total each of your quarterly amounts to arrive at the annual totals. To cross check your calculations, total the quarterly totals in the final column. This figure should equal the total for all of the annual totals in each category across the Annual Total row. If there is a discrepancy, check each of your figures until you discover the error.

ANNUAL INCOME SUMMARY

Year of:

Date	Taxable Income		Sales Tax		Non-Taxable Income		Total Income	
January								
February								
March								
1st Quarter								
April								
May								
June								
2nd Quarter								
July								
August								
September								
3rd Quarter								
October								
November								
December								
4th Quarter								
Annual Totals								

Tracking Credit Sales

The final component of your business income tracking system will be a logical method to track your credit sales. You will use a Daily, Weekly, or Monthly Credit Sales Record to track the actual sales on credit and Credit Sales Aging Report to track the payment on these sales. In addition, several forms are provided for the billing of these credit sales: an Invoice, Statement, Past Due Statement, and Credit Memo.

Daily, Weekly, or Monthly Credit Sales Records

To keep track of sales made to customers on credit or on account, follow these directions:

① Depending on your particular level of business activity, decide whether you will need to use a Daily, Weekly, or Monthly Credit Sales Record.

② Fill in the appropriate date or time period.

③ For each sale which is made on credit, fill in the following information from the customer Invoice (see Invoice instructions later in this Chapter):
  ♦ Invoice number,
  ♦ Date of the sale,
  ♦ Customer name,
  ♦ Total sales amount.

④ The final column is for recording the date that the credit sale has been paid in full.

⑤ The information from your Daily, Weekly, or Monthly Credit Sales Records will also be used to prepare your Credit Sales Aging Report on a monthly basis.

DAILY CREDIT SALES RECORD

Date:

INVOICE #	Sale Date	Customer	Sales Total		Date Paid

WEEKLY CREDIT SALES RECORD

Week of

INVOICE #	Sale Date	Customer	Sales Total		Date Paid

MONTHLY CREDIT SALES RECORD

Month of

INVOICE #	Sale Date	Customer	Sales Total		Date Paid

Credit Sales Aging Report

This report is used to track the current status of your credit sales or accounts receivables. Through the use of this form you will be able to track whether or not the people or companies that owe you money are falling behind on their payments. With this information, you will be able to determine how to handle these accounts: sending past due notices, halting sales to them, turning them over to a collection agency, etc. To use this form, do the following:

① Decide on which day of the month you would like to perform your credit sales aging calculations. Enter this date on the first line of the form.

② For each credit sales account, enter the name of the account from your Daily, Weekly, or Monthly Sales Records.

③ Under the Total column, enter the total current amount which is owed to you. If this figure is based on credit sales during the current month, enter this figure again in the Current column. Do this for each credit account.

④ Each month you will prepare a new Credit Sales Aging Report on a new sheet. On the same date in the next month, determine how much of the originally-owed balance has been paid off. Enter the amount of the unpaid balance from the previous month under the 30-60 days column. Enter any new credit sales for the month under the Current column. The figure under the Total column should be the total of all of the columns to the right of the Total column.

⑤ Each month, determine how much was paid on the account, deduct that amount from the oldest amount due, and shift the amounts due over one column to the right. Add any new credit sales to the Current column and total the amounts in the Total column.

⑥ After entering the information for each month, total each of the columns across the Total line at the bottom of the sheet. The Total column is 100% of the amount due. Calculate the percentage of 100% for each of the other columns to determine how much of your accounts receivable are 30, 60, 90, or more days overdue.

CREDIT SALES AGING REPORT

Date:

Account Name	Total	Current	30-60 days	60-90 days	90 days +
TOTALS					
PERCENT	100%				

Invoices and Statements

For credit sales, you will need to provide each customer with a current Invoice. You will also need to send them a Statement if the balance is not paid within the first 30 days. You will also need to send a Past Due Statement if the balance becomes overdue. Finally, a form is provided to record instances when a customer is given credit for a returned item. You will need to provide 2 copies of each of these forms: one for your records and one for the customer.

Invoices

The invoice is your key credit sales document. To prepare and track invoices, follow these directions:

① Make a number of copies of the invoice form. You can insert your business card in the upper left corner before copying. Number each form consecutively. Make a copy of the form when the form is sent out to the customer using either carbon paper or a copy machine.

② For each order, fill in the following information:
   * Date,
   * The name and address of who will be billed for the order,
   * The name and address where the order will be shipped,
   * The item numbers of the products or services sold,
   * The quantity ordered,
   * The description of the item,
   * The per unit price of the item,
   * The total amount billed (quantity times per unit price).

③ Sub-total all of the items where shown. Add any sales taxes and shipping costs and total the Balance.

④ Record the pertinent information from the Invoice on the appropriate Daily, Weekly, or Monthly Credit Sales Record sheet.

⑤ Record the pertinent information from the Invoice on the appropriate Daily, Weekly, or Monthly Income Record sheet.

⑥ Send one copy of the Invoice to the customer with the order and file the other copy in a file for your invoices.

INVOICE

Date:

Invoice #:

Bill To:

Ship To:

Item #	Quantity	Description	Price		Amount	

Sub-total

Tax

Shipping

BALANCE

Statements and Past Due Statements

Statements are used to send your credit customers a notice of the amount which is currently due. Statements are generally sent at 30 day intervals, beginning either 30 days after the invoice is sent or at the beginning of the next month or the next cycle for sending statements. Follow these instructions for using your statements:

① You should decide on a statement billing cycle. Generally, this is a specific date each month (for example: the 1st, or 10th, or 15th of each month).

② Make a copy of the Statement form using your business card in the upper left corner. Fill in the date and the account name and address.

③ In the body of the form, enter information from any Invoice which is still unpaid as of the date you are completing the statement. You should enter the following items for each unpaid Invoice:
  • The date of the invoice,
  • A description (including Invoice number) of the invoice,
  • Any payments received since the last statement or since the sale,
  • The amount still owed on that invoice.

④ When all of the invoice information for all of the customer's invoices has been entered, total the Amounts column and enter under Balance.

⑤ The information on the Statement can then be used to enter the information on your Credit Sales Aging Report.

⑥ The Past Due Statement is simply a version of the basic Statement which includes a notice that the account is past due. This Past Due Statement should be sent when the account becomes overdue. Fill it out in the same manner used for Statements.

STATEMENT

Date:

Account:

Date	Description	Payment		Amount	

Please Pay This BALANCE

PAST DUE

Date:
Account:

This Account is now Past Due. Please pay upon receipt to avoid collection costs.

Date	Description	Payment		Amount	

Please Pay This BALANCE

Credit Memo

The final form for tracking your business income is the Credit Memo. This form is used to provide you and your customer with a written record of any credit given for goods which have been returned by the customer. You will need to set a policy regarding when such credit will be given, whether limited to a certain time period after the sale, or for defects, or other limitations. To use the Credit Memo, follow these instructions:

① Make copies of the Credit Memo using your business card in the upper left corner. You will need to make two copies of the Credit Memo when filled in: one for your records and one for your customer to keep.

② Fill in the date, the number of the original invoice, and the customer's name and address.

③ Fill in the following information in the body of the Credit Memo:
  • Item number of item to be returned,
  • Quantity of items returned,
  • Description of item returned,
  • Unit price of item returned,
  • Total amount of credit (quantity times unit price).

④ Subtotal the credit for all items. Add any appropriate sales tax credit and total the amount under Credit. This is the amount which will be credited or refunded to the customer.

⑤ In the lower left box, indicate the reason for the return, any necessary approval, and the date of the approval.

⑥ Handle the Credit Memo like a negative Invoice. Record the amount of credit as a negative on the appropriate Daily or Weekly Income Record sheet.

⑦ Record the pertinent information from the Credit Memo as a negative amount on the appropriate Daily, Weekly, or Monthly Credit Sales Record sheet, if the Credit Memo applies to a previous sale on credit which was recorded on a Credit Sales Record.

CREDIT MEMO

Date:

Order #:

Credit To:

GOODS RETURNED

Item #	Quantity	Description	Price		Amount	

Reason for return:		**Sub-total**	
Approved by:		**Tax**	
Date:		**CREDIT**	

133

Business Income Checklist

❑ Track your cash handling.

❑ On a daily or weekly basis, prepare a Cash Report.

❑ As required, make any appropriate deposits of cash and checks to your Business Bank Account.

❑ Record any deposits in your Check Register.

❑ On a monthly basis, prepare a Monthly Cash Report Summary.

❑ Track your income.

❑ On a daily or weekly basis, record all non-taxable and taxable income taken in, and sales tax proceeds on an appropriate Income Record sheet.

❑ On a monthly basis, transfer information from your Income Records to your Monthly and Annual Income Summaries.

❑ Track your credit sales.

❑ For every sale on credit, prepare an Invoice and record the appropriate information on a Daily, Weekly, Monthly Credit Sales Record sheet and an appropriate Income Record sheet.

❑ On a monthly basis, prepare a Credit Sales Aging Report using the information from your Credit Sales Records and Statements.

❑ On a monthly basis, prepare Statements and Past Due Statements.

❑ As needed, prepare Credit Memos and record the information on the appropriate Income Record and Credit Sales Record, if applicable.

Chapter 9

Tracking Payroll

One of the most difficult and complex accounting functions that small businesses face is their payroll. Because of the various state and federal taxes which must be applied and because of the myriad government forms which must be prepared, the handling of a business payroll often causes accounting nightmares. Even if there is only one employee, there is a potential for problems.

First, lets examine the basics. If your business is a sole proprietorship and you are the only one who works in the business, there is no need for a formal payroll system. You may pay yourself on a periodic schedule, but these payments are not considered deductions for the business. They are simply draws and no taxes are withheld. You will need to file and pay estimated taxes as an individual on the amount of money that you expect your business to net each year. These payments are made quarterly and are handled on IRS Form 1040-ES: *Estimated Tax for Individuals*. This form is found in Chapter 14. You will also be required to pay a self-employment tax to the federal government. This is equivalent to a payroll deduction for Social Security and Medicare taxes. This is handled with IRS Schedule SE: *Self-Employment Tax* and is filed with your annual personal income taxes. This form is also found in Chapter 14.

If you operate as a partnership and there are no employees, the same rules apply. The partnership net income will be passed through to you as a partner and you will be liable for individual income taxes on your share. Any draws which you take against the partnership will not be considered business deductions for the business. If your business is a corporation, all pay must be handled as payroll, even if you are the only employee. The corporation is a separate entity and the corporation itself will be the employer. You and any other people which you hire will be the employees. Follow the instructions for business payroll explained later in this chapter.

If you operate as a sole-proprietorship or partnership and you will have employees, you must also follow the entire business payroll details which are explained in this chapter. Business payroll entails a great deal of paperwork and has numerous government tax filing deadlines. You will be required to make payroll tax deposits, file various quarterly payroll tax returns, and make additional end-of-the-year reports.

Initially, if you have any employees, you must take certain steps to set up your payroll and official status as an employer. The following information contains only the instructions for meeting federal requirements. Please check with your particular state and local governments for information regarding any additional payroll tax, state unemployment insurance, or worker's compensation requirements. The requirements below will apply to any business which decides to become an employer, whether it is a sole proprietorship, partnership, or S or C corporation.

Setting Up Your Payroll

① The first step in becoming an employer is to file IRS Form SS-4: *Application for Employer Identification Number* (FEIN). This will officially register your business with the federal government as an employer. This form and instructions are contained in Chapter 14.

② Next, each employee must fill in an IRS Form W-4: *Employee's Withholding Allowance Certificate*. This will provide you with the necessary information regarding withholding allowances to enable you to prepare your payroll.

③ You must then determine the gross salary or wage which each employee will earn. For each employee, complete a Payroll Record and prepare a Quarterly Payroll Time Sheet as explained later in this chapter.

④ You will then need to consult the tables in IRS Circular E: *Employer's Tax Guide*. From the tables in this publication, you will be able to determine the proper deductions for each employee for each pay period. If your employees are paid on an hourly basis and the number of hours worked are different each pay period, you will have to perform these calculation for each pay period.

⑤ Before you pay your employee, you should open a separate business bank account for handling your business payroll tax deductions and payments. This will allow you to immediately deposit all taxes due into this separate account and help prevent the lack of sufficient money available when the taxes are due.

⑥ Next you will pay your employee and record the deduction information on the employee's Payroll Record.

⑦ When you have completed paying all of your employees for the pay period, you will write a separate check for the total amount of all of your employee's deductions and for the total amount of any employer's share of taxes. You will then deposit this check into your business Payroll Tax Bank Account, which you set up in Item #5 above.

⑧ At the end of every month, you will need to transfer the information regarding employee deductions to your Payroll Depository Report and Annual Payroll Summary. A copy of these forms are included later in this chapter. You will then also calculate your employer share of Social Security and Medicare taxes. Each month (or quarterly if your tax liability is under $500.00 per quarter), you will need to deposit the correct amount of taxes due with the federal government. This is done either by making a monthly payment for the taxes due to your bank with a Tax Deposit Coupon (IRS form 8109) or by making the payment on a quarterly basis when you file IRS Form 941: *Employer's Quarterly Federal Tax Return*. A copy of this form is contained in Chapter 14.

⑨ On a quarterly or annual basis, you will also need to make a tax payment for Federal Unemployment Tax, using IRS Form 940 or IRS Form 940-EZ: *Employer's Annual Federal Unemployment (FUTA) Tax Return*. This tax is solely the responsibility of the employer and is not deducted from the employee's pay. Also on a quarterly basis, you will need to file IRS 941: *Employer's Quarterly Federal Tax Return*. If you have made monthly deposits of your taxes due, there will be no quarterly taxes to pay.

⑩   Finally, to complete your payroll, at the end of the year you must do the following:

  • Prepare IRS W-2 Forms (*Wage and Tax Statement*) for each employee,
  • File IRS Form W-3: *Transmittal of Wage and Tax Statements*.

Remember that your state and local tax authorities will generally have additional requirements and taxes which will need to be paid. In many jurisdictions, these requirements are tailored after the federal requirements and the procedures and due dates are similar.

Quarterly Payroll Time Sheet

On the following page is a Quarterly Payroll Time Sheet. If your employees are paid an hourly wage, you will prepare a sheet like this for each employee for each quarter during the year. On this sheet you will keep track of the following information:

  • Number of hours worked (daily, weekly, and quarterly),
  • Number of regular and overtime hours worked.

The information from this Payroll Time Sheet will be transferred to your individual Employee Payroll Record in order to calculate the employee's paycheck amounts. This is explained following the Payroll Time Sheet form.

QUARTERLY PAYROLL TIME SHEET

Employee:

Week of	Sun	Mon	Tue	Wed	Thu	Fri	Sat	Reg	OT	Total
Quarterly total										

Employee Payroll Record

You will use this form to track each employee's payroll information.

① For each employee, fill in the following information at the top of the form:
- Name and address of employee,
- Employee's Social Security number,
- Number of exemptions claimed by employee on Form W-4,
- Regular and Overtime wage rate,
- Pay period (ie. weekly, biweekly, monthly etc.).

② For each pay period, fill in the number of regular and overtime hours worked from the Employee's Quarterly Time Sheet. Multiply this amount times the employee's wage rate to determine the Gross pay. (For example: 40 hours at the regular wage of $8.00/hour = $320.00; plus 5 hours at the overtime wage rate of $12.00/hour = $60.00. Gross pay for the period is $320.00 + $60.00 = $380.00).

③ Determine the federal withholding tax deduction for the pay amount by consulting the withholding tax tables in IRS Circular E: *Employer's Tax Guide*. Enter this figure on the form. (For example: in 1995 for a single person with no dependents, claiming only one exemption, and paid weekly, the withholding tax for $380.00 would be $42.00).

④ Determine the employee's share of Social Security and Medicare deductions. As of 1995, the employee's Social Security share rate was 6.2% and the employee's Medicare share rate was 1.45%. Multiply these rates times the employees gross wages and enter in the appropriate place. (For example: for $380.00, the Social Security deduction would be $380.00 X .062 = $23.56 and the Medicare deduction would be $380.00 X .0145 = $5.51).

⑤ Determine any state or local taxes and enter in the appropriate column.

⑥ Subtract all of the deductions from the employee's gross wages to determine the employee's net pay. Enter this figure in the final column and prepare the employee's pay check using the deduction information from this sheet. Also prepare a check to your Payroll Tax Bank Account for a total of the federal withholding amount and 2 X the Social Security and Medicare amounts. This includes your employer share of these taxes. The employer's share of Social Security and Medicare taxes is equal to the employee's share.

PAYROLL RECORD

Employee Name:	Social Security #:
Address:	Number of Exemptions:
	Rate of Pay: Overtime:
	Pay Period:

Date	Check#	Period	Hours	OT	Gross	Fed.	SS	MC	State	Net
Period Totals										

Payroll Depository Record

You will be required to deposit taxes with the IRS on a monthly or quarterly basis (unless your total employment taxes totaled over $50,000.00 for the previous year, in which case you should obviously consult an accountant). If your employment taxes total less than $500.00 per quarter, you may pay your payroll tax liability when you quarterly file your Federal Form 941: *Employer's Quarterly Tax Return*. If your payroll tax liability is over $500.00 per quarter, you must deposit your payroll taxes on a monthly basis with a bank using a *Federal Tax Deposit Coupon* (IRS Form 8109). Copies of these two federal forms are contained in Chapter 14. To track your payroll tax liability, use the Payroll Depository Record following these instructions:

① On a monthly basis, total each column on all of your Employee Payroll Records. This will give you a figure for each employee's federal withholding tax, Social Security tax, and Medicare taxes for the month.

② Total all of the federal withholding taxes for all employees for the month and enter this figure in the appropriate column on the Payroll Depository Record.

③ Total all of Social Security and Medicare taxes for all of your employees for the entire month and enter this figure in the appropriate columns on the Payroll Depository Record. Note that SS/EE refers to Social Security/Employee's Share and that MC/EE refers to Medicare/Employee's Share.

④ Enter identical amounts in the SS/ER and MC/ER columns as you have entered in the SS/EE and MC/EE columns. The employer share of Social Security and Medicare is the same as the employee's share, but is not deducted from the employee's pay.

⑤ Total all of the deductions for the month. This is the amount of your total monthly federal payroll tax liability. If necessary, write a check to your local bank for this amount and deposit it using a *Federal Tax Deposit Coupon* (Form 8109).

⑥ If you must only file quarterly, total all three of your monthly amounts on a quarterly basis and pay this amount when you file your IRS Form 941: *Employer's Quarterly Federal Tax Return*. On a yearly basis, total all of the quarterly columns to arrive at your total annual federal payroll tax liability.

PAYROLL DEPOSITORY RECORD

Month	Fed W/H	SS/EE	SS/ER	MC/EE	MC/ER	Total
January						
February						
March						
1st Quarter						
1st Quarter Total Number of Employees:			**Total Wages Paid:**			
April						
May						
June						
2nd Quarter						
2nd Quarter Total Number of Employees:			**Total Wages Paid:**			
July						
August						
September						
3rd Quarter						
3rd Quarter Total Number of Employees:			**Total Wages Paid:**			
October						
November						
December						
4th Quarter						
4th Quarter Total Number of Employees:			**Total Wages Paid:**			
Yearly Total						
Yearly Total Number of Employees:			**Total Wages Paid:**			

Annual Payroll Summary

The final payroll form is used to total all of the payroll amounts for all employees on a monthly, quarterly, and annual basis. Much of the information on this form is similar to the information which you compiled for the Payroll Depository Record form. However, the purpose of this form is to provide you with a record of all of your payroll costs, including the payroll deduction costs. This form will be useful for both tax and planning purposes as you examine your business profitability on a quarterly and annual basis. Follow these directions to prepare this form:

① For each month, transfer the amounts for federal withholding from the Payroll Depository Record to this form.

② For each month, total the columns on your Payroll Depository form for SS/EE and SS/ER and also for MC/EE and MC/ER. You will then simply need to transfer the totals for Social Security and Medicare information to this form. Recall that SS refers to Social Security, MC refers to Medicare, EE refers to Employee, and ER refers to Employer.

③ For each month, total all of your employee's gross and net pay amounts from their individual Employee Payroll Records and transfer these totals to this form.

④ On a quarterly basis, total the columns to determine your quarterly payroll costs. Annually, total the quarterly amounts to determine your annual costs.

ANNUAL PAYROLL SUMMARY

	Gross	Fed.	SS	MC	State	Net
January						
February						
March						
1st Quarter Total						
April						
May						
June						
2nd Quarter Total						
July						
August						
September						
3rd Quarter Total						
October						
November						
December						
4th Quarter Total						
Yearly Total						

Payroll Checklist

❏ File IRS Form SS-4: *Application for Employer Identification Number* and obtain Federal Employer Identification Number.

❏ Obtain IRS Form W-4: *Employee's Withholding Allowance Certificate* for each employee.

❏ Set up Payroll Record and Quarterly Payroll Time sheet for each employee.

❏ Open separate business Payroll Tax Bank Account.

❏ Obtain IRS Circular E: *Employer's Tax Guide* and use tables to determine withholding tax amounts.

❏ Obtain information on any applicable state or local taxes.

❏ List withholding, Social Security, Medicare and any state or local deductions on employee's Payroll Record.

❏ Pay employees and deposit appropriate taxes in your Payroll Tax Bank Account.

❏ Fill in Payroll Depository Record and Annual Payroll Summary.

❏ Pay payroll taxes:

> ❏ Monthly using IRS Form 8109: *Federal Tax Deposit Coupon*, if your payroll tax liability is over $500 per quarter.

> ❏ Quarterly using IRS Form 941: *Employer's Quarterly Federal Tax Return*, if your payroll tax liability is under $500 per quarter.

> ❏ Annually, file IRS Form 940 or 940-EZ: *Employer's Annual Federal Unemployment (FUTA) Tax Return*.

❏ Annually, prepare and file IRS W-2 Forms: *Wage and Tax Statement* for each employee, and IRS Form W-3: *Transmittal of Wage and Tax Statements*.

Chapter 10

Preparing a Profit and Loss Statement

A profit and loss statement is the key financial statement for your business which presents how your business is performing over a period of time. The profit and loss statement illuminates both the amounts of money which your business has spent on expenses and the amounts of money that your business has taken in over a specific period of time. You may choose to prepare a profit and loss statement monthly, quarterly, or annually, depending on your particular needs. You will, at a minimum, need to have an annual profit and loss statement in order to stream-line your tax return preparation.

A profit and loss statement, however, provides much more than assistance in easing your tax preparation burdens. It allows you to clearly view the performance of your business over a particular time period. As you begin to collect a series of profit and loss statements, you will be able to conduct various analyses of your business. For example, you will be able to compare monthly performances over a single year to determine which month was the best or worst for your business. Quarterly results will also be able to be contrasted. The comparison of several annual expense and revenue figures will allow you to judge the growth or shrinkage of your business over time. Numerous other comparisons are possible, depending on your particular business. How have sales been influenced by advertising expenses? Are production costs higher this quarter than last? Do seasons have an impact on sales? Are certain expenses becoming a burden on the business? The profit and loss statement is one of the key financial statements for the analysis of your business. Along with the balance sheet, which is discussed in Chapter 11, the profit and loss statement should become an integral part of both your short and long-range business planning.

This chapter will explain how to compile the information which you will need to prepare your profit and loss statements. All of the necessary information to prepare your profit and loss statement will be obtained from the financial records which you have prepared using this book. No other sources will be necessary to complete your profit and loss statements. Various methods to analyze the information on your profit and loss statements will be outlined in Chapter 12.

There are several types of profit and loss statements provided for your use. The first two are Monthly and Quarterly Short Profit and Loss Statements. These are very simple forms which provide few details beyond your total income and expenses and your net pre-tax profit for the month. These Short Profit and Loss Statements are used primarily to determine any estimated tax liability. Monthly, Quarterly, and Annual Profit and Loss Statements are also included for those who wish to periodically extract more details from their records.

Finally, an Estimated Profit and Loss Statement is provided to allow you to estimate your future profits and losses over any time period. The Estimated Profit and Loss Statement can serve a valuable business planning service by allowing you to project estimated changes to your business over various time periods and examine what the results may be. Projections of various business plans can be examined in detail and decisions can then be made on the basis of clear pictures of future scenarios. Your estimates for your business profits and losses can take into account industry changes, economic factors, and personal business decisions. Your estimates are primarily for internal business planning purposes, although it may be useful to use an Estimated Profit and Loss Statement to convey your future business plans to others. As a trial exercise, you should prepare an Estimated Profit and Loss Statement using your best estimates before you even begin business. You may wish to prepare such pre-business statements for monthly, quarterly, and annual time periods.

Short Profit and Loss Statements

The first two forms are Monthly and Quarterly Short Profit and Loss Statements. These forms are useful if the only information that you wish to obtain regarding your business on a monthly or quarterly basis is the bottom line: the net pre-tax profit. This figure may be necessary to determine your individual or corporate estimated federal income tax liability. The use of this form also gives you a quick method to gauge the basic performance of your business. However, if you wish to have a more detailed and comprehensive presentation of your business income and expenses, please use the various Profit and Loss Statements provided next. You will always need to prepare a full Annual Profit and Loss Statement. To prepare a Short Profit and Loss Statement, follow these instructions:

① Choose either the Monthly or Quarterly Short Profit and Loss Statement. The first figure which you will need will be your Gross Sales Income. This figure will come from your monthly or quarterly Total Sales figures on your Annual Income Summary sheet. If your business is a pure service business, put your income on the Service Income Total line. If your business income comes from part sales and part service, place the appropriate figures on the correct lines.

② Next, if your business sells items from inventory, you will need to calculate your monthly or quarterly Cost of Goods Sold. You may need to do a quick inventory count in order to have the necessary figures to make this computation. Fill in the Cost of Goods Sold figure on the Profit and Loss Statement. If your business is a pure service business, skip this line. Determine your Net Sales Income by subtracting your Cost of Goods Sold from your Gross Sales Income.

③ Calculate your Total Income for the period by adding your Net Sales Income, your Total Service Income, and any Miscellaneous Income.

④ To obtain your Expenses figure, consult your Annual Expense Summary sheet. Transfer either the monthly or quarterly total for all of your expenses to the Short Profit and Loss Statement. Add any Miscellaneous Expenses.

⑤ Simply subtract your Total Expense figure from your Total Income figure to determine your Pre-Tax Profit for the time period. You may use this figure for a quick check of your business profitability or to determine your estimated income tax liability for the appropriate period.

MONTHLY SHORT PROFIT AND LOSS STATEMENT

For the month of:

	INCOME		
Income	Gross Sales Income:		
	Less Cost of Goods Sold		
	Net Sales Income Total		
	Service Income Total		
	Miscellaneous Income Total		
	Total Income		
	EXPENSES		
Expenses	General Expenses		
	Miscellaneous Expenses		
	Total Expenses		

Pre-Tax Profit (Income less Expenses)	

QUARTERLY SHORT PROFIT AND LOSS STATEMENT

For the quarter of:			
INCOME			
Income	Gross Sales Income:		
	Less Cost of Goods Sold		
	Net Sales Income Total		
	Service Income Total		
	Miscellaneous Income Total		
	Total Income		
EXPENSES			
Expenses	General Expenses		
	Miscellaneous Expenses		
	Total Expenses		
Pre-Tax Profit (Income less Expenses)			

Profit and Loss Statements

You may use this more detailed Profit and Loss Statement to obtain a clearer picture of your business performance. At a minimum, each year, at year end, you will need to prepare the Annual Profit and Loss Statement to assist you in tax preparation. If you desire, you may prepare a Monthly or Quarterly version of this form to help with your business planning. To prepare this form:

① Choose either the Monthly, Quarterly, or Annual Profit and Loss Statement. The first figure which you will need will be your Gross Sales Income. This figure will come from your monthly, quarterly, or annual Total Sales figures on your Annual Income Summary sheet. If your business is a pure service business, put your income on the Service Income Total line. If your business income comes from part sales and part service, place the appropriate figures on the correct lines.

② Next, if your business sells items from inventory, you will need to calculate your monthly, quarterly, or annual Cost of Goods Sold. Monthly or quarterly, you may need to do a quick inventory count in order to have the necessary figures to make this computation. Annually, you will need to perform a thorough inventory. Fill in the Cost of Goods Sold figure on the Profit and Loss Statement. If your business is a pure service business, skip this line. Determine your Net Sales Income by subtracting your Cost of Goods Sold from your Gross Sales Income.

③ Calculate your Total Income for the period by adding your Net Sales Income and your Total Service Income and any Miscellaneous Income (for example: interest earned on a checking account).

④ To obtain your Expenses figure, consult your Annual Expense Summary sheet. Fill in the appropriate Expense Account categories on the Profit and Loss Statement. If you have a large number of categories, you may need to prepare a second sheet. Transfer either the monthly, quarterly, or annual totals for each of your separate expense accounts to the Profit and Loss Statement. Add in any Miscellaneous Expenses.

⑤ Total all of your expenses and subtract your Total Expense figure from your Total Income figure to determine your Pre-Tax Profit for the time period. To analyze your Profit and Loss Statement, see Chapter 12.

MONTHLY PROFIT AND LOSS STATEMENT

For the month of:

INCOME			
Income	Gross Sales Income:		
	Less Cost of Goods Sold		
	Net Sales Income Total		
	Service Income Total		
	Miscellaneous Income Total		
	Total Income		
EXPENSES			
Expenses	Account #		
	Account #		
	Account #		
	Account #		
	Account #		
	Account #		
	Account #		
	Account #		
	Account #		
	Account #		
	Account #		
	Account #		
	Account #		
	General Expenses Total		
	Miscellaneous Expenses		
	Total Expenses		

Pre-Tax Profit (Income less Expenses)	

QUARTERLY PROFIT AND LOSS STATEMENT

For the quarter of:

INCOME			
Income	Gross Sales Income:		
	Less Cost of Goods Sold		
	Net Sales Income Total		
	Service Income Total		
	Miscellaneous Income Total		
	Total Income		

EXPENSES			
Expenses	Account #		
	Account #		
	Account #		
	Account #		
	Account #		
	Account #		
	Account #		
	Account #		
	Account #		
	Account #		
	Account #		
	Account #		
	Account #		
	General Expenses Total		
	Miscellaneous Expenses		
	Total Expenses		

Pre-Tax Profit (Income less Expenses)	

154

ANNUAL PROFIT AND LOSS STATEMENT

For the year of:

INCOME			
Income	Gross Sales Income:		
	Less Cost of Goods Sold		
	Net Sales Income Total		
	Service Income Total		
	Miscellaneous Income Total		
	Total Income		

EXPENSES			
Expenses	Account #		
	Account #		
	Account #		
	Account #		
	Account #		
	Account #		
	Account #		
	Account #		
	Account #		
	Account #		
	Account #		
	Account #		
	Account #		
	General Expenses Total		
	Miscellaneous Expenses		
	Total Expenses		

Pre-Tax Profit (Income less Expenses)	

155

Estimated Profit and Loss Statement

The Estimated Profit and Loss Statement differs from the other type of profit and loss statements in that the figures used are projections which you will estimate based on expected business income and expenses for a time period in the future. The value of this type of financial planning tool is to allow you to see how various scenarios will affect your business. You may prepare this form as either a monthly, quarterly, or annual projection. To prepare this form, do the following:

① The first figure which you will need will be your Gross Sales Income. Using either past Profit and Loss Statements or your Total Income figures on your Annual Income Summary sheet and future estimates of income, fill in this amount. If your business is a pure service business, put your estimated income on the Service Income Total line. If your business income comes from part sales and part service, place the appropriate figures on the correct lines.

② Next, if your business sells items from inventory, you will need to calculate your estimated Cost of Goods Sold. In order to have the necessary figures to make this computation, you will need to prepare a projection of your inventory costs and how many items you expect to sell. Fill in the Cost of Goods Sold figure on the Profit and Loss Statement. If your business is a pure service business, skip this line. Determine your Estimated Net Sales Income by subtracting your Cost of Goods Sold from your Gross Sales Income.

③ Calculate your Estimated Total Income for the period by adding your Net Sales Income and your Total Service Income and any estimated Miscellaneous Income (for example: interest earned on a checking account).

④ Fill in the appropriate Expense Account categories on the Estimated Profit and Loss Statement. If you have a large number of categories, you may need to prepare a second sheet. To obtain your Estimated General Expenses figure, consult your Annual Expense Summary sheet or prior Profit and Loss Statements. Based on your future projections, fill in the totals for each of your separate expense accounts. Add in any estimated Miscellaneous Expenses.

⑤ Total all of your expenses and subtract your Total Estimated Expense figure from your Total Estimated Income figure to determine your Estimated Pre-Tax Profit for the time period.

ESTIMATED PROFIT AND LOSS STATEMENT

For the period of:

	ESTIMATED INCOME		
Income	Estimated Gross Sales Income:		
	Less Estim. Cost of Goods Sold		
	Estimated Net Sales Income Total		
	Estimated Service Income Total		
	Estimated Miscellaneous Income Total		
	Estimated Total Income		
	ESTIMATED EXPENSES		
Expenses	Account #		
	Account #		
	Account #		
	Account #		
	Account #		
	Account #		
	Account #		
	Account #		
	Account #		
	Account #		
	Account #		
	Account #		
	Account #		
	Estimated General Expenses Total		
	Estimated Miscellaneous Expenses		
	Estimated Total Expenses		

Estimated Pre-Tax Profit (Income less Expenses)	

Profit and Loss Statement Checklist

❑ If you only need basic pre-tax profit information in order to determine your individual or corporate estimated tax liability, prepare a Short Profit and Loss Statement.

> ❑ Fill in your Gross Sales Income from your Annual Income Summary.

> ❑ Fill in Cost of Goods Sold and calculate Net Sales Income.

> ❑ Fill in any Service and Miscellaneous Income and calculate Total Income for the period.

> ❑ Fill in any Miscellaneous Income and calculate Total Expenses for the period.

> ❑ Calculate pre-tax profit for the time period.

❑ If you need more detailed information for business planning purposes, prepare a full Monthly or Quarterly Profit and Loss Statement. Every business should prepare a full Annual Profit and Loss Statement, at a minimum. Prepare an Estimated Profit and Loss Statement, if desired.

> ❑ Fill in your Gross Sales Income from your Annual Income Summary.

> ❑ Fill in Cost of Goods Sold and calculate Net Sales Income.

> ❑ Fill in any Service and Miscellaneous Income and calculate Total Income for the period.

> ❑ Fill in General Expenses information for each separate expense account from your Annual Expense Summary.

> ❑ Fill in any Miscellaneous Income and calculate Total Expenses for the period.

> ❑ Calculate pre-tax profit for the time period.

Special Instructions for Cash Method Accounting

The forms and instructions in this book are designed to be used primarily for accrual method accounting, as opposed to cash method. The accrual method of accounting records income when it is earned rather than when it is received and records expenses when they are incurred rather than when they are actually paid. In contrast, the cash method of accounting records income only when it is received and expenses only when they are actually paid. As explained in Chapter 1, businesses which have an inventory of any goods to be sold must keep their books using the accrual method. Only pure service businesses which do not offer any products for sale are eligible to use the cash method of accounting. If your business will likely ever offer any products for sale, you should elect to use the accrual method of accounting. Once a method has been chosen, you will need written IRS approval to switch to another method. All of the forms in this book will still be able to be used for those businesses who elect to use the cash method of accounting. Follow these minor alterations in how you handle your income and expenses:

① The major difference in accrual vs. cash accounting procedures regarding business expenses is that when using the cash method, unpaid expenses are not deductible as business expenses. Thus, all of your accounting procedures will be identical for cash and accrual except the treatment of your Accounts Payable. Recall that you record your unpaid bills as a current liability on an Accounts Payable Record. As you total your expenses at the end of the year, the unpaid bills and expenses which are recorded as accounts payable are simply not counted as current expenses for cash-method businesses. Only those business expenses which have actually been paid by the end of the year are deductible as business expenses for the year. The accounts payable figures are not used.

② The difference between cash and accrual method accounting in the area of income concerns the handling of your credit sales. Recall that you record all of your sales as income on your periodic Income Records. This includes both cash and credit sales. You also record your credit sales on your Credit Sales Records. For cash method businesses, you will simply not record any of your credit sales on your Income Records until they are actually paid. You will continue to record your credit sales as explained in Chapter 8. However, at tax time, you will not count any of your unpaid credit sales as business income. Only those sales for which you have actually taken in income will be counted. You may wish to re-title your Income Record sheets as Cash Income Records.

Your Credit Sales Records will also remain the same, but you will not transfer any of the credit sales to your (Cash) Income Records until they have been paid.

③ Refunds are handled a little differently for cash-method businesses. If the sale was for cash or was a credit sale which has been paid, record any refund as a negative sale. List the returned amount on your Income Record as a negative amount. This is the same as for accrual-method businesses. However, if the sale for which a refund is being made was a credit sale which has not yet been paid, simply list the refund as a negative credit sale. Do not make any entry on your Income Record. This is because since you have not recorded the income from the original sale, you may not record the refund as a deduction against the income.

④ Bad debts are also handled slightly differently for cash-method companies. Customers who were billed for a service, but who have not paid and whose accounts are deemed uncollectible are not "bad debts" for cash method businesses. The reason is that since the income from the account was never included as business income (remember: cash method only counts income when actually received), you can't count a bad debt deduction against that income. You simply never record the income as received. If you have received a check for a payment and included that payment as income, and later that check is returned as unpaid, you may then deduct that amount as a bad debt. The reasoning is the same: you included the check as income, thus you are entitled to a deduction to remove that income from your books because of the bounced check.

⑤ When you prepare your Profit and Loss Statements, cash-method businesses will not record any accounts payable (from their Accounts Payable Records) as expenses. Cash-method companies will also not use the accounts receivable figures (from their Credit Sales Records) to determine their current income. Expenses for a particular period will be limited to those expenses which have actually been paid (as shown on your Check Register and Petty Cash Register). Income for a particular period will be limited to that income which has actually been taken in (as shown on your Income Record and not your Credit Sales Record). Using these figures will give you an accurate Profit and Loss Statement for the period in question.

With these few simple alterations, you may use the forms and instructions in this book for cash-method accounting.

Chapter 11

Preparing a Balance Sheet

A profit and loss statement provides a view of business operations over a particular period of time. It allows a look at the income and expenses and profit or losses of the business during the time period. In contrast, a Balance Sheet is designed to be a look at the financial position of a company on a specific date. It shows what the business owns and owes on a fixed date. Its purpose is to depict the financial strength of a company as shown by its assets and liabilities. Recall that the assets - liabilities = equity (or net worth). Essentially, the Balance Sheet shows what the company would be worth if all of the assets were sold and all of the liabilities were paid off. A value is placed on each asset and each liability. These figures are then balanced by adjusting the value of the owner's equity figure in the equation.

In order to prepare a Balance Sheet for your business, you will need to update your Asset and Liability Accounts. Once you have updated these account balances, it will be a simple matter of transferring the balances to your Balance Sheet and performing the necessary calculations. On the next page, you will find the instructions for preparing Balance Sheets. Chapter 12 provides information on analyzing your Balance Sheets.

Balance Sheets

Your Balance Sheet will total your current and fixed assets and your current and long-term liabilities. You may choose to prepare a Balance Sheet monthly, quarterly, or annually. Forms for each time period are included. You will, at a minimum, need to prepare a Balance Sheet at year-end. For corporations and partnerships, this is a requirement. For sole-proprietorships, this is highly recommended. Obtain all of the figures you need on the same date after updating all of your accounts.

① Your Current Assets consist of the following items. Where to obtain the correct figure for the asset amount is shown after each item:
- Cash in Bank (from your Check Register Balance),
- Cash on Hand (from your Petty Cash Register and your Monthly Cash Report),
- Accounts Receivable (from your Credit Sales Aging Reports),
- Inventory (from a Physical Inventory Report annually or from a review of your Perpetual or Periodic Inventory monthly or quarterly),
- Pre-paid expense (These may be rent, insurance, pre-paid supplies, or similar items which have been paid for prior to their actual use. You will have to check through your Monthly Expense Summary to determine which items may be considered pre-paid expenses).

② Total all of your Current Assets on your Balance Sheet.

③ Your Fixed Assets consist of the following items. Where to obtain the correct figure for the asset amount is shown after each item:
- Equipment (from your Fixed Asset Account sheets. You will need to update these sheets to include any equipment purchased since your last update. Update from your Monthly Expense Record sheets);
- Autos and Trucks (from your Fixed Asset Account sheets. You will need to update these sheets to include any vehicles purchased since your last update. Update from your Monthly Expense Record sheets);
- Buildings (from your Fixed Asset Account sheets. You will need to update these sheets to include any buildings purchased since your last update. Update from your Monthly Expense Record sheets).

④ Total your Fixed Assets (except land) on your Balance Sheet. Now, returning to your Fixed Asset sheets, total all of the depreciation which you have previously deducted for all of your fixed assets (except land). Include in this figure any business deductions which you have taken for Section 179 write-offs of business equipment. Enter this total depreciation figure under Depreciation and subtract this figure from the total Fixed Assets (except land) figure.

⑤ Now, enter the value for any land which your business owns. Recall that land may not be depreciated. Add Fixed Asset amount less Depreciation and the value of the land. This is your total Fixed Asset value.

⑥ Add any Miscellaneous Assets not yet included. These may consist of stocks, bonds, or other business investments. Total your Current, Fixed, and Miscellaneous Assets to arrive at your total Assets figure.

⑦ Your Current Liabilities consist of the following items. Where to obtain the correct figure for the liability amount is shown after each item:
   * Accounts Payable (from your Accounts Payable Record sheets).
   * Taxes Payable (from two sources: your sales taxes payable figure will come from your Monthly Income Summary sheets and your payroll taxes payable will come from the Check Register of your special payroll tax bank account. Include any amounts which have been collected but not yet paid to the state or federal government.
   * Miscellaneous Current Liabilities (include here the principal due on any short-term notes payable. Also include any interest on credit purchases, notes, or loans which has accrued but not been paid. Also list the current amounts due on any long-term liabilities. Finally, list any payroll which has accrued but not yet been paid).

⑧ Your Long-Term Liabilities consist of the principal of any long-term note, loan, or mortgage due. Any current amounts due should be listed as a Current Liability.

⑨ Total your Current and Long-Term Liabilities to arrive at a Total Liabilities Figure.

⑩ Subtract your Total Liabilities from your Total Assets to arrive at your Owner's Equity. For a sole proprietor, this figure represents the Net Worth of your business. For a partnership, this figure represents the value of the partner's original investments plus any earnings and less any partner draws. For a corporation, this figure represents the total of contributions by the owners or stockholders plus earnings after paying any dividends. Total liabilities and owner's equity will always equal Total Assets.

MONTHLY BALANCE SHEET

As of _____

	ASSETS		
Current Assets	Cash in Bank		
	Cash on Hand		
	Accounts Receivable		
	Inventory		
	Prepaid Expenses		
	Total Current Assets		
Fixed Assets	Equipment (cost)		
	Autos and Trucks (cost)		
	Buildings (cost)		
	Total		
	Less depreciation		
	Net Total		
	Add Land (cost)		
	Total Fixed Assets		
	Total Miscellaneous Assets		
	Total Assets		
	LIABILITIES		
Current Liabilities	Accounts Payable		
	Taxes Payable		
	Total Current Liabilities		
Fixed Liabilities	Loans Payable (long-term)		
	Total Fixed Liabilities		
	Total Liabilities		
Owner's Equity	Net Worth or Capital Surplus + Stock		

QUARTERLY BALANCE SHEET

As of			
ASSETS			
Current Assets	Cash in Bank		
	Cash on Hand		
	Accounts Receivable		
	Inventory		
	Prepaid Expenses		
	Total Current Assets		
Fixed Assets	Equipment (cost)		
	Autos and Trucks (cost)		
	Buildings (cost)		
	Total		
	Less depreciation		
	Net Total		
	Add Land (cost)		
	Total Fixed Assets		
	Total Miscellaneous Assets		
	Total Assets		
LIABILITIES			
Current Liabilities	Accounts Payable		
	Taxes Payable		
	Total Current Liabilities		
Fixed Liabilities	Loans Payable (long-term)		
	Total Fixed Liabilities		
	Total Liabilities		
Owner's Equity	Net Worth or Capital Surplus + Stock		

ANNUAL BALANCE SHEET

As of

	ASSETS		
Current Assets	Cash in Bank		
	Cash on Hand		
	Accounts Receivable		
	Inventory		
	Prepaid Expenses		
	Total Current Assets		
Fixed Assets	Equipment (cost)		
	Autos and Trucks (cost)		
	Buildings (cost)		
	Total		
	Less depreciation		
	Net Total		
	Add Land (cost)		
	Total Fixed Assets		
	Total Miscellaneous Assets		
	Total Assets		
	LIABILITIES		
Current Liabilities	Accounts Payable		
	Taxes Payable		
	Total Current Liabilities		
Fixed Liabilities	Loans Payable (long-term)		
	Total Fixed Liabilities		
	Total Liabilities		
Owner's Equity	Net Worth or Capital Surplus + Stock		

Balance Sheet Checklist

❐ Decide on frequency for Balance Sheet preparation.

❐ Update your Current Asset accounts and transfer to Balance Sheet.

> ❐ Update your Cash in Bank (from Check Register).

> ❐ Update your Cash on Hand (Petty Cash Register and Monthly Cash Report).

> ❐ Update your Accounts Receivable (from Credit Sales Aging Report).

> ❐ Update your Inventory (from Physical, Perpetual, or Periodic Inventory report).

> ❐ Include any pre-paid expenses.

❐ Update Fixed Asset accounts and transfer to Balance Sheet.

> ❐ Enter any depreciation taken on Fixed Assets.

> ❐ Enter the value of any land owned by business.

❐ Update Current Liabilities and transfer to Balance Sheet.

> ❐ Update Accounts Payable (from Accounts Payable Record Sheets).

> ❐ Update Taxes Payable (from Monthly Payroll Tax Summary, Monthly Income Summary, or Check Register).

❐ Update Fixed Liabilities and transfer to Balance Sheet.

❐ Total all figures and calculate Owner's Equity.

Chapter 12

Analyzing the Financial Statements

Once you have prepared your Profit and Loss Statements and your Balance Sheets, you still need to know how to analyze them. You need to know how to effectively use the information they contain to more clearly understand your business. In this chapter, you will learn the use of simple ratio and proportion analysis in order to derive more meaning from your financial records. Looking at your assets, liabilities, income and expenses in different ways will allow you to exercise more control over your business finances.

Ratio analysis sounds intimidating. It isn't. Ratios are simply fractions used as a manner of comparison. We use them everyday to make different facts easier to understand. When you use 10 gallons of gas to drive 150 miles in your car, it is easier to explain if you say that your car gets 15 miles per gallon. 15 MPG is a ratio. It is derived from the simple fraction of 150/10 or 150 divided by 10. The answer of 15 is the ratio of miles driven to gas consumed or, simply put, miles per gallon. If you were to check your miles per gallon with every tankful of gasoline, you would have an effective method to check your car's performance. You would be performing a *ratio analysis* of your car's fuel consumption.

Ratios measure relationships between particular numbers. This manner of analyzing your business will allow to look at your operations in various manners. You will simply be using the figures on your two central financial records (your Profit and Loss Statement and your Balance Sheet). By periodically plugging figures from those two records into certain simple ratio equations, you will be able to track certain aspects of your business.

Let's look at a simple financial ratio: a comparison of the amount of debt of a business versus the amount of the net worth of a business. We will use the figures from our original business example: Smith's Gourmet Foods. Recall that in our first look at Smith's business, it had a net worth of $1,670.00 and Smith owed a total of $400.00 in total debt. The ratio equation that we will use is simply:

$$\text{Debt Ratio} = \text{Debt/Net Worth}$$

Plugging our financial figures into this equation, we get:

$$400/1670 = .2395 \text{ or about } 24\%.$$

This means that currently Smith's debt amounts to about 24% of her business net worth. This is a very stable situation. Smith could take these figures to a bank and, most likely, be able to borrow considerably more money to purchase additional equipment for expansion. If Smith tracks this particular ratio for several months or even years, she will be able to gain an understanding of how her debt and net worth are in proportion. If, for example, Smith chooses to take out another loan to buy additional equipment for $1,200.00, her total debt will increase by that amount and her net worth will stay the same. The new debt ratio would be:

$$1600/1670 = .958 \text{ or about } 96\%.$$

Smith's business debt is now fully 96% of its net worth. As long as she is able to bring in enough income to make timely payments on the loan for the new equipment, her business will still be financially sound. However, it would be unlikely that she would be given further loans for equipment unless she were able to decrease this percentage by either paying off a portion of the loan or increasing the business net worth in some way.

Simplified Small Business Accounting

Another way to use balance sheet figures to analyze a business is to look at the *current ratio*. This simply means how many times the current debts could be paid off with the current assets. Our equation for this is:

Current ratio = Current assets/Current debts

Again, for Smith's Gourmet Foods, we have the following figures:

Current ratio = $2,070.00/$400.00 = 5.175

Smith would be able to pay off her current debt about 5 times with her current assets. Her business is in a very sound cash position. A current ratio of 2 or more is considered adequate for most businesses: the ability to pay off current debts twice with current assets. If a business has a relatively unstable cash flow, however, it might be necessary to maintain a current ratio of more than 2.

Thus, based on our first two methods of analyzing the finances of our sample company, we have seen that it appears to be in sound financial shape. Its debt/net worth ratio is about 24% and its current ratio or ability to pay of current debts is a healthy 5.175.

We will look at 12 separate ways to use the figures from your Profit and Loss Statements and Balance Sheets to analyze your business. The first three methods will look at the profitability of your business: Net Profit Margin, Gross Profit Margin, and Return on Sales. The next six will examine the liquidity of your business or the ability of your business to meet its obligations: Current Ratio, Quick Ratio, Cash Turnover, and three separate Debt Ratios. The final three will look at the debt and investment aspects of your business: Collection Ratio, Investment Turnover, and Return on Investment. The meaning and use of each analysis method will be explained.

Each of these analysis methods consists of using figures from your Profit and Loss Statements or Balance Sheets in simple equations. Once you have performed the various analyses, you must then use the information which you have obtained to determine why the business trends which you have uncovered in your business have occurred. This will require an honest analysis of your business.

For each type of analysis, we will use the following figures from our sample company as examples:

Smith's Gourmet Foods
Profit and Loss Statement

Income:	1995	1996
Gross Sales:	$24,000.00	$30,000.00
Cost of Goods Sold:	$8,000.00	$16,000.00
Gross Profit:	$16,000.00	$14,000.00
Expenses:		
Advertising:	$1,200.00	$2,400.00
Bad Debt	$100.00	$400.00
Depreciation	$100.00	$200.00
Insurance	$200.00	$400.00
Interest	$150.00	$300.00
Repairs	$50.00	$150.00
Sales Tax	$1,200.00	$1,500.00
Supplies	$350.00	$700.00
Telephone	$400.00	$750.00
Wages	$4,000.00	$6,000.00
Total Expenses:	$7,750.00	$12,800.00
Net Profit before tax:	$8,250.00	$1,200.00

Smith's Gourmet Foods
Balance Sheet

Assets:	1995	1996
Current Assets:		
Cash	$100.00	$200.00
Accounts Receivable	$150.00	$450.00
Inventory	$350.00	$700.00
Total Current Assets:	$600.00	$1,350.00
Long-Term Assets:		
Equipment	$1,200.00	$2,400.00
Total Long-Term Assets:	$1,200.00	$2,400.00
Total Assets:	$1,800.00	$3,750.00
Liabilities:		
Current Liabilities:		
Notes Payable:	$100.00	$200.00
Accounts Payable:	$350.00	$1,000.00
Total Current Liabilities:	$450.00	$1,200.00
Long-Term Liabilities:		
Notes Payable:	$1,000.00	$2,000.00
Total Liabilities:	$1,450.00	$3,200.00
Net Worth:	$350.00	$550.00
Net Worth + Liabilities:	$1,800.00	$3,750.00

Net Profit Margin

The net profit margin that a business makes is determined by dividing its actual sales by its net profit figure without taking interest or income taxes into account. This figure will depend on earnings and expenses. By factoring out interest and taxes, you can use this figure to compare your business to other similar businesses without taking into account high debts or high income taxes. To perform this analysis, you will need to look at three figures from your Profit and Loss Statement:

- Gross Sales,
- Interest Expenses,
- Net Profit (before taxes).

The ratio that you will use is:

Net Profit - Interest/Gross Sales = Net Profit Margin
The higher the Net Profit Margin = the more profitable the business is.

To use the figures from our example, we would get:

$8,250.00 - $150.00/$24,000.00 = 33.75% for 1995
$1,200.00 - $300.00/$30,000.00 = 3% for 1996

For 1995, Smith made a 33.75% net profit on sales and in 1996, Smith's net profit margin dropped to 3%. This signals a danger sign for Smith. In 1996, although the amount of gross sales has gone up, the net profit has gone down. Smith must now carefully examine her business income and expenses to determine why this has happened.

Gross Profit Margin

The gross profit margin is an indication of the mark-up on goods that are sold to customers. It is only useful for businesses which sell goods from inventory. For this calculation, you will need the following figures from your Profit and Loss Statement:

- Gross Profit
- Gross Sales

The equation for gross profit margin is:

Gross Profit/Gross Sales = Gross Profit Margin
The higher the Gross Profit Margin the better for business.

Looking at our sample company, we see the following:

$16,000.00/$24,000.00 = 66.66% Gross Profit Margin for 1995
$14,000.00/$30,000.00 = 46.66% Gross Profit Margin for 1996

We can see that although the actual profit margin in 1996 is still relatively high at nearly 47%, it has fallen 20% in one year. This also signals Smith that something may be wrong. With this clue, we can examine the Profit and Loss Statements more closely. Looking at the Smith Profit and Loss Statement, we can see that the Cost of Goods Sold has doubled in one year (from $8,000.00 to $16,000.00), and yet Gross Sales have only increased 25% (from $24,000.00 to $30,000.00).

Smith must now attempt to determine what may have caused the cost of her goods sold to increase without a proportionate increase in sales income. Was food in inventory lost, stolen, or spoiled? Did her wholesale prices increase? Should she now increase her retail prices? This is where honest analysis of a business will come in. The use of financial ratios can give you insight into financial problems, but it will take your own knowledge of the business to determine how to solve the financial problems that may be uncovered.

Return on Sales Ratio

This ratio allows a business to determine how much net profit was derived from its gross sales. This ratio is very similar to the Net Profit Margin but it factors in all expenses, including interest. It provides an indication of whether your expenses are under control and also whether your business is generating enough income from sales to pay for its costs. The figures that you will need from your Profit and Loss Statement are:

- Gross Sales
- Net Profit before taxes

The equation for Return on Sales Ratio is:

Net Profit/Gross Sales = Return on Sales Ratio.
The higher the Return on Sales Ratio the better for business.

Plugging in our sample company's figures, we get:

$8,250.00/$24,000.00 = 34.375% for 1995
$1,200.00/$30,000.00 = 4% for 1996

We can see immediately that Smith has suffered a huge decrease in the rate of return on her sales, in fact an 800% drop. This signals a very serious problem for her business. Why? Although her gross sales are up in 1996 (from $24,000.00 to $30,000.00), her cost of goods sold are up even more (doubled from $8,000.00 to $16,000.00). In addition, her expenses have also nearly doubled (from $7,750.00 to $12,800.00). Thus, her expenses and goods costs are going up at a higher rate than her actual sales, leading to a precipitous drop in her net profit. She must either get her business expenses under control, increase her prices to account for higher cost of goods sold expenses, or find cheaper products to sell.

Current Ratio

The current ratio is the ability of a company to meet its short-term obligations. It measures how many times a company's current debt could be paid off by using its current assets. A general rule of thumb is that current assets should be about 2 times current debts. Too high a ratio man mean that too many assets are held in unproductive manners. Too low a ratio may mean that the business is too short on cash and may be unable to make timely payments to suppliers. The figures from your Balance Sheet which you will need are:

- Total Current Assets
- Total Current Liabilities

Current Assets/Current Liabilities = Current Ratio
Current Ratio should be around 2 on average.

Looking at our sample company, we see the following:

$600.00/$450.00 = 1.333 for 1995
$1,350.00/$1,200.00 = 1.125 for 1996

We can see that the Current Ratio for Smith's Gourmet Foods is falling slightly. A close examination shows that accounts payable for 1996 have nearly tripled. Although Current Assets have more than doubled , Current Liabilities have nearly tripled. If this trend continues, Smith will be in trouble.

We can also look at a similar ratio, termed a Quick Ratio. This is essentially a Current Ratio with inventory factored out of the equation. It should be held to under 1 to indicate a strong business.

Current Assets - Inventory/Current Debt = Quick Ratio

For Smith's Gourmet Foods, we see little change in the two-year period:

$600 - $350/$450 = .555 for 1995
$1,350 - $700/$1200 = .542 for 1996

175

Debt to Net Worth Ratio

This figure indicates the relationship between a business net worth and the debt which a business carries. It is an indication to banks and other creditors whether a business can handle additional debt. It is also a indication of business risk, in that a high debt to net worth ratio may indicate that the business is overly burdened by interest payments and hampered in its ability to borrow any additional funds which may be necessary. Too low a ratio, however, may indicate that a business is too conservative and could effectively borrow more funds to generate more profits. To calculate this ratio, use the following figures from your Balance Sheet:

- Total Liabilities
- Net Worth

The equation to use is as follows:

Total Debt/Net Worth = Total Debt Ratio
Over 1 indicates too much debt for net worth.

Using the figures for our sample company, we find that:

$1,450.00/350.00 = 4.14 Debt/Worth Ratio for 1995
$3,200.00/$550.00 = 5.82 Debt-Worth Ratio for 1996

Again, this calculation seems to indicate that Smith's Gourmet Foods may be in trouble financially. The 1995 Debt/Worth ratio is already to high and it increases in 1996. Smith's owes nearly 6 times as much as its Net Worth. Clearly, this company would not be a safe credit risk for new debt.

We could also look at the debt in terms of current and long-term liabilities by using similar equations:

Current Debt/Net Worth = Current Debt Ratio
Long-Term Debt/Net Worth = Long-Term Debt Ratio

Cash Turnover Ratio

The final liquidity ratio provides an indication of how often cash flow turns over to finance your sales. Your working cash is the amount of money which you need daily to operate your business: pay salaries, utilities, supplies, inventory, etc. If your cash supply is too tight this can restrict your ability to meet your current obligations. The figures you will need to make this calculation are:

- Current Assets
- Current Debt
- Gross Sales

The equation to determine your cash turnover is:

Gross Sales/Current Assets - Current Debt = Cash Turnover Ratio
Generally, your cash turnover should be between 4 and 7.

Lets look at Smith's Gourmet Foods figures:

$24,000/$600 - $450 = 160
$30,000/$1,350 - $1,200 = 200

We can easily see that Smith's Cash Turnover begins in 1995 at too high a rate and then increase in 1996. This indicates that the business operates on too little cash and may have a worsening ability to meet its obligations. It may soon be unable to pay its creditors, meet its salary obligations, or even buy additional inventory. There simply is not enough working capital in the form of cash available. Examining the Balance Sheet, we can see that Smith has let her available cash dwindle by not collecting her accounts receivable quickly enough and by not keeping up with her own bills (her accounts payable). This has led to her current cash poor position.

Collection Ratio

The collection ratio provides a clear indication of the average period of time that it takes to collect your accounts receivable or credit sales. The ratio shows the average number of days it takes for your business to get paid for credit sales. This figure should be near the point at which you declare an account overdue (for example: 30 days). Too long a period and you are overextending your credit and basically becoming a banker for your slow-paying customers. The figures you will need for this calculation are:

- Accounts Receivable
- Gross Sales

The equation for calculating your collection period success rate is:

Accounts Receivable X 365/Gross Sales = Average Collection Period
The period should be no more than 1.5 times your credit overdue period.

Let's see how Smith is doing in this regard:

$150 X 365/$24,000 = 2.28 days for 1995
$450 X 365/$30,000 = 5.475 for 1996

Although her overall collection period is very low, note that it more than doubled in one year. This is an indication that her customers are beginning to pay at a slower rate. If this continues, it may prove to be trouble for her, particularly in light of the other indications that her business is operating on a very tight cash flow. She may wish to exert more effort at getting prompt payment for her goods in order to keep her cash levels high enough to meet her obligations.

Investment Turnover Ratio

This figure indicates the ability of a business to use its assets to generate sales income. The ability to generate greater and greater sales from a stable asset base is a good indication of business health. If the ratio is going down, this may indicate that the growth of the business is not being met with a growth in sales proportionate to the investment in assets. The figures you will need for this calculation are:

- Gross Sales
- Long-Term Assets

The calculation is:

Gross Sales/Long-Term Assets = Investment Turnover Ratio
In general, the higher the ratio the stronger the business.

For Smith's Gourmet Foods, the figures look like this:

$24,000/$1,200 = 20 for 1995
$30,000/$2,400 = 12.5 for 1996

Again, we can see that Smith's financial position is weakening. Her ability to generate sales from her assets has fallen considerably in 1996. Despite having twice as many assets, she was only able to increase sales by 25%. If you couple this analysis with her increasing Cost of Goods Sold and expenses, you can readily see why her Net Profit has fallen from $8,250 in 1995 to only $1,200 in 1996. She was not able to translate her higher wage costs, increased equipment costs, and higher advertising into a proportionately higher sales income. If she hopes to continue as a viable business, she must get her expenses back in line with gross sales, generate more sales from her new equipment, rein in her Cost of Goods Sold, and, perhaps, increase her prices to bring in more income to her business.

Return on Investment

Our final financial ratio analysis tool is the return on investment ratio. This analysis provides a clear a indication of business profitability. It shows how much profit a business is able to generate in proportion to its net worth. This figure shows what level of actual return you are getting on the money which you have invested in your company. You should strive for a healthy return on your business investment or your business has little chance to grow. The figures you will need from both your Balance Sheet and Profit and Loss Statement are:

- ◆ Net Profit
- ◆ Net Worth

The calculation is:

Net Profit/Net Worth = Return on Investment
Your business should strive for at least a 12% return to be healthy.

Let's check on Smith's Gourmet Foods one final time:

$8,250/$350 = 2357% Return for 1995
$1,200/$550 = 218% Return for 1996

Although Smith has an extremely high return on her investment for both years, her return rate has fallen by 90% in one year. Also, it is clear that her high return rate stems from her extremely low actual Net Worth. Although she was able to generate a very high return for her low investment for both years, her rapidly falling profits and rising expenses are a clear indication of a business in trouble. She needs to use the information obtained from all of the ratios to carefully analyze what has gone wrong with her initially profitable business.

Ratio Comparison Chart

On the following page is a Ratio Comparison Chart for use in your business. It will allow you to compare key ratios over three time periods which you select (months, quarters, or years). By using this method of comparison you will be able to detect trends in your business, whether the trends involve profitability, liquidity, collections success, or general business prosperity.

To prepare your Ratio Comparison Chart, simply do the following:

① Decide which of the ratios will be most beneficial for your business to track.

② Determine over what time periods you will track the selected ratios.

③ Using the Comparison Chart, your Balance Sheets, and your Profit and Loss Statements, compute each selected ratio.

④ Repeat this for each time period.

⑤ Compare and contrast the business financial trends which become apparent in your Ratio Comparison Chart.

⑥ Using the information from the highlighted trends, carefully examine your Profit and Loss Statements and Balance Sheets to determine the business reasons behind the trends.

RATIO COMPARISON CHART

Ratio	Period	Period	Period
Net Profit Margin			
Gross Profit Margin			
Return on Sales			
Current Ratio			
Quick Ratio			
Total Debt/Net Worth			
Current Debt/Net Worth			
Long-Term Debt/Worth			
Cash Turnover Ratio			
Collection Ratio			
Investment Turnover			
Return on Investment			

Chapter 13

Mechanics and Schedules of Record-Keeping

Once you have read through this entire book, you should take the time to carefully analyze your business in light of its record-keeping needs. No two businesses will have identical financial record-keeping requirements. You must determine which financial facts and figures will be most important in the successful operation of your individual business. Keep in mind that as your business grows, your needs may change. In addition, as you become more familiar with your record-keeping, you may decide that you need additional methods of tracking certain aspects of your operations. You may decide that some of the information that you are collecting is unnecessary in your particular type of business. Don't be afraid to alter your record-keeping system as your business changes. Your system is only valuable to you if it fits your own needs.

Once you have attempted to analyze your record-keeping needs, you will need to actually set-up your financial record keeping system. The forms in this book are designed to be photo-copied and used in this system. The forms are not, however, designed to be torn out of this book (particularly if you are reading a library copy of this book!)

Setting Up Your Record-Keeping System

① Carefully go through this book and note which record-keeping forms you will need. A checklist of forms is provided at the end of this chapter. Your list may seem extensive. Many of the forms, however, may only be used once a year.

② Make a photo-copy of each of the necessary forms. Also make a photo-copy of each checklist that applies, and the Record-Keeping Schedule and specific Tax Schedule (see Chapter 14). If the form to be used is a monthly form, make 12 copies. If the form to be used is a quarterly form, make 4 copies. Make enough copies for one year's worth of records.

③ Purchase a three-ring binder and at least 15 tabbed dividers. Label the tabbed dividers in order as follows, deleting those items which do not apply to your particular business :
- Checklists and Schedules
- Business Chart of Accounts
- Check Register
- Petty Cash Register
- Assets
- Inventory
- Accounts Payable
- Liabilities
- Business Expenses
- Cash Reports
- Credit Sales
- Payroll
- Profit and Loss Statements
- Balance Sheets
- Ratio Comparison Charts

④ Three-hole punch all of the forms, schedules, and checklists. Place each form behind the appropriate divider in the binder. Label and fill in the preliminary information on the forms. Certain forms such as Invoices, Statements, and Past Due Statements will not be punched but will be kept in folders.

⑤ Now you are ready to begin filling in the forms. Beginning with your Business Chart of Accounts, follow the instructions in this book to initially prepare each form. Then follow the Schedule of Record-Keeping and Tax Schedule to keep up with your financial record- keeping tasks.

Financial Record-Keeping Schedules

Use these schedules of tasks to keep track of your schedule of record-keeping functions. Don't forget also to keep up with the Tax Schedule included in Chapter 14 for your particular type of business.

Daily Record-Keeping Tasks

- ☐ Record payments and deposits in Check Register.

- ☐ Record payments and additions in Petty Cash Register.

- ☐ Record any Inventory received.

- ☐ Prepare Daily Cash Report, if desired.

- ☐ Prepare Daily Income Report, if desired.

- ☐ Record any Invoices in Daily Credit Sales Record, if desired.

- ☐ Record Purchase Orders in Purchase Order Record.

- ☐ Record expenses in Daily Expense Record, if desired.

- ☐ Prepare and record any Credit Memos, if required.

- ☐ Fill in any Payroll time sheets.

Weekly Record-Keeping Tasks

❏ Prepare Weekly Cash Report, if desired.

❏ Prepare Weekly Income Report, if desired.

❏ Record any Invoices in Weekly Credit Sales Record, if desired.

❏ Record any accounts payable on your Accounts Payable Record and/or Individual Accounts Payable Record.

❏ Record expenses in Weekly Expense Record, if desired.

❏ Record travel expenses in Weekly Travel Expense Record, if desired.

❏ Record auto expenses in Weekly Auto Expense Record, if desired.

❏ Prepare payroll, if necessary.

❏ Make proper payroll deposits, if necessary.

Monthly Record-Keeping Tasks

❏ Reconcile your Check Register against your Bank Statement.

❏ Transfer the information from your Check Register and Petty Cash Register to your Expense Records.

❏ Record any Invoices in Monthly Credit Sales Record, if desired.

❏ Prepare Credit Sales Aging Report.

❏ Prepare and mail Statements and Past Due Statements.

❏ Prepare Monthly Cash Report Summary.

❏ Prepare Monthly Income Report Summary and transfer the information to your Annual Income Summary.

- ☐ Record monthly travel expenses in Monthly Travel Expense Record and transfer the information to your Annual Travel Expense Summary.

- ☐ Record monthly auto expenses in Monthly Auto Expense Record and transfer the information to your Annual Auto Expense Summary.

- ☐ Prepare a Monthly Expense Summary and Transfer the information to your Annual Expense Summary.

- ☐ Do a quick inventory check.

- ☐ Determine your Cost of Goods Sold, if desired.

- ☐ Prepare a Monthly Profit and Loss Statement, if desired.

- ☐ Check your progress against your Estimated Profit and Loss Statement.

- ☐ Update your Current Asset Accounts, if desired.

- ☐ Update your Fixed Asset Accounts, if desired.

- ☐ Update your Long-term Debts Record, if desired.

- ☐ Prepare a Monthly Balance Sheet, if desired.

- ☐ Prepare payroll, if necessary and transfer the information to your Annual Payroll Summary.

- ☐ Make proper payroll deposits, if necessary.

Quarterly Record-Keeping Tasks

- ☐ Do a quick inventory check.

- ☐ Determine your quarterly Cost of Goods Sold, if desired.

- ☐ Calculate quarterly totals on your Annual Income Summary.

- ☐ Calculate quarterly totals on your Annual Expense Summary.

- ☐ Calculate quarterly totals on your Annual Auto Expense Summary.

- ☐ Calculate quarterly totals on your Annual Travel Expense Summary.

- ☐ Calculate quarterly totals on your Annual Payroll Summary.

- ☐ Prepare a Quarterly Profit and Loss Statement, if desired.

- ☐ Check your progress against your Estimated Profit and Loss Statement.

- ☐ Update your Current Asset Accounts, if desired.

- ☐ Update your Fixed Asset Accounts, if desired.

- ☐ Update your Long-term Debts Record, if desired.

- ☐ Prepare a Quarterly Balance Sheet, if desired.

- ☐ Analyze your financial records using Ratio Comparison Chart, if desired.

Annual Record-Keeping Tasks

❐ Cash Basis businesses: Adjust your accounts for end-of-the-year as explained in Chapter 11.

❐ Finalize your Annual Income Summary.

❐ Finalize your Annual Expense Summary.

❐ Finalize your Annual Travel Expense Summary.

❐ Finalize your Annual Auto Expense Summary.

❐ Finalize your Annual Payroll Summary.

❐ Do a full Inventory using your Physical Inventory Report.

❐ Determine your Cost of Goods Sold.

❐ Prepare an Annual Profit and Loss Statement.

❐ Check your progress against your Estimated Profit and Loss Statement.

❐ Update your Current Asset Accounts.

❐ Update your Fixed Asset Accounts.

❐ Update your Long-term Debts Record.

❐ Prepare an Annual Balance Sheet.

❐ Analyze your financial records using Ratio Comparison Chart.

❐ Prepare an Estimated Profit and Loss Statement for the next year.

❐ Photo-copy the necessary forms for the next year's records.

❐ Set up all of the financial record-keeping for next year and file your old records and retain for 3 years.

Checklist of Financial Forms

- ❏ Chart of Accounts
- ❏ Check Register
- ❏ Monthly Bank Statement Reconciliation
- ❏ Petty Cash Register
- ❏ Current Asset Account
- ❏ Physical Inventory Report
- ❏ Periodic Inventory
- ❏ Perpetual Inventory
- ❏ Cost of Goods Sold
- ❏ Fixed Asset Account
- ❏ Accounts Payable Record
- ❏ Individual Accounts Payable Record
- ❏ Long-Term Debt Record
- ❏ Daily or Weekly Expense Record
- ❏ Monthly Expense Summary
- ❏ Annual Expense Summary
- ❏ Weekly or Monthly Travel Expense Record
- ❏ Annual Travel Expense Summary
- ❏ Weekly or Monthly Auto Expense Record
- ❏ Monthly Auto Expense Record
- ❏ Annual Auto Expense Summary
- ❏ Purchase Order
- ❏ Purchase Order Record
- ❏ Daily or Weekly Cash Report
- ❏ Monthly Cash Report Summary
- ❏ Daily or Weekly Income Record
- ❏ Monthly Income Summary
- ❏ Annual Income Summary
- ❏ Daily, Weekly, or Monthly Credit Sales Record
- ❏ Credit Sales Aging Report
- ❏ Invoice
- ❏ Statement
- ❏ Past Due Statement
- ❏ Credit Memo
- ❏ Quarterly Payroll Time Sheet
- ❏ Employee Payroll Record
- ❏ Payroll Depository Record
- ❏ Annual Payroll Summary
- ❏ Monthly or Quarterly Short Profit and Loss Statement
- ❏ Monthly, Quarterly, or Annual Profit and Loss Statement
- ❏ Estimated Profit and Loss Statement
- ❏ Monthly, Quarterly, or Annual Balance Sheet

Chapter 14

Business Tax Forms

In this chapter, you will find an array of the federal tax forms necessary for various business entities. The financial records which you will compile using the forms in this book will make your tax preparation much easier, whether you handle this yourself or it is handled by a tax professional. A basic comprehension of the information required on federal tax forms will help you understand why certain financial records are necessary. Understanding tax reporting will also assist you as you decide how to organize your business financial records.

For each of the four basic forms of business (sole-proprietorship, partnership, C corporation, and S corporation), a chart of tax forms will be provided which will detail which IRS forms may be necessary for each particular type of business. In addition, a schedule of tax filing for each type of business entity is also provided to assist you in keeping your tax reporting timely. Finally, a sample of each form is presented along with a discussion regarding which type of business needs to file the form, what information is necessary to complete the form, and where such information will be found in your business financial records. Finally, information regarding additional IRS information and publications is provided.

Sole Proprietorship Tax Forms

☐ Schedule C: *Profit or Loss From Business.* Must be filed with IRS 1040 by all sole proprietors, unless Schedule C-EZ is filed.

☐ Schedule C-EZ: *Net Profit From Business.* May be filed if gross receipts are under $25,000.00 and expenses are under $2,000.00.

☐ Schedule SE: *Self Employment Tax.* Required for any sole proprietor who shows $400+ income from their business on Schedule C or C-EZ.

☐ IRS Form 1040-ES: *Estimated Tax for Individuals.* Must be used by all sole proprietors who expect to make a profit requiring estimated taxes.

☐ IRS Form SS-4: *Application for Employer Identification Number.* Must be filed by all sole proprietors who will hire one or more employees.

☐ IRS Form W-2: *Wage and Tax Statement.* Must be filed by all sole proprietors who have one or more employees.

☐ IRS Form W-3: *Transmittal of Wage and Tax Statement.* Must be filed by all sole proprietors who have one or more employees.

☐ IRS Form W-4: *Employee's Withholding Allowance Certificate.* Must be provided to employees of sole proprietors. Not filed with the IRS.

☐ IRS Form 940 or 940-EZ: *Employer's Annual Federal Unemployment Tax Return.* Must be filed by all sole proprietors with employees.

☐ IRS Form 941: *Employer's Quarterly Federal Tax Return.* Must be filed by all sole proprietors who have one or more employees.

☐ IRS Form 8109: *Federal Tax Deposit Coupon.* Must be used by all sole proprietors with employees and tax liability over $500.00.

☐ IRS Form 8829: *Expenses for Business Use of Your Home,* if necessary. Filed with annual 1040

☐ Any required State and Local Income and Sales Tax forms.

Sole Proprietorship Monthly Tax Schedule

If you have employees, and your payroll tax liability is over $500 monthly, you must make monthly tax payments using Form 8109.

If required: file and pay any necessary state or local sales tax.

Sole Proprietorship Quarterly Tax Schedule

Pay any required estimated taxes using vouchers from IRS Form 1040-ES.

If you have employees: file IRS Form 941 and make any required payments of FICA and Withholding Taxes.

If you have employees and your unpaid FUTA tax liability is over $100, make FUTA deposit using IRS Form 8109.

If required: file and pay any necessary state or local sales tax.

Sole Proprietorship Annual Tax Schedule

If you have employees, prepare W-2 forms and provide to employees by January 31st and file Form W-3 and copies of all W-2 forms with IRS by January 31st.

If you have paid any independent contractors over $600 annually, prepare 1099 Forms and provide to recipient by January 31st and file Form 1096 and copies of all 1099 forms with IRS by January 31st.

Make required unemployment tax payment and file IRS Form 940 (or EZ).

File IRS Schedule SE with your annual 1040 Form.

File IRS Schedule C or C-EZ with your Annual 1040 form.

File IRS Form 8829 with your Annual 1040 Form, if necessary.

If required: file and pay any necessary state or local sales, income, or unemployment taxes.

Partnership Tax Forms

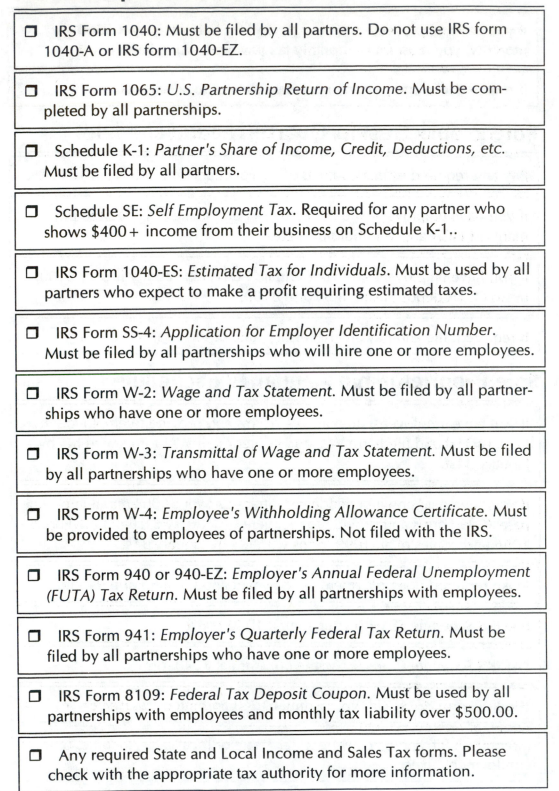

☐ IRS Form 1040: Must be filed by all partners. Do not use IRS form 1040-A or IRS form 1040-EZ.

☐ IRS Form 1065: *U.S. Partnership Return of Income.* Must be completed by all partnerships.

☐ Schedule K-1: *Partner's Share of Income, Credit, Deductions, etc.* Must be filed by all partners.

☐ Schedule SE: *Self Employment Tax.* Required for any partner who shows $400+ income from their business on Schedule K-1..

☐ IRS Form 1040-ES: *Estimated Tax for Individuals.* Must be used by all partners who expect to make a profit requiring estimated taxes.

☐ IRS Form SS-4: *Application for Employer Identification Number.* Must be filed by all partnerships who will hire one or more employees.

☐ IRS Form W-2: *Wage and Tax Statement.* Must be filed by all partnerships who have one or more employees.

☐ IRS Form W-3: *Transmittal of Wage and Tax Statement.* Must be filed by all partnerships who have one or more employees.

☐ IRS Form W-4: *Employee's Withholding Allowance Certificate.* Must be provided to employees of partnerships. Not filed with the IRS.

☐ IRS Form 940 or 940-EZ: *Employer's Annual Federal Unemployment (FUTA) Tax Return.* Must be filed by all partnerships with employees.

☐ IRS Form 941: *Employer's Quarterly Federal Tax Return.* Must be filed by all partnerships who have one or more employees.

☐ IRS Form 8109: *Federal Tax Deposit Coupon.* Must be used by all partnerships with employees and monthly tax liability over $500.00.

☐ Any required State and Local Income and Sales Tax forms. Please check with the appropriate tax authority for more information.

Partnership Monthly Tax Schedule

If you have employees, and your payroll tax liability is over $500 monthly, you must make monthly tax payments using Form 8109.

If required: file and pay any necessary state or local sales tax.

Partnership Quarterly Tax Schedule

Pay any required estimated taxes using vouchers from IRS Form 1040-ES.

If you have employees: file IRS Form 941 and make any required payments of FICA and Withholding Taxes.

If you have employees and your unpaid FUTA tax liability is over $100, make FUTA deposit using IRS Form 8109.

If required: file and pay any necessary state or local sales tax.

Partnership Annual Tax Schedule

If you have employees, prepare W-2 forms and provide to employees by January 31st and file Form W-3 and copies of all W-2 forms with IRS by January 31st.

If you have paid any independent contractors over $600 annually, prepare 1099 Forms and provide to recipient by January 31st and file Form 1096 and copies of all 1099 forms with IRS by January 31st.

Make required unemployment tax payment and file IRS Form 940 or EZ.

File IRS Schedule SE with your annual 1040 Form.

File IRS Form 1065 and Schedule K-1.

If you are required: file and pay any necessary state or local sales, income, or unemployment taxes.

C Corporation Tax Forms

❏ IRS Form 1040, 1040-A, 1040-EZ: One of these forms must be filed by all shareholders.

❏ IRS Form 1120 or 1120-A: *U.S. Corporation Income Tax Return*. One of these forms must be filed by all C corporations.

❏ IRS Form 1120-W: *Estimated Tax for Corporations (Worksheet)*. Must be completed by all corporations expecting a profit requiring estimated tax payments.

❏ IRS Form SS-4: *Application for Employer Identification Number*. Must be filed by all C corporations.

❏ IRS Form W-2: *Wage and Tax Statement*. Must be filed by all C corporations.

❏ IRS Form W-3: *Transmittal of Wage and Tax Statement*. Must be filed by all C corporations.

❏ IRS Form W-4: *Employee's Withholding Allowance Certificate*. Must be provided to employees of C corporations. It is not filed with the IRS.

❏ IRS Form 940 or 940-EZ: *Employer's Annual Federal Unemployment (FUTA) Tax Return*. Must be filed by all C corporations.

❏ IRS Form 941: *Employer's Quarterly Federal Tax Return*. Must be filed by all C corporations.

❏ IRS Form 8109: *Federal Tax Deposit Coupon*. Must be filed by all C corporations with a monthly tax liability over $500.00 .

❏ Any required State and Local Income and Sales Tax forms. Please check with the appropriate tax authority for more information.

C Corporation Monthly Tax Schedule

If corporate payroll tax liability is over $500 monthly, the corporation must make monthly tax payments using Form 8109.

If required: file and pay any necessary state or local sales tax.

C Corporation Quarterly Tax Schedule

Pay any required corporate estimated taxes using IRS Form 8109.

File IRS Form 941 and make any required payments of FICA and Withholding Taxes.

If corporate unpaid FUTA tax liability is over $100, make FUTA deposit using IRS Form 8109.

If required: file and pay any necessary state or local sales tax.

C Corporation Annual Tax Schedule

Prepare W-2 forms and provide to employees by January 31st and file Form W-3 and copies of all W-2 forms with IRS by January 31st.

If corporation has paid any independent contractors over $600 annually, prepare 1099 Forms and provide to recipient by January 31st and file Form 1096 and copies of all 1099 forms with IRS by January 31st.

Make required unemployment tax payment and file IRS Form 940 (or 940-EZ).

File IRS Form 1120 or 1120-A.

If required: file and pay any necessary state or local sales, income, or un-employment taxes.

S Corporation Tax Forms

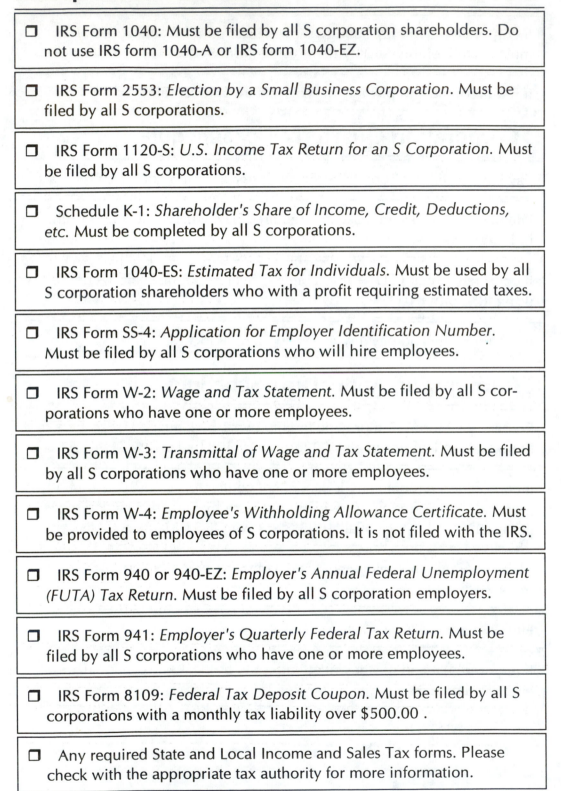

❐   IRS Form 1040: Must be filed by all S corporation shareholders. Do not use IRS form 1040-A or IRS form 1040-EZ.

❐   IRS Form 2553: *Election by a Small Business Corporation*. Must be filed by all S corporations.

❐   IRS Form 1120-S: *U.S. Income Tax Return for an S Corporation*. Must be filed by all S corporations.

❐   Schedule K-1: *Shareholder's Share of Income, Credit, Deductions, etc.* Must be completed by all S corporations.

❐   IRS Form 1040-ES: *Estimated Tax for Individuals*. Must be used by all S corporation shareholders who with a profit requiring estimated taxes.

❐   IRS Form SS-4: *Application for Employer Identification Number.* Must be filed by all S corporations who will hire employees.

❐   IRS Form W-2: *Wage and Tax Statement*. Must be filed by all S corporations who have one or more employees.

❐   IRS Form W-3: *Transmittal of Wage and Tax Statement*. Must be filed by all S corporations who have one or more employees.

❐   IRS Form W-4: *Employee's Withholding Allowance Certificate*. Must be provided to employees of S corporations. It is not filed with the IRS.

❐   IRS Form 940 or 940-EZ: *Employer's Annual Federal Unemployment (FUTA) Tax Return*. Must be filed by all S corporation employers.

❐   IRS Form 941: *Employer's Quarterly Federal Tax Return*. Must be filed by all S corporations who have one or more employees.

❐   IRS Form 8109: *Federal Tax Deposit Coupon*. Must be filed by all S corporations with a monthly tax liability over $500.00 .

❐   Any required State and Local Income and Sales Tax forms. Please check with the appropriate tax authority for more information.

S Corporation Monthly Tax Schedule

If corporation has employees, and corporate payroll tax liability is over $500 monthly, the corporation must make monthly tax payments using Form 8109.

If required: file and pay any necessary state or local sales tax.

S Corporation Quarterly Tax Schedule

Pay any required estimated taxes using vouchers from IRS Form 1040-ES.

If corporation has employees: file IRS Form 941 and make any required payments of FICA and Withholding Taxes.

If corporation has employees and corporate unpaid FUTA tax liability is over $100, make FUTA deposit using IRS Form 8109.

If required: file and pay any necessary state or local sales tax.

S Corporation Annual Tax Schedule

If corporation has employees, prepare W-2 forms and provide to employees by January 31st and file Form W-3 and copies of all W-2 forms with IRS by January 31st.

If corporation has paid any independent contractors over $600 annually, prepare 1099 Forms and provide to recipient by January 31st and file Form 1096 and copies of all 1099 forms with IRS by January 31st.

Make required unemployment tax payment and file IRS Form 940 (or 940-EZ).

File IRS Form 1120-S and Schedule K-1.

If required: file and pay any necessary state or local sales, income, or unemployment taxes.

Simplified Small Business Accounting

Form **SS-4**	**Application for Employer Identification Number**	EIN

Form **SS-4**
(Rev. December 1993)
Department of the Treasury
Internal Revenue Service

(For use by employers, corporations, partnerships, trusts, estates, churches, government agencies, certain individuals, and others. See instructions.)

OMB No. 1545-0003
Expires 12-31-96

Please type or print clearly.

1 Name of applicant (Legal name) (See instructions.)

2 Trade name of business, if different from name in line 1

3 Executor, trustee, "care of" name

4a Mailing address (street address) (room, apt., or suite no.)

5a Business address, if different from address in lines 4a and 4b

4b City, state, and ZIP code

5b City, state, and ZIP code

6 County and state where principal business is located

7 Name of principal officer, general partner, grantor, owner, or trustor—SSN required (See instructions.) ▶

8a Type of entity (Check only one box.) (See instructions.)
☐ Sole Proprietor (SSN) _____
☐ REMIC   ☐ Personal service corp.
☐ State/local government   ☐ National guard
☐ Other nonprofit organization (specify) _____
☐ Other (specify) ▶ _____

☐ Estate (SSN of decedent) _____
☐ Plan administrator-SSN _____
☐ Other corporation (specify) _____
☐ Federal government/military   ☐ Church or church controlled organization
(enter GEN if applicable) _____

☐ Trust
☐ Partnership
☐ Farmers' cooperative

8b If a corporation, name the state or foreign country (if applicable) where incorporated ▶

State

Foreign country

9 Reason for applying (Check only one box.)
☐ Started new business (specify) ▶ _____
☐ Hired employees
☐ Created a pension plan (specify type) ▶ _____
☐ Banking purpose (specify) ▶

☐ Changed type of organization (specify) ▶ _____
☐ Purchased going business
☐ Created a trust (specify) ▶ _____
☐ Other (specify) ▶

10 Date business started or acquired (Mo., day, year) (See instructions.)

11 Enter closing month of accounting year. (See instructions.)

12 First date wages or annuities were paid or will be paid (Mo., day, year). **Note:** *If applicant is a withholding agent, enter date income will first be paid to nonresident alien. (Mo., day, year)* . . . . ▶

13 Enter highest number of employees expected in the next 12 months. **Note:** *If the applicant does not expect to have any employees during the period, enter "0."* . . . . ▶

Nonagricultural	Agricultural	Household

14 Principal activity (See instructions.) ▶

15 Is the principal business activity manufacturing? . . . . ☐ Yes ☐ No
If "Yes," principal product and raw material used ▶

16 To whom are most of the products or services sold? Please check the appropriate box.   ☐ Business (wholesale)
☐ Public (retail)   ☐ Other (specify) ▶   ☐ N/A

17a Has the applicant ever applied for an identification number for this or any other business? . . . . ☐ Yes ☐ No
Note: *If "Yes," please complete lines 17b and 17c.*

17b If you checked the "Yes" box in line 17a, give applicant's legal name and trade name, if different than name shown on prior application.

Legal name ▶   Trade name ▶

17c Enter approximate date, city, and state where the application was filed and the previous employer identification number if known.

Approximate date when filed (Mo., day, year)	City and state where filed	Previous EIN

Under penalties of perjury, I declare that I have examined this application, and to the best of my knowledge and belief, it is true, correct, and complete.

Business telephone number (include area code)

Name and title (Please type or print clearly.) ▶

Signature ▶   Date ▶

Note: *Do not write below this line.   For official use only.*

Please leave blank ▶	Geo.	Ind.	Class	Size	Reason for applying

For Paperwork Reduction Act Notice, see attached instructions.   Cat. No. 16055N   Form **SS-4** (Rev. 12-93)

200

Form **1040**

Department of the Treasury—Internal Revenue Service

U.S. Individual Income Tax Return (O) **1994**

IRS Use Only—Do not write or staple in this space.

For the year Jan. 1–Dec. 31, 1994, or other tax year beginning , 1994, ending , 19 | OMB No. 1545-0074

Label

(See instructions on page 12.)

Use the IRS label. Otherwise, please print or type.

LABEL HERE

Your first name and initial | Last name | Your social security number

If a joint return, spouse's first name and initial | Last name | Spouse's social security number

Home address (number and street). If you have a P.O. box, see page 12. | Apt. no.

City, town or post office, state, and ZIP code. If you have a foreign address, see page 12.

For Privacy Act and Paperwork Reduction Act Notice, see page 4.

Presidential Election Campaign
(See page 12.)

| | Yes | No | Note: *Checking "Yes" will not change your tax or reduce your refund.* |

Do you want $3 to go to this fund? . . . .

If a joint return, does your spouse want $3 to go to this fund? . . . .

Filing Status

(See page 12.)

Check only one box.

1 Single

2 Married filing joint return (even if only one had income)

3 Married filing separate return. Enter spouse's social security no. above and full name here. ▶ _____

4 Head of household (with qualifying person). (See page 13.) If the qualifying person is a child but not your dependent, enter this child's name here. ▶ _____

5 Qualifying widow(er) with dependent child (year spouse died ▶ 19). (See page 13.)

Exemptions

(See page 13.)

If more than six dependents, see page 14.

6a **Yourself.** If your parent (or someone else) can claim you as a dependent on his or her tax return, **do not** check box 6a. But be sure to check the box on line 33b on page 2 }

b **Spouse** . . . .

c **Dependents:**

(1) Name (first, initial, and last name)	(2) Check if under age 1	(3) If age 1 or older, dependent's social security number	(4) Dependent's relationship to you	(5) No. of months lived in your home in 1994

d If your child didn't live with you but is claimed as your dependent under a pre-1985 agreement, check here ▶ ☐

e Total number of exemptions claimed . . . .

No. of boxes checked on 6a and 6b _____

No. of your children on 6c who:
- **lived with you** _____
- **didn't live with you due to divorce or separation (see page 14)** _____

Dependents on 6c not entered above _____

Add numbers entered on lines above ▶ ☐

Income

Attach Copy B of your Forms W-2, W-2G, and 1099-R here.

If you did not get a W-2, see page 15.

Enclose, but do not attach, any payment with your return.

7 Wages, salaries, tips, etc. Attach Form(s) W-2 . . . . | 7

8a **Taxable** interest income (see page 15). Attach Schedule B if over $400 . . . . | 8a

b **Tax-exempt** interest (see page 16). DON'T include on line 8a | 8b |

9 Dividend income. Attach Schedule B if over $400 . . . . | 9

10 Taxable refunds, credits, or offsets of state and local income taxes (see page 16) . . | 10

11 Alimony received . . . . | 11

12 Business income or (loss). Attach Schedule C or C-EZ . . . . . | 12

13 Capital gain or (loss). If required, attach Schedule D (see page 16) . . | 13

14 Other gains or (losses). Attach Form 4797 . . . . | 14

15a Total IRA distributions . | 15a | | b Taxable amount (see page 17) | 15b

16a Total pensions and annuities | 16a | | b Taxable amount (see page 17) | 16b

17 Rental real estate, royalties, partnerships, S corporations, trusts, etc. Attach Schedule E | 17

18 Farm income or (loss). Attach Schedule F . . . . | 18

19 Unemployment compensation (see page 18) . . . . | 19

20a Social security benefits | 20a | | b Taxable amount (see page 18) | 20b

21 Other income. List type and amount—see page 18 . . . . | 21

22 Add the amounts in the far right column for lines 7 through 21. This is your **total income** ▶ | 22

Adjustments to Income

Caution: See instructions . . ▶

23a Your IRA deduction (see page 19) . . . . . . | 23a |

b Spouse's IRA deduction (see page 19) . . . . . | 23b |

24 Moving expenses. Attach Form 3903 or 3903-F . . . | 24 |

25 One-half of self-employment tax . . . . | 25 |

26 Self-employed health insurance deduction (see page 21) | 26 |

27 Keogh retirement plan and self-employed SEP deduction | 27 |

28 Penalty on early withdrawal of savings . . . . | 28 |

29 Alimony paid. Recipient's SSN ▶ | 29 |

30 Add lines 23a through 29. These are your **total adjustments** . . . . | 30

Adjusted Gross Income

31 Subtract line 30 from line 22. This is your **adjusted gross income.** If less than $25,296 and a child lived with you (less than $9,000 if a child didn't live with you), see "Earned Income Credit" on page 27 ▶ | 31

Cat. No. 11320B

Form **1040** (1994)

Simplified Small Business Accounting

Tax Compu-tation (See page 23.)	32	Amount from line 31 (adjusted gross income)	32	
	33a	Check if: ☐ **You** were 65 or older, ☐ Blind; ☐ **Spouse** was 65 or older, ☐ Blind.		
		Add the number of boxes checked above and enter the total here . . . ▶ **33a**		
	b	If your parent (or someone else) can claim you as a dependent, check here . ▶ **33b** ☐		
	c	If you are married filing separately and your spouse itemizes deductions or you are a dual-status alien, see page 23 and check here . . . . ▶ **33c** ☐		
	34	Enter the **larger** of your: **Itemized deductions** from Schedule A, line 29, **OR** **Standard deduction** shown below for your filing status. **But if you checked any box on line 33a or b,** go to page 23 to find your standard deduction. If you checked box 33c, your standard deduction is zero. • Single—$3,800 • Head of household—$5,600 • Married filing jointly or Qualifying widow(er)—$6,350 • Married filing separately—$3,175	34	
	35	Subtract line 34 from line 32	35	
	36	If line 32 is $83,850 or less, multiply $2,450 by the total number of exemptions claimed on line 6e. If line 32 is over $83,850, see the worksheet on page 24 for the amount to enter .	36	
If you want the IRS to figure your tax, see page 24.	37	**Taxable income.** Subtract line 36 from line 35. If line 36 is more than line 35, enter -0-	37	
	38	Tax. Check if from **a** ☐ Tax Table, **b** ☐ Tax Rate Schedules, **c** ☐ Capital Gain Tax Worksheet, or **d** ☐ Form 8615 (see page 24). Amount from Form(s) 8814 ▶ **e** _____	38	
	39	Additional taxes. Check if from **a** ☐ Form 4970 **b** ☐ Form 4972 . . .	39	
	40	Add lines 38 and 39 . . . . ▶	40	
Credits (See page 24.)	41	Credit for child and dependent care expenses. Attach Form 2441	41	
	42	Credit for the elderly or the disabled. Attach Schedule R .	42	
	43	Foreign tax credit. Attach Form 1116	43	
	44	Other credits (see page 25). Check if from **a** ☐ Form 3800 **b** ☐ Form 8396 **c** ☐ Form 8801 **d** ☐ Form (specify) _____	44	
	45	Add lines 41 through 44	45	
	46	Subtract line 45 from line 40. If line 45 is more than line 40, enter -0- . . . . . ▶	46	
Other Taxes (See page 25.)	47	Self-employment tax. Attach Schedule SE	47	
	48	Alternative minimum tax. Attach Form 6251	48	
	49	Recapture taxes. Check if from **a** ☐ Form 4255 **b** ☐ Form 8611 **c** ☐ Form 8828	49	
	50	Social security and Medicare tax on tip income not reported to employer. Attach Form 4137 .	50	
	51	Tax on qualified retirement plans, including IRAs. If required, attach Form 5329 . .	51	
	52	Advance earned income credit payments from Form W-2	52	
	53	Add lines 46 through 52. This is your **total tax** . . . . ▶	53	
Payments Attach Forms W-2, W-2G, and 1099-R on the front.	54	Federal income tax withheld. If any is from Form(s) 1099, check ▶ ☐	54	
	55	1994 estimated tax payments and amount applied from 1993 return .	55	
	56	**Earned income credit.** If required, attach Schedule EIC (see page 27). Nontaxable earned income: amount ▶ _____ and type ▶	56	
	57	Amount paid with Form 4868 (extension request)	57	
	58	Excess social security and RRTA tax withheld (see page 32) .	58	
	59	Other payments. Check if from **a** ☐ Form 2439 **b** ☐ Form 4136	59	
	60	Add lines 54 through 59. These are your **total payments** . . . . . . ▶	60	
Refund or Amount You Owe	61	If line 60 is more than line 53, subtract line 53 from line 60. This is the amount you **OVERPAID**. ▶	61	
	62	Amount of line 61 you want **REFUNDED TO YOU**. . . . . ▶	62	
	63	Amount of line 61 you want **APPLIED TO YOUR 1995 ESTIMATED TAX** ▶ **63**		
	64	If line 53 is more than line 60, subtract line 60 from line 53. This is the **AMOUNT YOU OWE.** For details on how to pay, including what to write on your payment, see page 32 . . .	64	
	65	Estimated tax penalty (see page 33). Also include on line 64 **65**		

Sign Here Keep a copy of this return for your records.	Under penalties of perjury, I declare that I have examined this return and accompanying schedules and statements, and to the best of my knowledge and belief, they are true, correct, and complete. Declaration of preparer (other than taxpayer) is based on all information of which preparer has any knowledge.		
	Your signature	Date	Your occupation
	Spouse's signature. If a joint return, BOTH must sign.	Date	Spouse's occupation

Paid Preparer's Use Only	Preparer's signature ▶	Date	Check if self-employed ☐	Preparer's social security no.
	Firm's name (or yours if self-employed) and address ▶		E.I. No.	
			ZIP code	

✵ *Printed on recycled paper*

202

Form **1040-ES**

Department of the Treasury
Internal Revenue Service

Estimated Tax for Individuals

This package is primarily for first-time filers of estimated tax.

OMB No. 1545-0087

1995

1995 Estimated Tax Worksheet (keep for your records)

1	Enter amount of adjusted gross income you expect in 1995 (see instructions)	**1**	
2	• If you plan to itemize deductions, enter the estimated total of your itemized deductions. **Caution:** If line 1 above is over $114,700 ($57,350 if married filing separately), your deduction may be reduced. See Pub. 505 for details. • If you do not plan to itemize deductions, see **Standard Deduction for 1995** on page 2, and enter your standard deduction here.	**2**	
3	Subtract line 2 from line 1	**3**	
4	Exemptions. Multiply $2,500 by the number of personal exemptions. If you can be claimed as a dependent on another person's 1995 return, your personal exemption is not allowed. **Caution:** If line 1 above is over $172,050 ($143,350 if head of household; $114,700 if single; $86,025 if married filing separately), get Pub. 505 to figure the amount to enter	**4**	
5	Subtract line 4 from line 3	**5**	
6	**Tax.** Figure your tax on the amount on line 5 by using the 1995 Tax Rate Schedules on page 2. DO NOT use the Tax Table or the Tax Rate Schedules in the 1994 Form 1040 or Form 1040A instructions. **Caution:** If you have a net capital gain and line 5 is over $94,250 ($80,750 if head of household; $56,550 if single; $47,125 if married filing separately), get Pub. 505 to figure the tax	**6**	
7	Additional taxes (see instructions)	**7**	
8	Add lines 6 and 7	**8**	
9	Credits (see instructions). Do not include any income tax withholding on this line . . .	**9**	
10	Subtract line 9 from line 8. Enter the result, but not less than zero	**10**	
11	Self-employment tax. Estimate of 1995 net earnings from self-employment $................; if **$61,200 or less,** multiply the amount by 15.3%; if **more than $61,200,** multiply the amount by 2.9%, add $7,588.80 to the result, and enter the total. **Caution:** If you also have wages subject to social security tax, get Pub. 505 to figure the amount to enter.	**11**	
12	Other taxes (see instructions).	**12**	
13a	Add lines 10 through 12	**13a**	
b	Earned income credit and credit from **Form 4136**	**13b**	
c	Subtract line 13b from line 13a. Enter the result, but not less than zero. **THIS IS YOUR TOTAL 1995 ESTIMATED TAX** . . . . ▶	**13c**	

		14a		
14a	Multiply line 13c by 90% (66⅔% for farmers and fishermen) . . .			
b	Enter 100% of the tax shown on your 1994 tax return (110% of that amount if you are not a farmer or a fisherman and the adjusted gross income shown on that return is more than $150,000 or, if married filing separately for 1995, more than $75,000)	14b		

c	Enter the **smaller** of line 14a or 14b. **THIS IS YOUR REQUIRED ANNUAL PAYMENT TO AVOID A PENALTY** . . . . ▶	**14c**	
	Caution: Generally, if you do not prepay (through income tax withholding and estimated tax payments) at least the amount on line 14c, you may owe a penalty for not paying enough estimated tax. To avoid a penalty, make sure your estimate on line 13c is as accurate as possible. Even if you pay the required annual payment, you may still owe tax when you file your return. If you prefer, you may pay the amount shown on line 13c. For more details, get Pub. 505.		
15	Income tax withheld and estimated to be withheld during 1995 (including income tax withholding on pensions, annuities, certain deferred income, etc.)	**15**	
16	Subtract line 15 from line 14c. (**Note:** If zero or less, or line 13c minus line 15 is less than $500, stop here. You are not required to make estimated tax payments.)	**16**	
17	If the first payment you are required to make is due April 17, 1995, enter ¼ of line 16 (minus any 1994 overpayment that you are applying to this installment) here and on your payment voucher(s)	**17**	

Simplified Small Business Accounting

SCHEDULE C	Profit or Loss From Business	OMB No. 1545-0074

SCHEDULE C
(Form 1040)

Department of the Treasury
Internal Revenue Service   (O)

Profit or Loss From Business
(Sole Proprietorship)
▶ Partnerships, joint ventures, etc., must file Form 1065.
▶ Attach to Form 1040 or Form 1041.   ▶ See Instructions for Schedule C (Form 1040).

OMB No. 1545-0074

1994

Attachment
Sequence No. **09**

Name of proprietor	Social security number (SSN)

A Principal business or profession, including product or service (see page C-1)

B Enter principal business code
(see page C-6) ▶

C Business name. If no separate business name, leave blank.

D Employer ID number (EIN), if any

E Business address (including suite or room no.) ▶ ....
City, town or post office, state, and ZIP code

F Accounting method: (1) ☐ Cash   (2) ☐ Accrual   (3) ☐ Other (specify) ▶ ....

G Method(s) used to
value closing inventory: (1) ☐ Cost   (2) ☐ Lower of cost or market   (3) ☐ Other (attach explanation)   (4) ☐ Does not apply (if checked, skip line H) | Yes | No |

H Was there any change in determining quantities, costs, or valuations between opening and closing inventory? If "Yes," attach explanation

I Did you "materially participate" in the operation of this business during 1994? If "No," see page C-2 for limit on losses.

J If you started or acquired this business during 1994, check here ....▶ ☐

Part I   Income

1	Gross receipts or sales. **Caution:** If this income was reported to you on Form W-2 and the "Statutory employee" box on that form was checked, see page C-2 and check here ....▶ ☐	1	
2	Returns and allowances	2	
3	Subtract line 2 from line 1	3	
4	Cost of goods sold (from line 40 on page 2)	4	
5	**Gross profit.** Subtract line 4 from line 3	5	
6	Other income, including Federal and state gasoline or fuel tax credit or refund (see page C-2) . .	6	
7	**Gross income.** Add lines 5 and 6 ....▶	7	

Part II   Expenses. Enter expenses for business use of your home **only** on line 30.

8	Advertising	8	19 Pension and profit-sharing plans	19	
9	Bad debts from sales or services (see page C-3) ..	9	20 Rent or lease (see page C-4):		
			a Vehicles, machinery, and equipment .	20a	
10	Car and truck expenses (see page C-3) ..	10	b Other business property ..	20b	
11	Commissions and fees..	11	21 Repairs and maintenance ..	21	
12	Depletion....	12	22 Supplies (not included in Part III) .	22	
13	Depreciation and section 179 expense deduction (not included in Part III) (see page C-3) ..	13	23 Taxes and licenses	23	
			24 Travel, meals, and entertainment:		
			a Travel	24a	
14	Employee benefit programs (other than on line 19) ...	14	b Meals and entertainment .		
15	Insurance (other than health) .	15	c Enter 50% of line 24b subject to limitations (see page C-4) .		
16	Interest:				
a	Mortgage (paid to banks, etc.) .	16a	d Subtract line 24c from line 24b	24d	
b	Other	16b	25 Utilities	25	
17	Legal and professional services	17	26 Wages (less employment credits) .	26	
18	Office expense	18	27 Other expenses (from line 46 on page 2)	27	

28	**Total expenses** before expenses for business use of home. Add lines 8 through 27 in columns. ▶	28	
29	Tentative profit (loss). Subtract line 28 from line 7	29	
30	Expenses for business use of your home. Attach **Form 8829**	30	
31	**Net profit or (loss).** Subtract line 30 from line 29.		
	• If a profit, enter on **Form 1040, line 12,** and ALSO on **Schedule SE, line 2** (statutory employees, see page C-5). Estates and trusts, enter on Form 1041, line 3.	31	
	• If a loss, you MUST go on to line 32.		
32	If you have a loss, check the box that describes your investment in this activity (see page C-5).		
	• If you checked 32a, enter the loss on **Form 1040, line 12,** and ALSO on **Schedule SE, line 2** (statutory employees, see page C-5). Estates and trusts, enter on Form 1041, line 3.	32a ☐ All investment is at risk.	
	• If you checked 32b, you MUST attach **Form 6198.**	32b ☐ Some investment is not at risk.	

For Paperwork Reduction Act Notice, see Form 1040 instructions.   Cat. No. 11334P   Schedule C (Form 1040) 1994

·

Part III   **Cost of Goods Sold** (see page C-5)

33	Inventory at beginning of year. If different from last year's closing inventory, attach explanation . .	**33**
34	Purchases less cost of items withdrawn for personal use	**34**
35	Cost of labor. Do not include salary paid to yourself	**35**
36	Materials and supplies	**36**
37	Other costs	**37**
38	Add lines 33 through 37	**38**
39	Inventory at end of year	**39**
40	**Cost of goods sold.** Subtract line 39 from line 38. Enter the result here and on page 1, line 4 . .	**40**

Part IV   **Information on Your Vehicle. Complete this part ONLY if you are claiming car or truck expenses on line 10 and are not required to file Form 4562 for this business. See the instructions for line 13 on page C-3 to find out if you must file.**

41   When did you place your vehicle in service for business purposes? (month, day, year) ▶ ..../........../...... .

42   Of the total number of miles you drove your vehicle during 1994, enter the number of miles you used your vehicle for:

a Business .... **b** Commuting .... **c** Other ....

43   Do you (or your spouse) have another vehicle available for personal use? . . . . ☐ Yes   ☐ No

44   Was your vehicle available for use during off-duty hours? . . . . ☐ Yes   ☐ No

45a   Do you have evidence to support your deduction? . . . . ☐ Yes   ☐ No
 b   If "Yes," is the evidence written? . . . . ☐ Yes   ☐ No

Part V   **Other Expenses.** List below business expenses not included on lines 8–26 or line 30.

....	
....	
....	
....	
....	
....	
....	
....	
....	

46	**Total other expenses.** Enter here and on page 1, line 27	**46**

Printed on recycled paper   ☆ U.S. GPO:1994-375-198

Simplified Small Business Accounting

SCHEDULE C-EZ (Form 1040) Department of the Treasury Internal Revenue Service (O)	**Net Profit From Business** (Sole Proprietorship) ▶ Partnerships, joint ventures, etc., must file Form 1065. ▶ Attach to Form 1040 or Form 1041. ▶ See instructions on back.	OMB No. 1545-0074 **1994** Attachment Sequence No. **09A**

Name of proprietor	Social security number (SSN)

Part I   General Information

You May Use This Schedule Only If You:	• Had gross receipts from your business of $25,000 or less. • Had business expenses of $2,000 or less. • Use the cash method of accounting. • Did not have an inventory at any time during the year. • Did not have a net loss from your business. • Had only one business as a sole proprietor.	And You:	• Had no employees during the year. • Are not required to file **Form 4562,** Depreciation and Amortization, for this business. See the instructions for Schedule C, line 13, on page C-3 to find out if you must file. • Do not deduct expenses for business use of your home. • Do not have prior year unallowed passive activity losses from this business.

A	Principal business or profession, including product or service	**B Enter principal business code** (see page C-6) ▶
C	Business name. If no separate business name, leave blank.	**D Employer ID number (EIN), if any**

E   Business address (including suite or room no.). Address not required if same as on Form 1040, page 1.

City, town or post office, state, and ZIP code

Part II   Figure Your Net Profit

1	**Gross receipts.** If more than $25,000, you **must** use Schedule C. **Caution:** *If this income was reported to you on Form W-2 and the "Statutory employee" box on that form was checked, see **Statutory Employees** in the instructions for Schedule C, line 1, on page C-2 and check here* . . . . ▶ ☐	**1**
2	**Total expenses.** If more than $2,000, you **must** use Schedule C. See instructions	**2**
3	**Net profit.** Subtract line 2 from line 1. If less than zero, you **must** use Schedule C. Enter on **Form 1040, line 12,** and ALSO on **Schedule SE, line 2.** (Statutory employees **do not** report this amount on Schedule SE, line 2. Estates and trusts, enter on Form 1041, line 3.)	**3**

Part III   Information on Your Vehicle. Complete this part **ONLY** if you are claiming car or truck expenses on line 2.

4   When did you place your vehicle in service for business purposes? (month, day, year) ▶ ..... / ..... / ....

5   Of the total number of miles you drove your vehicle during 1994, enter the number of miles you used your vehicle for:

a   Business ....   b   Commuting   c   Other ....

6   Do you (or your spouse) have another vehicle available for personal use? . . . .   ☐ Yes   ☐ No

7   Was your vehicle available for use during off-duty hours? . . . .   ☐ Yes   ☐ No

8a   Do you have evidence to support your deduction? . . . .   ☐ Yes   ☐ No

  b   If "Yes," is the evidence written? . . . .   ☐ Yes   ☐ No

For Paperwork Reduction Act Notice, see Form 1040 instructions.   Cat. No. 14374D   **Schedule C-EZ (Form 1040) 1994**

SCHEDULE SE	Self-Employment Tax	OMB No. 1549-0074
(Form 1040)	► See Instructions for Schedule SE (Form 1040).	**1994**
Department of the Treasury Internal Revenue Service (O)	► Attach to Form 1040.	Attachment Sequence No. **17**

Name of person with **self-employment** income (as shown on Form 1040)	Social security number of person with **self-employment** income ►	: : :

Who Must File Schedule SE

You must file Schedule SE if:

- You had net earnings from self-employment from other than church employee income (line 4 of Short Schedule SE or line 4c of Long Schedule SE) of $400 or more, **OR**
- You had church employee income of $108.28 or more. Income from services you performed as a minister or a member of a religious order **is not** church employee income. See page SE-1.

Note: *Even if you have a loss or a small amount of income from self-employment, it may be to your benefit to file Schedule SE and use either "optional method" in Part II of Long Schedule SE. See page SE-2.*

Exception. If your only self-employment income was from earnings as a minister, member of a religious order, or Christian Science practitioner, **and** you filed Form 4361 and received IRS approval not to be taxed on those earnings, **do not** file Schedule SE. Instead, write "Exempt–Form 4361" on Form 1040, line 47.

May I Use Short Schedule SE or MUST I Use Long Schedule SE?

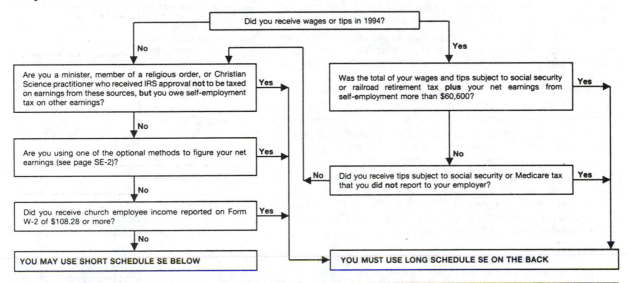

Section A—Short Schedule SE. Caution: *Read above to see if you can use Short Schedule SE.*

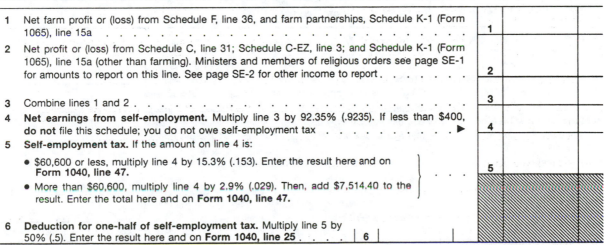

1	Net farm profit or (loss) from Schedule F, line 36, and farm partnerships, Schedule K-1 (Form 1065), line 15a	1
2	Net profit or (loss) from Schedule C, line 31; Schedule C-EZ, line 3; and Schedule K-1 (Form 1065), line 15a (other than farming). Ministers and members of religious orders see page SE-1 for amounts to report on this line. See page SE-2 for other income to report	2
3	Combine lines 1 and 2	3
4	**Net earnings from self-employment.** Multiply line 3 by 92.35% (.9235). If less than $400, **do not** file this schedule; you do not owe self-employment tax . . . . ►	4
5	**Self-employment tax.** If the amount on line 4 is: • $60,600 or less, multiply line 4 by 15.3% (.153). Enter the result here and on **Form 1040, line 47.** • More than $60,600, multiply line 4 by 2.9% (.029). Then, add $7,514.40 to the result. Enter the total here and on **Form 1040, line 47.**	5
6	**Deduction for one-half of self-employment tax.** Multiply line 5 by 50% (.5). Enter the result here and on **Form 1040, line 25**	6

For Paperwork Reduction Act Notice, see Form 1040 instructions.   Cat. No. 11358Z   Schedule SE (Form 1040) 1994

Simplified Small Business Accounting

Name of person with **self-employment** income (as shown on Form 1040)	Social security number of person with **self-employment** income ▶		

Section B—Long Schedule SE

Part I   Self-Employment Tax

> **Note:** *If your only income subject to self-employment tax is church employee income, skip lines 1 through 4b. Enter -0-on line 4c and go to line 5a. Income from services you performed as a minister or a member of a religious order* **is not** *church employee income. See page SE-1.*

A   If you are a minister, member of a religious order, or Christian Science practitioner **and** you filed Form 4361, but you had $400 or more of **other** net earnings from self-employment, check here and continue with Part I. . . . . . ▶ ☐

1	Net farm profit or (loss) from Schedule F, line 36, and farm partnerships, Schedule K-1 (Form 1065), line 15a. **Note:** *Skip this line if you use the farm optional method. See page SE-3* . .	**1**	
2	Net profit or (loss) from Schedule C, line 31; Schedule C-EZ, line 3; and Schedule K-1 (Form 1065), line 15a (other than farming). Ministers and members of religious orders see page SE-1 for amounts to report on this line. See page SE-2 for other income to report. **Note:** *Skip this line if you use the nonfarm optional method. See page SE-3.*	**2**	
3	Combine lines 1 and 2	**3**	
4a	If line 3 is more than zero, multiply line 3 by 92.35% (.9235). Otherwise, enter amount from line 3	**4a**	
b	If you elected one or both of the optional methods, enter the total of lines 15 and 17 here . .	**4b**	
c	Combine lines 4a and 4b. If less than $400, **do not** file this schedule; you do not owe self-employment tax. **Exception.** If less than $400 and you had church employee income, enter -0- and continue . ▶	**4c**	
5a	Enter your church employee income from Form W-2. **Caution:** *See page SE-1 for definition of church employee income* **5a**	**5b**	
b	Multiply line 5a by 92.35% (.9235). If less than $100, enter -0-		
6	**Net earnings from self-employment.** Add lines 4c and 5b	**6**	
7	Maximum amount of combined wages and self-employment earnings subject to social security tax or the 6.2% portion of the 7.65% railroad retirement (tier 1) tax for 1994	**7**	60,600	00
8a	Total social security wages and tips (total of boxes 3 and 7 on Form(s) W-2) and railroad retirement (tier 1) compensation. **8a**		
b	Unreported tips subject to social security tax (from Form 4137, line 9) **8b**		
c	Add lines 8a and 8b	**8c**	
9	Subtract line 8c from line 7. If zero or less, enter -0- here and on line 10 and go to line 11 . ▶	**9**	
10	Multiply the **smaller** of line 6 or line 9 by 12.4% (.124)	**10**	
11	Multiply line 6 by 2.9% (.029).	**11**	
12	**Self-employment tax.** Add lines 10 and 11. Enter here and on **Form 1040, line 47**	**12**	
13	**Deduction for one-half of self-employment tax.** Multiply line 12 by 50% (.5). Enter the result here and on **Form 1040, line 25** **13**		

Part II   Optional Methods To Figure Net Earnings (See page SE-2.)

Farm Optional Method. You may use this method **only** if:			
● Your gross farm income[1] was not more than $2,400, **or**			
● Your gross farm income[1] was more than $2,400 and your net farm profits[2] were less than $1,733.			
14 Maximum income for optional methods	**14**	1,600	00
15 Enter the **smaller** of: two-thirds (⅔) of gross farm income[1] (not less than zero) **or** $1,600. Also, include this amount on line 4b above	**15**		
Nonfarm Optional Method. You may use this method **only** if:			
● Your net nonfarm profits[3] were less than $1,733 and also less than 72.189% of your gross nonfarm income,[4] **and**			
● You had net earnings from self-employment of at least $400 in 2 of the prior 3 years.			
Caution: *You may use this method no more than five times.*			
16 Subtract line 15 from line 14	**16**		
17 Enter the **smaller** of: two-thirds (⅔) of gross nonfarm income[4] (not less than zero) **or** the amount on line 16. Also, include this amount on line 4b above	**17**		

[1] From Schedule F, line 11, and Schedule K-1 (Form 1065), line 15b.   [3] From Schedule C, line 31; Schedule C-EZ, line 3; and Schedule K-1 (Form 1065), line 15a.
[2] From Schedule F, line 36, and Schedule K-1 (Form 1065), line 15a.   [4] From Schedule C, line 7; Schedule C-EZ, line 1; and Schedule K-1 (Form 1065), line 15c.

✱ Printed on recycled paper   ☆ U.S. GPO:1994-375-219

Form **1065**

Department of the Treasury
Internal Revenue Service

U.S. Partnership Return of Income

For calendar year 1994, or tax year beginning .... , 1994, and ending .... , 19 ....
▶ See separate instructions.

OMB No. 1545-0099

1994

A Principal business activity	Use the IRS label. Other-wise, please print or type.	Name of partnership	D Employer identification number
B Principal product or service		Number, street, and room or suite no. (If a P.O. box, see page 9 of the instructions.)	E Date business started
C Business code number		City or town, state, and ZIP code	F Total assets (see **Specific Instructions**) $

G Check applicable boxes: (1) ☐ Initial return (2) ☐ Final return (3) ☐ Change in address (4) ☐ Amended return
H Check accounting method: (1) ☐ Cash (2) ☐ Accrual (3) ☐ Other (specify) ▶ ....
I Number of Schedules K-1. Attach one for each person who was a partner at any time during the tax year ▶ ....

Caution: *Include* **only** *trade or business income and expenses on lines 1a through 22 below. See the instructions for more information.*

Income

1a Gross receipts or sales	1a		
b Less returns and allowances	1b	1c	
2 Cost of goods sold (Schedule A, line 8)		2	
3 Gross profit. Subtract line 2 from line 1c		3	
4 Ordinary income (loss) from other partnerships, estates, and trusts (attach schedule)		4	
5 Net farm profit (loss) (attach Schedule F (Form 1040))		5	
6 Net gain (loss) from Form 4797, Part II, line 20		6	
7 Other income (loss) (see instructions) (attach schedule)		7	
8 **Total income (loss).** Combine lines 3 through 7		8	

Deductions (see instructions for limitations)

9 Salaries and wages (other than to partners) (less employment credits)		9	
10 Guaranteed payments to partners		10	
11 Repairs and maintenance		11	
12 Bad debts		12	
13 Rent		13	
14 Taxes and licenses		14	
15 Interest		15	
16a Depreciation (see instructions)	16a		
b Less depreciation reported on Schedule A and elsewhere on return	16b	16c	
17 Depletion (**Do not deduct oil and gas depletion.**)		17	
18 Retirement plans, etc.		18	
19 Employee benefit programs		19	
20 Other deductions (attach schedule)		20	
21 **Total deductions.** Add the amounts shown in the far right column for lines 9 through 20		21	
22 **Ordinary income (loss)** from trade or business activities. Subtract line 21 from line 8		22	

Please Sign Here

Under penalties of perjury, I declare that I have examined this return, including accompanying schedules and statements, and to the best of my knowledge and belief, it is true, correct, and complete. Declaration of preparer (other than general partner) is based on all information of which preparer has any knowledge.

▶ Signature of general partner or limited liability company member ▶ Date

Paid Preparer's Use Only

Preparer's signature ▶	Date	Check if self-employed ▶ ☐	Preparer's social security no.
Firm's name (or yours if self-employed) and address ▶		E.I. No. ▶	
		ZIP code ▶	

For Paperwork Reduction Act Notice, see page 1 of separate instructions.   Cat. No. 11390Z   Form **1065** (1994)

Simplified Small Business Accounting

Schedule A	Cost of Goods Sold

1	Inventory at beginning of year	1	
2	Purchases less cost of items withdrawn for personal use	2	
3	Cost of labor.	3	
4	Additional section 263A costs (see instructions) *(attach schedule)*	4	
5	Other costs *(attach schedule)*	5	
6	**Total.** Add lines 1 through 5	6	
7	Inventory at end of year	7	
8	**Cost of goods sold.** Subtract line 7 from line 6. Enter here and on page 1, line 2	8	

9a Check all methods used for valuing closing inventory:
    (i) ☐ Cost
    (ii) ☐ Lower of cost or market as described in Regulations section 1.471-4
    (iii) ☐ Writedown of "subnormal" goods as described in Regulations section 1.471-2(c)
    (iv) ☐ Other (specify method used and attach explanation) ▶ ....
  b Check this box if the LIFO inventory method was adopted this tax year for any goods *(if checked, attach Form 970)* . . ▶ ☐
  c Do the rules of section 263A (for property produced or acquired for resale) apply to the partnership? . . ☐Yes ☐No
  d Was there any change in determining quantities, cost, or valuations between opening and closing inventory? ☐Yes ☐No
    If "Yes," attach explanation.

Schedule B	Other Information

		Yes	No
1	What type of entity is filing this return? Check the applicable box ▶ ☐ General partnership ☐ Limited partnership ☐ Limited liability company		
2	Are any partners in this partnership also partnerships?		
3	Is this partnership a partner in another partnership?		
4	Is this partnership subject to the consolidated audit procedures of sections 6221 through 6233? If "Yes," see **Designation of Tax Matters Partner** below		
5	Does this partnership meet **ALL THREE** of the following requirements?		
a	The partnership's total receipts for the tax year were less than $250,000;		
b	The partnership's total assets at the end of the tax year were less than $600,000; **AND**		
c	Schedules K-1 are filed with the return and furnished to the partners on or before the due date (including extensions) for the partnership return.		
	If "Yes," the partnership is not required to complete Schedules L, M-1, and M-2; Item F on page 1 of Form 1065; or Item J on Schedule K-1		
6	Does this partnership have any foreign partners?		
7	Is this partnership a publicly traded partnership as defined in section 469(k)(2)?		
8	Has this partnership filed, or is it required to file, **Form 8264,** Application for Registration of a Tax Shelter? . .		
9	At any time during calendar year 1994, did the partnership have an interest in or a signature or other authority over a financial account in a foreign country (such as a bank account, securities account, or other financial account)? (See the instructions for exceptions and filing requirements for Form TD F 90-22.1.) If "Yes," enter the name of the foreign country. ▶		
10	Was the partnership the grantor of, or transferor to, a foreign trust that existed during the current tax year, whether or not the partnership or any partner has any beneficial interest in it? If "Yes," you may have to file Forms 3520, 3520-A, or 926		
11	Was there a distribution of property or a transfer (e.g., by sale or death) of a partnership interest during the tax year? If "Yes," you may elect to adjust the basis of the partnership's assets under section 754 by attaching the statement described under **Elections Made By the Partnership**		

Designation of Tax Matters Partner (See instructions.)
Enter below the general partner designated as the tax matters partner (TMP) for the tax year of this return:

Name of designated TMP ▶ _____	Identifying number of TMP ▶ _____
Address of designated TMP ▶ _____	

Form 1065 (1994)   Page **3**

Schedule K   Partners' Shares of Income, Credits, Deductions, etc.

	(a) Distributive share items		(b) Total amount

Income (Loss)

1 Ordinary income (loss) from trade or business activities (page 1, line 22) ... **1**
2 Net income (loss) from rental real estate activities (attach Form 8825) ... **2**
3a Gross income from other rental activities ... **3a**
b Expenses from other rental activities (attach schedule) ... **3b**
c Net income (loss) from other rental activities. Subtract line 3b from line 3a ... **3c**
4 Portfolio income (loss) (see instructions): a Interest income ... **4a**
b Dividend income ... **4b**
c Royalty income ... **4c**
d Net short-term capital gain (loss) (attach Schedule D (Form 1065)) ... **4d**
e Net long-term capital gain (loss) (attach Schedule D (Form 1065)) ... **4e**
f Other portfolio income (loss) (attach schedule) ... **4f**
5 Guaranteed payments to partners ... **5**
6 Net gain (loss) under section 1231 (other than due to casualty or theft) (attach Form 4797) ... **6**
7 Other income (loss) (attach schedule) ... **7**

Deductions

8 Charitable contributions (see instructions) (attach schedule) ... **8**
9 Section 179 expense deduction (attach Form 4562) ... **9**
10 Deductions related to portfolio income (see instructions) (itemize) ... **10**
11 Other deductions (attach schedule) ... **11**

Investment Interest

12a Interest expense on investment debts ... **12a**
b (1) Investment income included on lines 4a, 4b, 4c, and 4f above ... **12b(1)**
(2) Investment expenses included on line 10 above ... **12b(2)**

Credits

13a Credit for income tax withheld ... **13a**
b Low-income housing credit (see instructions):
(1) From partnerships to which section 42(j)(5) applies for property placed in service before 1990 ... **13b(1)**
(2) Other than on line 13b(1) for property placed in service before 1990 ... **13b(2)**
(3) From partnerships to which section 42(j)(5) applies for property placed in service after 1989 ... **13b(3)**
(4) Other than on line 13b(3) for property placed in service after 1989 ... **13b(4)**
c Qualified rehabilitation expenditures related to rental real estate activities (attach Form 3468) ... **13c**
d Credits (other than credits shown on lines 13b and 13c) related to rental real estate activities (see instructions) ... **13d**
e Credits related to other rental activities (see instructions) ... **13e**
14 Other credits (see instructions) ... **14**

Self-Employment

15a Net earnings (loss) from self-employment ... **15a**
b Gross farming or fishing income ... **15b**
c Gross nonfarm income ... **15c**

Adjustments and Tax Preference Items

16a Depreciation adjustment on property placed in service after 1986 ... **16a**
b Adjusted gain or loss ... **16b**
c Depletion (other than oil and gas) ... **16c**
d (1) Gross income from oil, gas, and geothermal properties ... **16d(1)**
(2) Deductions allocable to oil, gas, and geothermal properties ... **16d(2)**
e Other adjustments and tax preference items (attach schedule) ... **16e**

Foreign Taxes

17a Type of income ▶ .... b Foreign country or U.S. possession ▶ ....
c Total gross income from sources outside the United States (attach schedule) ... **17c**
d Total applicable deductions and losses (attach schedule) ... **17d**
e Total foreign taxes (check one): ▶ ☐ Paid ☐ Accrued ... **17e**
f Reduction in taxes available for credit (attach schedule) ... **17f**
g Other foreign tax information (attach schedule) ... **17g**

Other

18a Total expenditures to which a section 59(e) election may apply ... **18a**
b Type of expenditures ▶ ....
19 Tax-exempt interest income ... **19**
20 Other tax-exempt income ... **20**
21 Nondeductible expenses ... **21**
22 Other items and amounts required to be reported separately to partners (see instructions) (attach schedule)

Analysis

23a Income (loss). Combine lines 1 through 7 in column (b). From the result, subtract the sum of lines 8 through 12a, 17e, and 18a ... **23a**

b Analysis by type of partner:	(a) Corporate	(b) Individual		(c) Partnership	(d) Exempt organization	(e) Nominee/Other
		i. Active	ii. Passive			
(1) General partners						
(2) Limited partners						

Simplified Small Business Accounting

Note: If Question 5 of Schedule B is answered "Yes," the partnership is not required to complete Schedules L, M-1, and M-2.

Schedule L — Balance Sheets

Assets	Beginning of tax year		End of tax year	
	(a)	(b)	(c)	(d)
1 Cash				
2a Trade notes and accounts receivable				
b Less allowance for bad debts				
3 Inventories				
4 U.S. government obligations				
5 Tax-exempt securities				
6 Other current assets (attach schedule)				
7 Mortgage and real estate loans				
8 Other investments (attach schedule)				
9a Buildings and other depreciable assets				
b Less accumulated depreciation				
10a Depletable assets				
b Less accumulated depletion				
11 Land (net of any amortization)				
12a Intangible assets (amortizable only)				
b Less accumulated amortization				
13 Other assets (attach schedule)				
14 Total assets				
Liabilities and Capital				
15 Accounts payable				
16 Mortgages, notes, bonds payable in less than 1 year				
17 Other current liabilities (attach schedule)				
18 All nonrecourse loans				
19 Mortgages, notes, bonds payable in 1 year or more				
20 Other liabilities (attach schedule)				
21 Partners' capital accounts				
22 Total liabilities and capital				

Schedule M-1 — Reconciliation of Income (Loss) per Books With Income (Loss) per Return (see instructions)

1 Net income (loss) per books		6 Income recorded on books this year not included on Schedule K, lines 1 through 7 (itemize):	
2 Income included on Schedule K, lines 1 through 4, 6, and 7, not recorded on books this year (itemize):		a Tax-exempt interest $	
3 Guaranteed payments (other than health insurance)		7 Deductions included on Schedule K, lines 1 through 12a, 17e, and 18a, not charged against book income this year (itemize):	
4 Expenses recorded on books this year not included on Schedule K, lines 1 through 12a, 17e, and 18a (itemize):		a Depreciation $	
a Depreciation $		....	
b Travel and entertainment $		8 Add lines 6 and 7	
5 Add lines 1 through 4		9 Income (loss) (Schedule K, line 23a). Subtract line 8 from line 5	

Schedule M-2 — Analysis of Partners' Capital Accounts

1 Balance at beginning of year		6 Distributions: a Cash	
2 Capital contributed during year		b Property	
3 Net income (loss) per books		7 Other decreases (itemize):	
4 Other increases (itemize):			
5 Add lines 1 through 4		8 Add lines 6 and 7	
		9 Balance at end of year. Subtract line 8 from line 5	

Printed on recycled paper

*U.S.GPO:1994-375-264

212

SCHEDULE K-1
(Form 1065)
Department of the Treasury
Internal Revenue Service

Partner's Share of Income, Credits, Deductions, etc.
▶ See separate instructions.
For calendar year 1994 or tax year beginning   , 1994, and ending   , 19

OMB No. 1545-0099

1994

Partner's identifying number ▶	Partnership's identifying number ▶
Partner's name, address, and ZIP code	Partnership's name, address, and ZIP code

A This partner is a ☐ general partner   ☐ limited partner
     ☐ limited liability company member

B What type of entity is this partner?   ▶ ....

C Is this partner a ☐ domestic or a ☐ foreign partner?

D Enter partner's percentage of:

	(i) Before change or termination	(ii) End of year
Profit sharing	.... %	...... %
Loss sharing	.... %	...... %
Ownership of capital	.... %	...... %

E IRS Center where partnership filed return:

F Partner's share of liabilities (see instructions):

Nonrecourse . . . . $ ....

Qualified nonrecourse financing . $ ....

Other . . . . $ ....

G Tax shelter registration number . ▶ ....

H Check here if this partnership is a publicly traded partnership as defined in section 469(k)(2) . . . . ☐

I Check applicable boxes: (1) ☐ Final K-1 (2) ☐ Amended K-1

J Analysis of partner's capital account:

(a) Capital account at beginning of year	(b) Capital contributed during year	(c) Partner's share of lines 3, 4, and 7, Form 1065, Schedule M-2	(d) Withdrawals and distributions	(e) Capital account at end of year (combine columns (a) through (d))
			( )	

	(a) Distributive share item		(b) Amount	(c) 1040 filers enter the amount in column (b) on:
Income (Loss)	**1** Ordinary income (loss) from trade or business activities . . .	**1**		See Partner's Instructions for Schedule K-1 (Form 1065).
	2 Net income (loss) from rental real estate activities	**2**		
	3 Net income (loss) from other rental activities	**3**		
	4 Portfolio income (loss):			
	a Interest	**4a**		Sch. B, Part I, line 1
	b Dividends	**4b**		Sch. B, Part II, line 5
	c Royalties	**4c**		Sch. E, Part I, line 4
	d Net short-term capital gain (loss)	**4d**		Sch. D, line 5, col. (f) or (g)
	e Net long-term capital gain (loss).	**4e**		Sch. D, line 13, col. (f) or (g)
	f Other portfolio income (loss) (attach schedule) . . .	**4f**		Enter on applicable line of your return.
	5 Guaranteed payments to partner	**5**		See Partner's Instructions for Schedule K-1 (Form 1065)
	6 Net gain (loss) under section 1231 (other than due to casualty or theft)	**6**		
	7 Other income (loss) (attach schedule)	**7**		Enter on applicable line of your return.
Deduc-tions	**8** Charitable contributions (see instructions) (attach schedule) . .	**8**		Sch. A, line 15 or 16
	9 Section 179 expense deduction	**9**		See Partner's Instructions for Schedule K-1 (Form 1065).
	10 Deductions related to portfolio income (attach schedule) . . .	**10**		
	11 Other deductions (attach schedule).	**11**		
Investment Interest	**12a** Interest expense on investment debts	**12a**		Form 4952, line 1
	b (1) Investment income included on lines 4a, 4b, 4c, and 4f above	**b(1)**		See Partner's Instructions for Schedule K-1 (Form 1065).
	(2) Investment expenses included on line 10 above	**b(2)**		
Credits	**13a** Credit for income tax withheld	**13a**		See Partner's Instructions for Schedule K-1 (Form 1065).
	b Low-income housing credit:			
	(1) From section 42(j)(5) partnerships for property placed in service before 1990	**b(1)**		
	(2) Other than on line 13b(1) for property placed in service before 1990	**b(2)**		Form 8586, line 5
	(3) From section 42(j)(5) partnerships for property placed in service after 1989	**b(3)**		
	(4) Other than on line 13b(3) for property placed in service after 1989	**b(4)**		
	c Qualified rehabilitation expenditures related to rental real estate activities (see instructions)	**13c**		See Partner's Instructions for Schedule K-1 (Form 1065).
	d Credits (other than credits shown on lines 13b and 13c) related to rental real estate activities (see instructions)	**13d**		
	e Credits related to other rental activities (see instructions) . . .	**13e**		
	14 Other credits (see instructions)	**14**		

For Paperwork Reduction Act Notice, see Instructions for Form 1065.   Cat. No. 11394R   **Schedule K-1 (Form 1065) 1994**

Simplified Small Business Accounting

	(a) Distributive share item		(b) Amount	(c) 1040 filers enter the amount in column (b) on:
Self-employment	15a Net earnings (loss) from self-employment	15a		Sch. SE, Section A or B
	b Gross farming or fishing income	15b		See Partner's Instructions for Schedule K-1 (Form 1065).
	c Gross nonfarm income	15c		
Adjustments and Tax Preference Items	16a Depreciation adjustment on property placed in service after 1986	16a		See Partner's Instructions for Schedule K-1 (Form 1065) and Instructions for Form 6251.
	b Adjusted gain or loss	16b		
	c Depletion (other than oil and gas)	16c		
	d (1) Gross income from oil, gas, and geothermal properties	d(1)		
	(2) Deductions allocable to oil, gas, and geothermal properties	d(2)		
	e Other adjustments and tax preference items (attach schedule)	16e		
Foreign Taxes	17a Type of income ▶			Form 1116, check boxes
	b Name of foreign country or U.S. possession ▶			
	c Total gross income from sources outside the United States (attach schedule)	17c		Form 1116, Part I
	d Total applicable deductions and losses (attach schedule)	17d		
	e Total foreign taxes (check one): ▶ ☐ Paid ☐ Accrued	17e		Form 1116, Part II
	f Reduction in taxes available for credit (attach schedule)	17f		Form 1116, Part III
	g Other foreign tax information (attach schedule)	17g		See Instructions for Form 1116.
Other	18a Total expenditures to which a section 59(e) election may apply	18a		See Partner's Instructions for Schedule K-1 (Form 1065).
	b Type of expenditures ▶			
	19 Tax-exempt interest income	19		Form 1040, line 8b
	20 Other tax-exempt income	20		See Partner's Instructions for Schedule K-1 (Form 1065).
	21 Nondeductible expenses	21		
	22 Recapture of low-income housing credit:			Form 8611, line 8
	a From section 42(j)(5) partnerships	22a		
	b Other than on line 22a	22b		

Supplemental Information

23 Supplemental information required to be reported separately to each partner (attach additional schedules if more space is needed):

Form **1120**		U.S. Corporation Income Tax Return		OMB No. 1545-0123	

Department of the Treasury
Internal Revenue Service

For calendar year 1994 or tax year beginning .... , 1994, ending .... , 19 ...
▶ Instructions are separate. See page 1 for Paperwork Reduction Act Notice.

19 94

A Check if a:		Use IRS label. Other-wise, please print or type.	Name		B Employer identification number
1 Consolidated return (attach Form 851) ☐					
2 Personal holding co. (attach Sch. PH) ☐			Number, street, and room or suite no. (If a P.O. box, see page 6 of instructions.)		C Date incorporated
3 Personal service corp. (as defined in Temporary Regs. sec. 1.441-4T— see instructions) ☐			City or town, state, and ZIP code		D Total assets (see Specific Instructions)

E Check applicable boxes: (1) ☐ Initial return (2) ☐ Final return (3) ☐ Change of address $

Income	1a	Gross receipts or sales ____ b Less returns and allowances ____ c Bal ▶			1c	
	2	Cost of goods sold (Schedule A, line 8)			2	
	3	Gross profit. Subtract line 2 from line 1c			3	
	4	Dividends (Schedule C, line 19)			4	
	5	Interest			5	
	6	Gross rents			6	
	7	Gross royalties			7	
	8	Capital gain net income (attach Schedule D (Form 1120))			8	
	9	Net gain or (loss) from Form 4797, Part II, line 20 (attach Form 4797)			9	
	10	Other income (see instructions—attach schedule)			10	
	11	**Total income.** Add lines 3 through 10 . . . . ▶			11	
Deductions (See instructions for limitations on deductions.)	12	Compensation of officers (Schedule E, line 4)			12	
	13	Salaries and wages (less employment credits)			13	
	14	Repairs and maintenance			14	
	15	Bad debts			15	
	16	Rents			16	
	17	Taxes and licenses			17	
	18	Interest			18	
	19	Charitable contributions (see instructions for 10% limitation) . .			19	
	20	Depreciation (attach Form 4562)	20			
	21	Less depreciation claimed on Schedule A and elsewhere on return . . .	21a		21b	
	22	Depletion			22	
	23	Advertising			23	
	24	Pension, profit-sharing, etc., plans			24	
	25	Employee benefit programs			25	
	26	Other deductions (attach schedule)			26	
	27	**Total deductions.** Add lines 12 through 26 . . . . . . ▶			27	
	28	Taxable income before net operating loss deduction and special deductions. Subtract line 27 from line 11			28	
	29	**Less:** a Net operating loss deduction (see instructions)	29a			
		b Special deductions (Schedule C, line 20)	29b		29c	
Tax and Payments	30	**Taxable income.** Subtract line 29c from line 28			30	
	31	**Total tax** (Schedule J, line 10)			31	
	32	**Payments:** a 1993 overpayment credited to 1994	32a			
	b	1994 estimated tax payments . .	32b			
	c	Less 1994 refund applied for on Form 4466	32c ( ) d Bal ▶	32d		
	e	Tax deposited with Form 7004		32e		
	f	Credit from regulated investment companies (attach Form 2439) . . .		32f		
	g	Credit for Federal tax on fuels (attach Form 4136). See instructions . .	32g	32h		
	33	Estimated tax penalty (see instructions). Check if Form 2220 is attached . . . . . ▶ ☐			33	
	34	**Tax due.** If line 32h is smaller than the total of lines 31 and 33, enter amount owed			34	
	35	**Overpayment.** If line 32h is larger than the total of lines 31 and 33, enter amount overpaid . . .			35	
	36	Enter amount of line 35 you want: **Credited to 1995 estimated tax** ▶ Refunded ▶			36	

Please Sign Here

Under penalties of perjury, I declare that I have examined this return, including accompanying schedules and statements, and to the best of my knowledge and belief, it is true, correct, and complete. Declaration of preparer (other than taxpayer) is based on all information of which preparer has any knowledge.

▶ Signature of officer	Date	▶ Title

Paid Preparer's Use Only	Preparer's signature ▶	Date	Check if self-employed ☐	Preparer's social security number
	Firm's name (or yours if self-employed) and address ▶		E.I. No. ▶	
			ZIP code ▶	

Cat. No. 11450Q

Simplified Small Business Accounting

Schedule A   Cost of Goods Sold (See instructions.)

1 Inventory at beginning of year	1	
2 Purchases	2	
3 Cost of labor	3	
4 Additional section 263A costs (attach schedule)	4	
5 Other costs (attach schedule)	5	
6 **Total.** Add lines 1 through 5	6	
7 Inventory at end of year	7	
8 **Cost of goods sold.** Subtract line 7 from line 6. Enter here and on page 1, line 2	8	

9a Check all methods used for valuing closing inventory:

☐ Cost   ☐ Lower of cost or market as described in Regulations section 1.471-4

☐ Writedown of subnormal goods as described in Regulations section 1.471-2(c)

☐ Other (Specify method used and attach explanation.) ▶ ....

b Check if the LIFO inventory method was adopted this tax year for any goods (if checked, attach Form 970) . . . . . ▶ ☐

c If the LIFO inventory method was used for this tax year, enter percentage (or amounts) of closing inventory computed under LIFO . . . . | 9c | |

d Do the rules of section 263A (for property produced or acquired for resale) apply to the corporation? . . . . . ☐ Yes ☐ No

e Was there any change in determining quantities, cost, or valuations between opening and closing inventory? If "Yes," attach explanation . . . . ☐ Yes ☐ No

Schedule C   Dividends and Special Deductions (See instructions.)

	(a) Dividends received	(b) %	(c) Special deductions (a) × (b)
1 Dividends from less-than-20%-owned domestic corporations that are subject to the 70% deduction (other than debt-financed stock)		70	
2 Dividends from 20%-or-more-owned domestic corporations that are subject to the 80% deduction (other than debt-financed stock)		80	
3 Dividends on debt-financed stock of domestic and foreign corporations (section 246A)		see instructions	
4 Dividends on certain preferred stock of less-than-20%-owned public utilities . .		42	
5 Dividends on certain preferred stock of 20%-or-more-owned public utilities . . .		48	
6 Dividends from less-than-20%-owned foreign corporations and certain FSCs that are subject to the 70% deduction		70	
7 Dividends from 20%-or-more-owned foreign corporations and certain FSCs that are subject to the 80% deduction		80	
8 Dividends from wholly owned foreign subsidiaries subject to the 100% deduction (section 245(b))		100	
9 **Total.** Add lines 1 through 8. See instructions for limitation			
10 Dividends from domestic corporations received by a small business investment company operating under the Small Business Investment Act of 1958		100	
11 Dividends from certain FSCs that are subject to the 100% deduction (section 245(c)(1))		100	
12 Dividends from affiliated group members subject to the 100% deduction (section 243(a)(3))		100	
13 Other dividends from foreign corporations not included on lines 3, 6, 7, 8, or 11 . .			
14 Income from controlled foreign corporations under subpart F (attach Form(s) 5471) .			
15 Foreign dividend gross-up (section 78)			
16 IC-DISC and former DISC dividends not included on lines 1, 2, or 3 (section 246(d)) .			
17 Other dividends			
18 Deduction for dividends paid on certain preferred stock of public utilities			
19 **Total dividends.** Add lines 1 through 17. Enter here and on line 4, page 1 . . ▶			

20 **Total special deductions.** Add lines 9, 10, 11, 12, and 18. Enter here and on line 29b, page 1 . . . . . . ▶

Schedule E   Compensation of Officers (See instructions for line 12, page 1.)

Complete Schedule E only if total receipts (line 1a plus lines 4 through 10 on page 1, Form 1120) are $500,000 or more.

(a) Name of officer	(b) Social security number	(c) Percent of time devoted to business	Percent of corporation stock owned		(f) Amount of compensation
			(d) Common	(e) Preferred	
1		%	%	%	
		%	%	%	
		%	%	%	
		%	%	%	
		%	%	%	

2 Total compensation of officers . . . .

3 Compensation of officers claimed on Schedule A and elsewhere on return . . . .

4 Subtract line 3 from line 2. Enter the result here and on line 12, page 1 . . . .

Form 1120 (1994)　　　　　　　　　　　　　　　　　　　　　　　　　Page **3**

Schedule J　Tax Computation (See instructions.)

1 Check if the corporation is a member of a controlled group (see sections 1561 and 1563) . . . . . ▶ ☐

2a If the box on line 1 is checked, enter the corporation's share of the $50,000, $25,000, and $9,925,000 taxable income brackets (in that order):

(1) $ _____   (2) $ _____   (3) $ _____

b Enter the corporation's share of:
(1) Additional 5% tax (not more than $11,750) $ _____
(2) Additional 3% tax (not more than $100,000) $ _____

3 Income tax. Check this box if the corporation is a qualified personal service corporation as defined in section 448(d)(2) (see instructions on page 14). . . . . ▶ ☐ | **3**

4a Foreign tax credit (attach Form 1118) . . . . | **4a**
b Possessions tax credit (attach Form 5735) . . . . | **4b**
c Orphan drug credit (attach Form 6765) . . . . . . | **4c**
d Check: ☐ Nonconventional source fuel credit ☐ QEV credit (attach Form 8834) | **4d**
e General business credit. Enter here and check which forms are attached:
☐ 3800 ☐ 3468 ☐ 5884 ☐ 6478 ☐ 6765 ☐ 8586 ☐ 8830
☐ 8826 ☐ 8835 ☐ 8844 ☐ 8845 ☐ 8846 ☐ 8847 . . . | **4e**
f Credit for prior year minimum tax (attach Form 8827) . . . . | **4f**

5 **Total credits.** Add lines 4a through 4f . . . . | **5**
6 Subtract line 5 from line 3 . . . . | **6**
7 Personal holding company tax (attach Schedule PH (Form 1120)) . . . | **7**
8 Recapture taxes. Check if from: ☐ Form 4255 ☐ Form 8611 . . . | **8**
9a Alternative minimum tax (attach Form 4626) . . . . . . | **9a**
b Environmental tax (attach Form 4626) . . . . . . | **9b**
10 **Total tax.** Add lines 6 through 9b. Enter here and on line 31, page 1 . . . . | **10**

Schedule K　Other Information (See pages 17 and 18 of instructions.)

		Yes	No
1	Check method of accounting: **a** ☐ Cash		
	b ☐ Accrual **c** ☐ Other (specify) ▶		
2	Refer to page 19 of the instructions and state the principal:		
a	Business activity code no. ▶		
b	Business activity ▶		
c	Product or service ▶		
3	Did the corporation at the end of the tax year own, directly or indirectly, 50% or more of the voting stock of a domestic corporation? (For rules of attribution, see section 267(c).)		
	If "Yes," attach a schedule showing: (a) name and identifying number, (b) percentage owned, and (c) taxable income or (loss) before NOL and special deductions of such corporation for the tax year ending with or within your tax year.		
4	Is the corporation a subsidiary in an affiliated group or a parent-subsidiary controlled group?		
	If "Yes," enter employer identification number and name of the parent corporation ▶		
5	Did any individual, partnership, corporation, estate or trust at the end of the tax year own, directly or indirectly, 50% or more of the corporation's voting stock? (For rules of attribution, see section 267(c).)		
	If "Yes," attach a schedule showing name and identifying number. (Do not include any information already entered in 4 above.) Enter percentage owned ▶		
6	During this tax year, did the corporation pay dividends (other than stock dividends and distributions in exchange for stock) in excess of the corporation's current and accumulated earnings and profits? (See secs. 301 and 316.)		
	If "Yes," file Form 5452. If this is a consolidated return, answer here for the parent corporation and on **Form 851,** Affiliations Schedule, for each subsidiary.		

		Yes	No
7	Was the corporation a U.S. shareholder of any controlled foreign corporation? (See sections 951 and 957.) . . .		
	If "Yes," attach Form 5471 for each such corporation. Enter number of Forms 5471 attached ▶		
8	At any time during the 1994 calendar year, did the corporation have an interest in or a signature or other authority over a financial account in a foreign country (such as a bank account, securities account, or other financial account)? .		
	If "Yes," the corporation may have to file Form TD F 90-22.1. If "Yes," enter name of foreign country ▶		
9	Was the corporation the grantor of, or transferor to, a foreign trust that existed during the current tax year, whether or not the corporation has any beneficial interest in it? If "Yes," the corporation may have to file Forms 926, 3520, or 3520-A		
10	Did one foreign person at any time during the tax year own, directly or indirectly, at least 25% of: (a) the total voting power of all classes of stock of the corporation entitled to vote, or (b) the total value of all classes of stock of the corporation? If "Yes,"		
a	Enter percentage owned ▶		
b	Enter owner's country ▶		
c	The corporation may have to file Form 5472. Enter number of Forms 5472 attached ▶		
11	Check this box if the corporation issued publicly offered debt instruments with original issue discount . ▶ ☐		
	If so, the corporation may have to file Form 8281.		
12	Enter the amount of tax-exempt interest received or accrued during the tax year ▶ $		
13	If there were 35 or fewer shareholders at the end of the tax year, enter the number ▶		
14	If the corporation has an NOL for the tax year and is electing to forego the carryback period, check here ▶ ☐		
15	Enter the available NOL carryover from prior tax years (Do not reduce it by any deduction on line 29a.) ▶ $		

Simplified Small Business Accounting

Schedule L	**Balance Sheets**	Beginning of tax year		End of tax year	
	Assets	(a)	(b)	(c)	(d)
1	Cash				
2a	Trade notes and accounts receivable . . .				
b	Less allowance for bad debts	( )		( )	
3	Inventories				
4	U.S. government obligations				
5	Tax-exempt securities (see instructions) . .				
6	Other current assets (attach schedule) . .				
7	Loans to stockholders				
8	Mortgage and real estate loans				
9	Other investments (attach schedule) . .				
10a	Buildings and other depreciable assets . .				
b	Less accumulated depreciation	( )		( )	
11a	Depletable assets				
b	Less accumulated depletion	( )		( )	
12	Land (net of any amortization)				
13a	Intangible assets (amortizable only) . . .				
b	Less accumulated amortization	( )		( )	
14	Other assets (attach schedule)				
15	Total assets				
	Liabilities and Stockholders' Equity				
16	Accounts payable				
17	Mortgages, notes, bonds payable in less than 1 year				
18	Other current liabilities (attach schedule) . .				
19	Loans from stockholders				
20	Mortgages, notes, bonds payable in 1 year or more				
21	Other liabilities (attach schedule)				
22	Capital stock: a Preferred stock . . .				
	b Common stock . . .				
23	Paid-in or capital surplus				
24	Retained earnings—Appropriated (attach schedule)				
25	Retained earnings—Unappropriated . . .				
26	Less cost of treasury stock		( )		( )
27	Total liabilities and stockholders' equity . .				

Note: *You are not required to complete Schedules M-1 and M-2 below if the total assets on line 15, column (d) of Schedule L are less than $25,000.*

Schedule M-1	**Reconciliation of Income (Loss) per Books With Income per Return** (See instructions.)

1	Net income (loss) per books		7	Income recorded on books this year not included on this return (itemize):	
2	Federal income tax				
3	Excess of capital losses over capital gains .			Tax-exempt interest $	
4	Income subject to tax not recorded on books this year (itemize):			....	
	....		8	Deductions on this return not charged against book income this year (itemize):	
5	Expenses recorded on books this year not deducted on this return (itemize):		a	Depreciation . . . . $	
a	Depreciation . . . $		b	Contributions carryover $	
b	Contributions carryover $			....	
c	Travel and entertainment $			....	
	....		9	Add lines 7 and 8	
6	Add lines 1 through 5		10	Income (line 28, page 1)—line 6 less line 9	

Schedule M-2	**Analysis of Unappropriated Retained Earnings per Books (Line 25, Schedule L)**

1	Balance at beginning of year		5	Distributions: a Cash	
2	Net income (loss) per books			b Stock	
3	Other increases (itemize):			c Property	
	....		6	Other decreases (itemize):	
	....			....	
	....		7	Add lines 5 and 6	
4	Add lines 1, 2, and 3		8	Balance at end of year (line 4 less line 7)	

   *U.S. Government Printing Office: 1994 — 375-287

| Form **1120-A**
Department of the Treasury
Internal Revenue Service | **U.S. Corporation Short-Form Income Tax Return**
See separate instructions to make sure the corporation qualifies to file Form 1120-A.
For calendar year 1994 or tax year beginning .... , 1994, ending................ , 19..... | OMB No. 1545-0890
1994 |

A Check this box if the corp. is a personal service corp. (as defined in Temporary Regs. section 1.441-4T—see instructions) ▶ ☐

Use IRS label. Otherwise, please print or type.	Name
	Number, street, and room or suite no. (If a P.O. box, see page 6 of instructions.)
	City or town, state, and ZIP code

B Employer identification number

C Date incorporated

D Total assets (see Specific Instructions) $

E Check applicable boxes: **(1)** ☐ Initial return **(2)** ☐ Change of address

F Check method of accounting: **(1)** ☐ Cash **(2)** ☐ Accrual **(3)** ☐ Other (specify) . . ▶

Income

1a	Gross receipts or sales [ ] **b** Less returns and allowances [ ] **c** Balance ▶	1c	
2	Cost of goods sold (see instructions)	2	
3	Gross profit. Subtract line 2 from line 1c	3	
4	Domestic corporation dividends subject to the 70% deduction	4	
5	Interest	5	
6	Gross rents	6	
7	Gross royalties	7	
8	Capital gain net income (attach Schedule D (Form 1120))	8	
9	Net gain or (loss) from Form 4797, Part II, line 20 (attach Form 4797)	9	
10	Other income (see instructions)	10	
11	**Total income.** Add lines 3 through 10 ▶	11	

Deductions
(See instructions for limitations on deductions.)

12	Compensation of officers (see instructions)	12	
13	Salaries and wages (less employment credits)	13	
14	Repairs and maintenance	14	
15	Bad debts	15	
16	Rents	16	
17	Taxes and licenses	17	
18	Interest	18	
19	Charitable contributions (see instructions for 10% limitation)	19	
20	Depreciation (attach Form 4562) [20]		
21	Less depreciation claimed elsewhere on return [21a]	21b	
22	Other deductions (attach schedule)	22	
23	**Total deductions.** Add lines 12 through 22 ▶	23	
24	Taxable income before net operating loss deduction and special deductions. Subtract line 23 from line 11	24	
25	**Less: a** Net operating loss deduction (see instructions) [25a]		
	b Special deductions (see instructions) [25b]	25c	

26	**Taxable income.** Subtract line 25c from line 24	26	
27	**Total tax** (from page 2, Part I, line 7)	27	
28	**Payments:**		
	a 1993 overpayment credited to 1994 [28a]		
	b 1994 estimated tax payments [28b]		
	c Less 1994 refund applied for on Form 4466 [28c ( )] Bal ▶ [28d]		
	e Tax deposited with Form 7004 [28e]		
	f Credit from regulated investment companies (attach Form 2439) [28f]		
	g Credit for Federal tax on fuels (attach Form 4136). See instructions [28g]		
	h Total payments. Add lines 28d through 28g	28h	
29	Estimated tax penalty (see instructions). Check if Form 2220 is attached ▶ ☐	29	
30	**Tax due.** If line 28h is smaller than the total of lines 27 and 29, enter amount owed	30	
31	**Overpayment.** If line 28h is larger than the total of lines 27 and 29, enter amount overpaid	31	
32	Enter amount of line 31 you want: **Credited to 1995 estimated tax** ▶ [ ] Refunded ▶	32	

Tax and Payments

Please Sign Here

Under penalties of perjury, I declare that I have examined this return, including accompanying schedules and statements, and to the best of my knowledge and belief, it is true, correct, and complete. Declaration of preparer (other than taxpayer) is based on all information of which preparer has any knowledge.

▶ _____ _____ ▶ _____
Signature of officer   Date   Title

Paid Preparer's Use Only	Preparer's signature ▶	Date	Check if self-employed ▶ ☐	Preparer's social security number
	Firm's name (or yours if self-employed) and address ▶		E.I. No. ▶	
			ZIP code ▶	

For Paperwork Reduction Act Notice, see page 1 of the instructions.　　Cat. No. 11456E　　Form **1120-A** (1994)

Simplified Small Business Accounting

Part I Tax Computation (See instructions.)

1	Income tax. If the corporation is a qualified personal service corporation (see page 14), check here ▶ ☐	1
2a	General business credit. Check if from: ☐ Form 3800 ☐ Form 3468 ☐ Form 5884 ☐ Form 6478 ☐ Form 6765 ☐ Form 8586 ☐ Form 8830 ☐ Form 8826 ☐ Form 8835 ☐ Form 8844 ☐ Form 8845 ☐ Form 8846 ☐ Form 8847	2a
b	Credit for prior year minimum tax (attach Form 8827)	2b
3	**Total credits.** Add lines 2a and 2b	3
4	Subtract line 3 from line 1	4
5	Recapture taxes. Check if from: ☐ Form 4255 ☐ Form 8611	5
6	Alternative minimum tax (attach Form 4626)	6
7	**Total tax.** Add lines 4 through 6. Enter here and on line 27, page 1	7

Part II Other Information (See instructions.)

1 Refer to page 19 of the instructions and state the principal:

  a Business activity code no. ▶ ....

  b Business activity ▶ ....

  c Product or service ▶ ....

2 Did any individual, partnership, estate, or trust at the end of the tax year own, directly or indirectly, 50% or more of the corporation's voting stock? (For rules of attribution, see section 267(c).) . . . . ☐ Yes ☐ No

  If "Yes," attach a schedule showing name and identifying number.

3 Enter the amount of tax-exempt interest received or accrued during the tax year . . . . ▶ |$

4 Enter amount of cash distributions and the book value of property (other than cash) distributions made in this tax year . . . . ▶ |$

5a If an amount is entered on line 2, page 1, see the worksheet on page 12 for amounts to enter below:

  (1) Purchases . . . .

  (2) Additional sec. 263A costs (see instructions—attach schedule)

  (3) Other costs (attach schedule)

  b Do the rules of section 263A (for property produced or acquired for resale) apply to the corporation? . . . . . . ☐ Yes ☐ No

6 At any time during the 1994 calendar year, did the corporation have an interest in or a signature or other authority over a financial account in a foreign country (such as a bank account, securities account, or other financial account)? If "Yes," the corporation may have to file Form TD F 90-22.1 . . . . ☐ Yes ☐ No

  If "Yes," enter the name of the foreign country ▶ ....

Part III Balance Sheets

		(a) Beginning of tax year		(b) End of tax year	
Assets	1 Cash				
	2a Trade notes and accounts receivable				
	b Less allowance for bad debts	(	)	(	)
	3 Inventories				
	4 U.S. government obligations				
	5 Tax-exempt securities (see instructions) . . .				
	6 Other current assets (attach schedule)				
	7 Loans to stockholders				
	8 Mortgage and real estate loans				
	9a Depreciable, depletable, and intangible assets .				
	b Less accumulated depreciation, depletion, and amortization	(	)	(	)
	10 Land (net of any amortization)				
	11 Other assets (attach schedule)				
	12 Total assets				
Liabilities and Stockholders' Equity	13 Accounts payable				
	14 Other current liabilities (attach schedule) . . .				
	15 Loans from stockholders				
	16 Mortgages, notes, bonds payable				
	17 Other liabilities (attach schedule)				
	18 Capital stock (preferred and common stock) . .				
	19 Paid-in or capital surplus				
	20 Retained earnings				
	21 Less cost of treasury stock	(	)	(	)
	22 Total liabilities and stockholders' equity				

Part IV Reconciliation of Income (Loss) per Books With Income per Return (You are not required to complete Part IV if the total assets on line 12, column (b), Part III are less than $25,000.)

1 Net income (loss) per books			6 Income recorded on books this year not included on this return (itemize)................		
2 Federal income tax.					
3 Excess of capital losses over capital gains. .			7 Deductions on this return not charged against book income this year (itemize)....................		
4 Income subject to tax not recorded on books this year (itemize)			....		
5 Expenses recorded on books this year not deducted on this return (itemize)			8 Income (line 24, page 1). Enter the sum of lines 1 through 5 less the sum of lines 6 and 7 . .		

✺ *Printed on recycled paper*   ☆ U.S. GPO: 1994-375-292

220

Form **1120S**

Department of the Treasury
Internal Revenue Service

U.S. Income Tax Return for an S Corporation

▶ Do not file this form unless the corporation has timely filed
Form 2553 to elect to be an S corporation.
▶ See separate instructions.

OMB No. 1545-0130

1994

For calendar year 1994, or tax year beginning _____ , 1994, and ending _____ , 19 ____

A Date of election as an S corporation	Use IRS label. Other-wise, please print or type.	Name	C Employer identification number
		Number, street, and room or suite no. (If a P.O. box, see page 9 of the instructions.)	D Date incorporated
B Business code no. (see Specific Instructions)		City or town, state, and ZIP code	E Total assets (see Specific Instructions) $

F Check applicable boxes: (1) ☐ Initial return (2) ☐ Final return (3) ☐ Change in address (4) ☐ Amended return
G Check this box if this S corporation is subject to the consolidated audit procedures of sections 6241 through 6245 (see instructions before checking this box) . ▶ ☐
H Enter number of shareholders in the corporation at end of the tax year . . . . ▶

Caution: *Include only trade or business income and expenses on lines 1a through 21. See the instructions for more information.*

Income

1a	Gross receipts or sales	b Less returns and allowances _____ c Bal ▶	1c
2	Cost of goods sold (Schedule A, line 8)		2
3	Gross profit. Subtract line 2 from line 1c		3
4	Net gain (loss) from Form 4797, Part II, line 20 *(attach Form 4797)*		4
5	Other income (loss) (see instructions) *(attach schedule)* . . .		5
6	**Total income (loss).** Combine lines 3 through 5 . . . . ▶		6

Deductions (See instructions for limitations.)

7	Compensation of officers		7
8	Salaries and wages (less employment credits)		8
9	Repairs and maintenance		9
10	Bad debts		10
11	Rents		11
12	Taxes and licenses		12
13	Interest		13
14a	Depreciation (see instructions)	14a	
b	Depreciation claimed on Schedule A and elsewhere on return	14b	
c	Subtract line 14b from line 14a		14c
15	Depletion (**Do not deduct oil and gas depletion.**)		15
16	Advertising		16
17	Pension, profit-sharing, etc., plans		17
18	Employee benefit programs		18
19	Other deductions (see instructions) *(attach schedule)*		19
20	**Total deductions.** Add the amounts shown in the far right column for lines 7 through 19 . ▶		20
21	Ordinary income (loss) from trade or business activities. Subtract line 20 from line 6 . . .		21

Tax and Payments

22	Tax: a Excess net passive income tax *(attach schedule)*. . .	22a	
b	Tax from Schedule D (Form 1120S)	22b	
c	Add lines 22a and 22b (see instructions for additional taxes) . . .		22c
23	Payments: a 1994 estimated tax payments and amount applied from 1993 return	23a	
b	Tax deposited with Form 7004	23b	
c	Credit for Federal tax paid on fuels *(attach Form 4136)* . . .	23c	
d	Add lines 23a through 23c		23d
24	Estimated tax penalty (see instructions). Check if Form 2220 is attached. . . . . . . ▶☐		24
25	**Tax due.** If the total of lines 22c and 24 is larger than line 23d, enter amount owed. See instructions for depositary method of payment . . . . ▶		25
26	**Overpayment.** If line 23d is larger than the total of lines 22c and 24, enter amount overpaid ▶		26
27	Enter amount of line 26 you want: **Credited to 1995 estimated tax** ▶ _____ **Refunded** ▶		27

Please Sign Here

Under penalties of perjury, I declare that I have examined this return, including accompanying schedules and statements, and to the best of my knowledge and belief, it is true, correct, and complete. Declaration of preparer (other than taxpayer) is based on all information of which preparer has any knowledge.

▶ _____   _____   ▶ _____
Signature of officer   Date   Title

Paid Preparer's Use Only

Preparer's signature ▶		Date		Check if self-employed ▶ ☐	Preparer's social security number
Firm's name (or yours if self-employed) and address ▶				E.I. No. ▶	
				ZIP code ▶	

For Paperwork Reduction Act Notice, see page 1 of separate instructions.   Cat. No. 11510H   Form **1120S** (1994)

Simplified Small Business Accounting

Schedule A   Cost of Goods Sold (See instructions.)

1 Inventory at beginning of year	**1**	
2 Purchases.	**2**	
3 Cost of labor	**3**	
4 Additional section 263A costs (see instructions) *(attach schedule)*	**4**	
5 Other costs *(attach schedule)*.	**5**	
6 **Total.** Add lines 1 through 5	**6**	
7 Inventory at end of year	**7**	
8 **Cost of goods sold.** Subtract line 7 from line 6. Enter here and on page 1, line 2	**8**	

9a Check all methods used for valuing closing inventory:

    (i) ☐ Cost

    (ii) ☐ Lower of cost or market as described in Regulations section 1.471-4

    (iii) ☐ Writedown of "subnormal" goods as described in Regulations section 1.471-2(c)

    (iv) ☐ Other (specify method used and attach explanation) ▶ ....

  b Check if the LIFO inventory method was adopted this tax year for any goods *(if checked, attach Form 970).* . . . . . . ▶ ☐

  c If the LIFO inventory method was used for this tax year, enter percentage (or amounts) of closing
    inventory computed under LIFO . . . . | **9c** |

  d Do the rules of section 263A (for property produced or acquired for resale) apply to the corporation? . . . . ☐ Yes ☐ No

  e Was there any change in determining quantities, cost, or valuations between opening and closing inventory? . . ☐ Yes ☐ No
    If "Yes," attach explanation.

Schedule B   Other Information

	Yes	No
1 Check method of accounting: **(a)** ☐ Cash **(b)** ☐ Accrual **(c)** ☐ Other (specify) ▶		
2 Refer to the list in the instructions and state the corporation's principal: **(a)** Business activity ▶ .... **(b)** Product or service ▶		
3 Did the corporation at the end of the tax year own, directly or indirectly, 50% or more of the voting stock of a domestic corporation? (For rules of attribution, see section 267(c).) If "Yes," attach a schedule showing: **(a)** name, address, and employer identification number and **(b)** percentage owned.		
4 Was the corporation a member of a controlled group subject to the provisions of section 1561?		
5 At any time during calendar year 1994, did the corporation have an interest in or a signature or other authority over a financial account in a foreign country (such as a bank account, securities account, or other financial account)? (See instructions for exceptions and filing requirements for Form TD F 90-22.1.) . . . . If "Yes," enter the name of the foreign country ▶		
6 Was the corporation the grantor of, or transferor to, a foreign trust that existed during the current tax year, whether or not the corporation has any beneficial interest in it? If "Yes," the corporation may have to file Forms 3520, 3520-A, or 926		
7 Check this box if the corporation has filed or is required to file **Form 8264,** Application for Registration of a Tax Shelter . . . . ▶ ☐		
8 Check this box if the corporation issued publicly offered debt instruments with original issue discount . . ▶ ☐ If so, the corporation may have to file **Form 8281,** Information Return for Publicly Offered Original Issue Discount Instruments.		
9 If the corporation: **(a)** filed its election to be an S corporation after 1986, **(b)** was a C corporation before it elected to be an S corporation **or** the corporation acquired an asset with a basis determined by reference to its basis (or the basis of any other property) in the hands of a C corporation, and **(c)** has net unrealized built-in gain (defined in section 1374(d)(1)) in excess of the net recognized built-in gain from prior years, enter the net unrealized built-in gain reduced by net recognized built-in gain from prior years (see instructions) . . . . ▶ $		
10 Check this box if the corporation had subchapter C earnings and profits at the close of the tax year (see instructions) . . . . ▶ ☐		

Designation of Tax Matters Person (See instructions.)

Enter below the shareholder designated as the tax matters person (TMP) for the tax year of this return:

Name of designated TMP ▶	Identifying number of TMP ▶

Address of
designated TMP ▶

Form 1120S (1994)   Page **3**

Schedule K   **Shareholders' Shares of Income, Credits, Deductions, etc.**

	(a) Pro rata share items		(b) Total amount	
Income (Loss)	**1** Ordinary income (loss) from trade or business activities (page 1, line 21)	**1**		
	2 Net income (loss) from rental real estate activities *(attach Form 8825)*	**2**		
	3a Gross income from other rental activities `3a`			
	b Expenses from other rental activities *(attach schedule)* `3b`			
	c Net income (loss) from other rental activities. Subtract line 3b from line 3a	**3c**		
	4 Portfolio income (loss):			
	a Interest income	**4a**		
	b Dividend income	**4b**		
	c Royalty income	**4c**		
	d Net short-term capital gain (loss) *(attach Schedule D (Form 1120S))*	**4d**		
	e Net long-term capital gain (loss) *(attach Schedule D (Form 1120S))*	**4e**		
	f Other portfolio income (loss) *(attach schedule)*	**4f**		
	5 Net gain (loss) under section 1231 (other than due to casualty or theft) *(attach Form 4797)*	**5**		
	6 Other income (loss) *(attach schedule)*	**6**		
Deductions	**7** Charitable contributions (see instructions) *(attach schedule)*	**7**		
	8 Section 179 expense deduction *(attach Form 4562)*.	**8**		
	9 Deductions related to portfolio income (loss) (see instructions) (itemize)	**9**		
	10 Other deductions *(attach schedule)*	**10**		
Investment Interest	**11a** Interest expense on investment debts	**11a**		
	b (1) Investment income included on lines 4a, 4b, 4c, and 4f above	**11b(1)**		
	(2) Investment expenses included on line 9 above	**11b(2)**		
Credits	**12a** Credit for alcohol used as a fuel *(attach Form 6478)*	**12a**		
	b Low-income housing credit (see instructions):			
	(1) From partnerships to which section 42(j)(5) applies for property placed in service before 1990	**12b(1)**		
	(2) Other than on line 12b(1) for property placed in service before 1990.	**12b(2)**		
	(3) From partnerships to which section 42(j)(5) applies for property placed in service after 1989	**12b(3)**		
	(4) Other than on line 12b(3) for property placed in service after 1989	**12b(4)**		
	c Qualified rehabilitation expenditures related to rental real estate activities *(attach Form 3468)*	**12c**		
	d Credits (other than credits shown on lines 12b and 12c) related to rental real estate activities (see instructions).	**12d**		
	e Credits related to other rental activities (see instructions)	**12e**		
	13 Other credits (see instructions)	**13**		
Adjustments and Tax Preference Items	**14a** Depreciation adjustment on property placed in service after 1986	**14a**		
	b Adjusted gain or loss	**14b**		
	c Depletion (other than oil and gas)	**14c**		
	d (1) Gross income from oil, gas, or geothermal properties	**14d(1)**		
	(2) Deductions allocable to oil, gas, or geothermal properties	**14d(2)**		
	e Other adjustments and tax preference items *(attach schedule)*	**14e**		
Foreign Taxes	**15a** Type of income ▶			
	b Name of foreign country or U.S. possession ▶			
	c Total gross income from sources outside the United States *(attach schedule)*	**15c**		
	d Total applicable deductions and losses *(attach schedule)*	**15d**		
	e Total foreign taxes (check one): ▶ ☐ Paid ☐ Accrued	**15e**		
	f Reduction in taxes available for credit *(attach schedule)*	**15f**		
	g Other foreign tax information *(attach schedule)*	**15g**		
Other	**16a** Total expenditures to which a section 59(e) election may apply	**16a**		
	b Type of expenditures ▶			
	17 Tax-exempt interest income	**17**		
	18 Other tax-exempt income	**18**		
	19 Nondeductible expenses	**19**		
	20 Total property distributions (including cash) other than dividends reported on line 22 below	**20**		
	21 Other items and amounts required to be reported separately to shareholders (see instructions) *(attach schedule)*			
	22 Total dividend distributions paid from accumulated earnings and profits	**22**		
	23 **Income (loss).** (Required only if Schedule M-1 must be completed.) Combine lines 1 through 6 in column (b). From the result, subtract the sum of lines 7 through 11a, 15e, and 16a	**23**		

Simplified Small Business Accounting

Schedule L	Balance Sheets	Beginning of tax year		End of tax year	
	Assets	(a)	(b)	(c)	(d)
1	Cash				
2a	Trade notes and accounts receivable				
b	Less allowance for bad debts				
3	Inventories				
4	U.S. Government obligations				
5	Tax-exempt securities				
6	Other current assets (attach schedule)				
7	Loans to shareholders				
8	Mortgage and real estate loans				
9	Other investments (attach schedule)				
10a	Buildings and other depreciable assets				
b	Less accumulated depreciation				
11a	Depletable assets				
b	Less accumulated depletion				
12	Land (net of any amortization)				
13a	Intangible assets (amortizable only)				
b	Less accumulated amortization				
14	Other assets (attach schedule)				
15	Total assets				
	Liabilities and Shareholders' Equity				
16	Accounts payable				
17	Mortgages, notes, bonds payable in less than 1 year				
18	Other current liabilities (attach schedule)				
19	Loans from shareholders				
20	Mortgages, notes, bonds payable in 1 year or more				
21	Other liabilities (attach schedule)				
22	Capital stock				
23	Paid-in or capital surplus				
24	Retained earnings				
25	Less cost of treasury stock		( )		( )
26	Total liabilities and shareholders' equity				

Schedule M-1	Reconciliation of Income (Loss) per Books With Income (Loss) per Return (You are not required to complete this schedule if the total assets on line 15, column (d), of Schedule L are less than $25,000.)

1	Net income (loss) per books		5	Income recorded on books this year not included on Schedule K, lines 1 through 6 (itemize):
2	Income included on Schedule K, lines 1 through 6, not recorded on books this year (itemize):		a	Tax-exempt interest $ ....
3	Expenses recorded on books this year not included on Schedule K, lines 1 through 11a, 15e, and 16a (itemize):		6	Deductions included on Schedule K, lines 1 through 11a, 15e, and 16a, not charged against book income this year (itemize):
a	Depreciation $		a	Depreciation $ ....
b	Travel and entertainment $			
			7	Add lines 5 and 6
4	Add lines 1 through 3		8	Income (loss) (Schedule K, line 23). Line 4 less line 7

Schedule M-2	Analysis of Accumulated Adjustments Account, Other Adjustments Account, and Shareholders' Undistributed Taxable Income Previously Taxed (See instructions.)

		(a) Accumulated adjustments account	(b) Other adjustments account	(c) Shareholders' undistributed taxable income previously taxed
1	Balance at beginning of tax year			
2	Ordinary income from page 1, line 21			
3	Other additions			
4	Loss from page 1, line 21	( )		
5	Other reductions	( )	( )	
6	Combine lines 1 through 5			
7	Distributions other than dividend distributions			
8	Balance at end of tax year. Subtract line 7 from line 6			

| SCHEDULE K-1
(Form 1120S)
Department of the Treasury
Internal Revenue Service | Shareholder's Share of Income, Credits, Deductions, etc.
▶ See separate instructions.
For calendar year 1994 or tax year
beginning   , 1994, and ending   , 19 | OMB No. 1545-0130
1994 |

Shareholder's identifying number ▶	Corporation's identifying number ▶
Shareholder's name, address, and ZIP code	Corporation's name, address, and ZIP code

A Shareholder's percentage of stock ownership for tax year (see Instructions for Schedule K-1) . . . . ▶ .... %

B Internal Revenue Service Center where corporation filed its return ▶ ....

C Tax shelter registration number (see Instructions for Schedule K-1) . . . . ▶ ....

D Check applicable boxes: **(1)** ☐ Final K-1   **(2)** ☐ Amended K-1

	(a) Pro rata share items		(b) Amount	(c) Form 1040 filers enter the amount in column (b) on:
Income (Loss)	**1** Ordinary income (loss) from trade or business activities . . .	**1**		See Shareholder's Instructions for Schedule K-1 (Form 1120S).
	2 Net income (loss) from rental real estate activities	**2**		
	3 Net income (loss) from other rental activities	**3**		
	4 Portfolio income (loss):			
	a Interest	**4a**		Sch. B, Part I, line 1
	b Dividends	**4b**		Sch. B, Part II, line 5
	c Royalties	**4c**		Sch. E, Part I, line 4
	d Net short-term capital gain (loss).	**4d**		Sch. D, line 5, col. (f) or (g)
	e Net long-term capital gain (loss)	**4e**		Sch. D, line 13, col. (f) or (g)
	f Other portfolio income (loss) *(attach schedule)*	**4f**		(Enter on applicable line of your return.)
	5 Net gain (loss) under section 1231 (other than due to casualty or theft)	**5**		See Shareholder's Instructions for Schedule K-1 (Form 1120S)
	6 Other income (loss) *(attach schedule)*	**6**		(Enter on applicable line of your return.)
Deductions	**7** Charitable contributions (see instructions) *(attach schedule)* .	**7**		Sch. A, line 15 or 16
	8 Section 179 expense deduction	**8**		See Shareholder's Instructions for Schedule K-1 (Form 1120S).
	9 Deductions related to portfolio income (loss) *(attach schedule)* .	**9**		
	10 Other deductions *(attach schedule)*	**10**		
Investment Interest	**11a** Interest expense on investment debts	**11a**		Form 4952, line 1
	b (1) Investment income included on lines 4a, 4b, 4c, and 4f above	**b(1)**		See Shareholder's Instructions for Schedule K-1 (Form 1120S).
	(2) Investment expenses included on line 9 above	**b(2)**		
Credits	**12a** Credit for alcohol used as fuel	**12a**		Form 6478, line 10
	b Low-income housing credit:			
	(1) From section 42(j)(5) partnerships for property placed in service before 1990.	**b(1)**		Form 8586, line 5
	(2) Other than on line 12b(1) for property placed in service before 1990	**b(2)**		
	(3) From section 42(j)(5) partnerships for property placed in service after 1989	**b(3)**		
	(4) Other than on line 12b(3) for property placed in service after 1989	**b(4)**		
	c Qualified rehabilitation expenditures related to rental real estate activities (see instructions).	**12c**		See Shareholder's Instructions for Schedule K-1 (Form 1120S).
	d Credits (other than credits shown on lines 12b and 12c) related to rental real estate activities (see instructions) . . .	**12d**		
	e Credits related to other rental activities (see instructions) . .	**12e**		
	13 Other credits (see instructions)	**13**		
Adjustments and Tax Preference Items	**14a** Depreciation adjustment on property placed in service after 1986	**14a**		See Shareholder's Instructions for Schedule K-1 (Form 1120S) and Instructions for Form 6251
	b Adjusted gain or loss	**14b**		
	c Depletion (other than oil and gas)	**14c**		
	d (1) Gross income from oil, gas, or geothermal properties . . .	**d(1)**		
	(2) Deductions allocable to oil, gas, or geothermal properties	**d(2)**		
	e Other adjustments and tax preference items *(attach schedule)* .	**14e**		

For Paperwork Reduction Act Notice, see page 1 of Instructions for Form 1120S.   Cat. No. 11520D   **Schedule K-1 (Form 1120S) 1994**

Simplified Small Business Accounting

Schedule K-1 (Form 1120S) (1994)

Page **2**

	(a) Pro rata share items		(b) Amount	(c) Form 1040 filers enter the amount in column (b) on:
Foreign Taxes	**15a** Type of income ▶			Form 1116, Check boxes
	b Name of foreign country or U.S. possession ▶			
	c Total gross income from sources outside the United States *(attach schedule)*	15c		Form 1116, Part I
	d Total applicable deductions and losses *(attach schedule)*	15d		
	e Total foreign taxes (check one): ▶ ☐ Paid ☐ Accrued	15e		Form 1116, Part II
	f Reduction in taxes available for credit *(attach schedule)*	15f		Form 1116, Part III
	g Other foreign tax information *(attach schedule)*	15g		See Instructions for Form 1116
Other	**16a** Total expenditures to which a section 59(e) election may apply	16a		See Shareholder's Instructions for Schedule K-1 (Form 1120S).
	b Type of expenditures ▶			
	17 Tax-exempt interest income	17		Form 1040, line 8b
	18 Other tax-exempt income	18		
	19 Nondeductible expenses	19		
	20 Property distributions (including cash) other than dividend distributions reported to you on Form 1099-DIV	20		See Shareholder's Instructions for Schedule K-1 (Form 1120S).
	21 Amount of loan repayments for "Loans From Shareholders"	21		
	22 Recapture of low-income housing credit:			
	a From section 42(j)(5) partnerships	22a		Form 8611, line 8
	b Other than on line 22a	22b		

23 Supplemental information required to be reported separately to each shareholder *(attach additional schedules if more space is needed):*

Supplemental Information

GPO : 1994 O - 375-319

226

Form 1120-W
(WORKSHEET)
Department of the Treasury
Internal Revenue Service

Estimated Tax for Corporations

For calendar year 1995, or tax year beginning .... , 1995, and ending .... , 19 .....

(Keep for the corporation's records—Do *not* send to the Internal Revenue Service)

OMB No. 1545-0975

1995

1	Taxable income expected in the tax year	1
	(Qualified personal service corporations (defined in the instructions), skip lines 2 through 13 and go to line 14.)	
2	Enter the smaller of line 1 or $50,000. (Members of a controlled group, see instructions.). . .	2
3	Subtract line 2 from line 1	3
4	Enter the smaller of line 3 or $25,000. (Members of a controlled group, see instructions.). . .	4
5	Subtract line 4 from line 3	5
6	Enter the smaller of line 5 or $9,925,000. (Members of a controlled group, see instructions.) .	6
7	Subtract line 6 from line 5	7
8	Multiply line 2 by 15%	8
9	Multiply line 4 by 25%	9
10	Multiply line 6 by 34%	10
11	Multiply line 7 by 35%	11
12	If line 1 is greater than $100,000, enter the smaller of 5% of the excess over $100,000 or $11,750. Otherwise, enter -0-. (Members of a controlled group, see instructions.)	12
13	If line 1 is greater than $15 million, enter the smaller of 3% of the excess over $15 million or $100,000. Otherwise, enter -0-. (Members of a controlled group, see instructions.) . .	13
14	**Total.** Add lines 8 through 13. (Qualified personal service corporations, multiply line 1 by 35%.)	14
15	Estimated tax credits (see instructions)	15
16	Subtract line 15 from line 14	16
17	Recapture taxes	17
18a	Alternative minimum tax (see instructions)	18a
b	Environmental tax (see instructions)	18b
19	**Total.** Add lines 16 through 18b	19
20	Credit for Federal tax paid on fuels (see instructions)	20
21	Subtract line 20 from line 19. **Note:** *If the result is less than $500, the corporation is not required to make estimated tax payments.*	21
22a	Enter the tax shown on the corporation's 1994 tax return. **CAUTION: See instructions before completing this line**	22a
b	Enter the smaller of line 21 or line 22a. If the corporation is required to skip line 22a, enter the amount from line 21 on line 22b	22b

		(a)	(b)	(c)	(d)
23	**Installment due dates** (See instructions.) . . . . ▶				
24	**Required installments.** Enter 25% of line 22b in columns **(a)** through **(d)** unless **a** or **b** below applies. (See instructions.)				
a	**Annualized income installment method and/or adjusted seasonal installment method.** Complete Schedule A. (See instructions.)				
b	**"Large corporations."** (See instructions.)				

For Paperwork Reduction Act Notice, see the instructions on page 4.　　Cat. No. 11525G　　Form **1120-W** (1995)

Simplified Small Business Accounting

| Schedule A | Required Installments Using the Annualized Income Installment Method and/or the Adjusted Seasonal Installment Method Under Section 6655(e). (See instructions.) |

Part I—Annualized Income Installment Method

			(a)	(b)	(c)	(d)
1	Annualization period (see instructions).	1	First ____ months	First ____ months	First ____ months	First ____ months
2	Enter taxable income for each period.	2				
3	Annualization amount (see instructions).	3				
4	Multiply line 2 by line 3.	4				
5	Figure the tax on the amount in each column on line 4 by following the same steps used to figure the tax for line 14, page 1 of Form 1120-W.	5				
6	Enter other taxes for each payment period (see instructions).	6				
7	Total tax. Add lines 5 and 6.	7				
8	For each period, enter the same type of credits as allowed on lines 15 and 20, page 1 of Form 1120-W (see instructions).	8				
9	Total tax after credits. Subtract line 8 from line 7. If zero or less, enter -0-.	9				
10	Applicable percentage.	10	25%	50%	75%	100%
11	Multiply line 9 by line 10.	11				
12	Add the amounts in all preceding columns of line 41 (see instructions).	12	////////			
13	Subtract line 12 from line 11. If zero or less, enter -0-.	13				

Part II—Adjusted Seasonal Installment Method
(Use this method only if the base period percentage for any 6 consecutive months is at least 70%.)

			(a)	(b)	(c)	(d)
14	Enter taxable income for the following periods:		First 3 months	First 5 months	First 8 months	First 11 months
a	Tax year beginning in 1992	14a				
b	Tax year beginning in 1993	14b				
c	Tax year beginning in 1994	14c				
15	Enter taxable income for each period for the tax year beginning in 1995.	15				
16	Enter taxable income for the following periods:		First 4 months	First 6 months	First 9 months	Entire year
a	Tax year beginning in 1992	16a				
b	Tax year beginning in 1993	16b				
c	Tax year beginning in 1994	16c				
17	Divide the amount in each column on line 14a by the amount in column (d) on line 16a.	17				
18	Divide the amount in each column on line 14b by the amount in column (d) on line 16b.	18				
19	Divide the amount in each column on line 14c by the amount in column (d) on line 16c.	19				

228

Form 1120-W (WORKSHEET) 1995   Page **3**

		(a) First 4 months	(b) First 6 months	(c) First 9 months	(d) Entire year
20	Add lines 17 through 19. **20**				
21	Divide line 20 by 3. **21**				
22	Divide line 15 by line 21. **22**				
23	Figure the tax on the amount on line 22 by following the same steps used to figure the tax for line 14, page 1 of Form 1120-W. **23**				
24	Divide the amount in columns (a) through (c) on line 16a by the amount in column (d) on line 16a. **24**				/////
25	Divide the amount in columns (a) through (c) on line 16b by the amount in column (d) on line 16b. **25**				/////
26	Divide the amount in columns (a) through (c) on line 16c by the amount in column (d) on line 16c. **26**				/////
27	Add lines 24 through 26. **27**				/////
28	Divide line 27 by 3. **28**				/////
29	Multiply the amount in columns (a) through (c) of line 23 by the amount in the corresponding column of line 28. In column (d), enter the amount from line 23, column (d). **29**				
30	Enter other taxes for each payment period (see instructions). **30**				
31	Total tax. Add lines 29 and 30. **31**				
32	For each period, enter the same type of credits as allowed on lines 15 and 20, page 1 of Form 1120-W (see instructions). **32**				
33	Total tax after credits. Subtract line 32 from line 31. If zero or less, enter -0-. **33**				
34	Add the amounts in all preceding columns of line 41 (see instructions). **34**	/////			
35	Subtract line 34 from line 33. If zero or less, enter -0-. **35**				

Part III—Required Installments

		1st installment	2nd installment	3rd installment	4th installment
36	If only one of the above parts is completed, enter the amount in each column from line 13 or line 35. If both parts are completed, enter the **smaller** of the amounts in each column from line 13 or line 35. **36**				
37	Divide line 22b, page 1 of Form 1120-W, by 4 and enter the result in each column. (**Note:** *"Large corporations," see the instructions for line 24b for the amount to enter.*) **37**				
38	Enter the amount from line 40 for the preceding column. **38**	/////			
39	Add lines 37 and 38. **39**				
40	If line 39 is more than line 36, subtract line 36 from line 39. Otherwise, enter -0-. **40**				/////
41	**Required installments.** Enter the **smaller** of line 36 or line 39 here and on line 24, page 1 of Form 1120-W. **41**				

Simplified Small Business Accounting

Form **940**

Department of the Treasury
Internal Revenue Service   (O)

**Employer's Annual Federal
Unemployment (FUTA) Tax Return**

▶ **For Paperwork Reduction Act Notice, see separate Instructions.**

OMB No. 1545-0028

1994

T	
FF	
FD	
FP	
I	
T	

Name (as distinguished from trade name)   Calendar year

Trade name, if any

Address and ZIP code   Employer identification number

A Are you required to pay unemployment contributions to only one state? (If no, skip questions B and C.) . .   ☐ Yes ☐ No

B Did you pay all state unemployment contributions by January 31, 1995? (If a 0% experience rate is granted, check "Yes.") (If no, skip question C.) . . . .   ☐ Yes ☐ No

C Were all wages that were taxable for FUTA tax also taxable for your state's unemployment tax? . . . . .   ☐ Yes ☐ No

If you answered "No" to any of these questions, you must file Form 940. If you answered "Yes" to all the questions, you may file Form 940-EZ, which is a simplified version of Form 940. You can get Form 940-EZ by calling 1-800-TAX-FORM (1-800-829-3676).

If you will not have to file returns in the future, check here, complete, and sign the return . . . . ▶ ☐

If this is an Amended Return, check here . . . . ▶ ☐

Part I	**Computation of Taxable Wages**

1 Total payments (including exempt payments) during the calendar year for services of employees . **1**

2 Exempt payments. (Explain each exemption shown, attach additional sheets if necessary.) ▶ --

--   Amount paid   **2**

3 Payments of more than $7,000 for services. Enter only amounts over the first $7,000 paid to each employee. Do not include payments from line 2. The $7,000 amount is the Federal wage base. Your state wage base may be different. **Do not use the state wage limitation**   **3**

4 Total exempt payments (add lines 2 and 3) **4**

5 **Total taxable wages** (subtract line 4 from line 1) . . . . ▶   **5**

Be sure to complete both sides of this return and sign in the space provided on the back.   Cat. No. 11234O   Form **940** (1994)

DO NOT DETACH

Form **940-V**

Department of the Treasury
Internal Revenue Service

Form 940 Payment Voucher

1994

Complete boxes 1, 2, 6, and 7. **Do not send cash and do not staple your payment to this voucher.** Make your check or money order payable to the **Internal Revenue Service.** If tax due is over $100, make the deposit with Form 8109.

1 Your employer identification number	2 Enter the first four letters of your business name	3 MFT	4 Tax year	5 Transaction code
		1 0	9 4 1 2	6 1 0
	6 Your business name and address		7 Amount of payment	
Do not staple your payment to this voucher.			$.
Do not send cash.	

230

Form 940 (1994) | Page **2**

Part II   Tax Due or Refund

1   Gross FUTA tax. Multiply the wages in Part I, line 5, by .062 . . . . | **1**

2   Maximum credit. Multiply the wages in Part I, line 5, by .054 . . . | **2** |

3   **Computation of tentative credit** (Note: *All taxpayers must complete the applicable columns.*)

(a) Name of state	(b) State reporting number(s) as shown on employer's state contribution returns	(c) Taxable payroll (as defined in state act)	(d) State experience rate period		(e) State experience rate	(f) Contributions if rate had been 5.4% (col. (c) x .054)	(g) Contributions payable at experience rate (col. (c) x col. (e))	(h) Additional credit (col. (f) minus col.(g)). If 0 or less, enter -0-.	(i) Contributions actually paid to state
			From	To					

3a   Totals . . . ▶

3b   Total tentative credit (add line 3a, columns (h) and (i) only—see instructions for limitations on late payments) ▶

4

5

6   **Credit:** Enter the smaller of the amount in Part II, line 2, or line 3b. . . . . | **6**

7   **Total FUTA tax** (subtract line 6 from line 1) . . . . | **7**

8   Total FUTA tax deposited for the year, including any overpayment applied from a prior year . . | **8**

9   **Balance due** (subtract line 8 from line 7). This should be $100 or less. Pay to the Internal Revenue Service. See page 3 of the Instructions for Form 940 for details . . . . ▶ | **9**

10   **Overpayment** (subtract line 7 from line 8). Check if it is to be: ☐ **Applied to next return,** or ☐ **Refunded** . . . . ▶ | **10**

Part III   Record of Quarterly Federal Unemployment Tax Liability *(Do not include state liability)*

Quarter	First	Second	Third	Fourth	Total for year
Liability for quarter					

Under penalties of perjury, I declare that I have examined this return, including accompanying schedules and statements, and to the best of my knowledge and belief, it is true, correct, and complete, and that no part of any payment made to a state unemployment fund claimed as a credit was or is to be deducted from the payments to employees.

Signature ▶   Title (Owner, etc.) ▶   Date ▶

Simplified Small Business Accounting

Form **940-EZ**

Department of the Treasury
Internal Revenue Service (O)

**Employer's Annual Federal
Unemployment (FUTA) Tax Return**

OMB No. 1545-1110

19**94**

T	
FF	
FD	
FP	
I	
T	

Name (as distinguished from trade name)

Calendar year

Trade name, if any

Address and ZIP code

Employer identification number

*Follow the chart under **Who May Use Form 940-EZ** on page 2. If you cannot use Form 940-EZ, you must use Form 940 instead.*

A   Enter the amount of contributions paid to your state unemployment fund. (See instructions for line A on page 4.) ▶ $ ....

B   (1) Enter the name of the state where you have to pay contributions . . . . ▶ ....
      (2) Enter your state reporting number as shown on state unemployment tax return. ▶

If you will not have to file returns in the future, check here (see **Who Must File**, on page 2) **complete, and sign the return** . . . . . ▶ ☐

If this is an Amended Return check here . . . . ▶ ☐

Part I   Taxable Wages and FUTA Tax

1	Total payments (including payments shown on lines 2 and 3) during the calendar year for services of employees		**1**		
			Amount paid		
2	Exempt payments. (Explain all exempt payments, attaching additional sheets if necessary.) ▶		**2**		
3	Payments for services of more than $7,000. Enter only amounts over the first $7,000 paid to each employee. Do not include any exempt payments from line 2. Do not use your state wage limitation. The $7,000 amount is the Federal wage base. Your state wage base may be different		**3**		
4	Total exempt payments (add lines 2 and 3)		**4**		
5	**Total taxable wages** (subtract line 4 from line 1) . . . . ▶		**5**		
6	FUTA tax. Multiply the wages on line 5 by .008 and enter here. (If the result is over $100, also complete Part II.) ▶		**6**		
7	Total FUTA tax deposited for the year, including any overpayment applied from a prior year (from your records)		**7**		
8	**Amount you owe** (subtract line 7 from line 6). This should be $100 or less. Pay to "Internal Revenue Service." ▶		**8**		
9	Overpayment (subtract line 6 from line 7). Check if it is to be: ☐ **Applied to next return,** or ☐ Refunded ▶		**9**		

Part II   Record of Quarterly Federal Unemployment Tax Liability (Do not include state liability.) Complete only if line 6 is over $100.

Quarter	First (Jan. 1 – Mar. 31)	Second (Apr. 1 – June 30)	Third (July 1 – Sept. 30)	Fourth (Oct. 1 – Dec. 31)	Total for year
Liability for quarter					

Under penalties of perjury, I declare that I have examined this return, including accompanying schedules and statements, and, to the best of my knowledge and belief, it is true, correct, and complete, and that no part of any payment made to a state unemployment fund claimed as a credit was, or is to be, deducted from the payments to employees.

Signature ▶   Title (Owner, etc.) ▶   Date ▶

Cat. No. 10983G

Form **940-EZ** (1994)

DO NOT DETACH

Form **940-V-EZ**

Department of the Treasury
Internal Revenue Service

Form 940-EZ Payment Voucher

19**94**

Complete boxes 1, 2, 6, and 7. **Do not send cash and do not staple your payment to this voucher.** Make your check or money order, with your employer identification number clearly written on it, payable to the **Internal Revenue Service.**

1 Your employer identification number	2 Enter the first four letters of your business name	3 MFT	4 Tax year	5 Transaction code
		1 0	9 4 1 2	6 1 0
	6 Your name and address		7 Amount of payment	
			$.	
Do not staple your payment to this voucher.			Do not send cash.	

232

Form **941**
(Rev. April 1994)
Department of the Treasury
Internal Revenue Service (O)

4141

Employer's Quarterly Federal Tax Return

▶ **See separate instructions for information on completing this return.**
Please type or print.

Enter state code for state in which deposits made ▶ (see page 2 of instructions).

Name (as distinguished from trade name)	Date quarter ended
Trade name, if any	Employer identification number
Address (number and street)	City, state, and ZIP code

OMB No. 1545-0029

T
FF
FD
FP
I
T

If address is different from prior return, check here ▶

IRS Use

```
1  1  1   1   1  1  1  1  1   2   3  3  3  3  3  3   4  4  4
5  5  5    6    7    8  8  8  8  8   9  9  9   10 10 10 10 10 10 10 10 10 10
```

If you do not have to file returns in the future, check here ▶ ☐ and enter date final wages paid ▶

If you are a seasonal employer, see **Seasonal employers** on page 2 and check here (see instructions) ▶ ☐

1	Number of employees (except household) employed in the pay period that includes March 12th ▶		
2	Total wages and tips subject to withholding, plus other compensation	2	
3	Total income tax withheld from wages, tips, and sick pay	3	
4	Adjustment of withheld income tax for preceding quarters of calendar year	4	
5	Adjusted total of income tax withheld (line 3 as adjusted by line 4—see instructions) . . .	5	
6a	Taxable social security wages . . . . . . $ _____ × 12.4% (.124) =	6a	
b	Taxable social security tips . . . . $ _____ × 12.4% (.124) =	6b	
7	Taxable Medicare wages and tips . . . . . $ _____ × 2.9% (.029) =	7	
8	Total social security and Medicare taxes (add lines 6a, 6b, and 7). Check here if wages are not subject to social security and/or Medicare tax . . . . ▶ ☐	8	
9	Adjustment of social security and Medicare taxes (see instructions for required explanation) Sick Pay $ _____ ± Fractions of Cents $ _____ ± Other $ _____ =	9	
10	Adjusted total of social security and Medicare taxes (line 8 as adjusted by line 9—see instructions)	10	
11	**Total taxes** (add lines 5 and 10)	11	
12	Advance earned income credit (EIC) payments made to employees, if any	12	
13	Net taxes (subtract line 12 from line 11). **This should equal line 17, column (d) below** (or line D of Schedule B (Form 941))	13	
14	Total deposits for quarter, including overpayment applied from a prior quarter	14	
15	**Balance due** (subtract line 14 from line 13). Pay to Internal Revenue Service	15	

16 **Overpayment,** if line 14 is more than line 13, enter excess here ▶ $ _____
and check if to be: ☐ Applied to next return **OR** ☐ Refunded.

- **All filers:** If line 13 is less than $500, you need not complete line 17 or Schedule B.
- **Semiweekly depositors:** Complete Schedule B and check here . . . . ▶ ☐
- **Monthly depositors:** Complete line 17, columns (a) through (d) and check here . . . . . ▶ ☐

17 Monthly Summary of Federal Tax Liability.

(a) First month liability	(b) Second month liability	(c) Third month liability	(d) Total liability for quarter

Sign Here

Under penalties of perjury, I declare that I have examined this return, including accompanying schedules and statements, and to the best of my knowledge and belief, it is true, correct, and complete.

Signature ▶ _____ Print Your Name and Title ▶ _____ Date ▶ _____

For Paperwork Reduction Act Notice, see page 1 of separate instructions.   Cat. No. 17001Z   Form **941** (Rev. 4-94)

*U.S. Government Printing Office: 1995 — 387-095/00360

DO NOT STAPLE   6969

Form **1096**	**Annual Summary and Transmittal of U.S. Information Returns**	OMB No. 1545-0108
Department of the Treasury Internal Revenue Service		**1994**

┌─────────────────────────────────────┐
│ FILER'S name   │
│   │
│ Street address (including room or suite number) │
│   │
│ City, state, and ZIP code   │
└─────────────────────────────────────┘

If you are not using a preprinted label, enter in box 1 or 2 below the identification number you used as the filer on the information returns being transmitted. Do not fill in both boxes 1 and 2.

Name of person to contact if the IRS needs more information

Telephone number
(   )

For Official Use Only

1 Employer identification number	2 Social security number	3 Total number of forms	4 Federal income tax withheld $	5 Total amount reported with this Form 1096 $

Enter an "X" in only one box below to indicate the type of form being filed.

If this is your FINAL return, enter an "X" here ▶ ☐

W-2G 32	1098 81	1099-A 80	1099-B 79	1099-C 85	1099-DIV 91	1099-G 86	1099-INT 92	1099-MISC 95	1099-OID 96	1099-PATR 97	1099-R 98	1099-S 75	5498 28
☐	☐	☐	☐	☐	☐	☐	☐	☐	☐	☐	☐	☐	☐

Please return this entire page to the Internal Revenue Service. Photocopies are NOT acceptable.

Under penalties of perjury, I declare that I have examined this return and accompanying documents, and, to the best of my knowledge and belief, they are true, correct, and complete.

Signature ▶   Title ▶   Date ▶

Instructions

Purpose of Form.—Use this form to transmit paper Forms 1099, 1098, 5498, and W-2G to the Internal Revenue Service. DO NOT USE FORM 1096 TO TRANSMIT MAGNETIC MEDIA. See **Form 4804**, Transmittal of Information Returns Reported Magnetically/Electronically.

Use of Preprinted Label.—If you received a preprinted label from the IRS with Package 1099, place the label in the name and address area of this form inside the brackets. Make any necessary changes to your name and address on the label. However, do not use the label if the taxpayer identification number (TIN) shown is incorrect. **Do not prepare your own label. Use only the IRS-prepared label that came with your Package 1099.**

If you are not using a preprinted label, enter the filer's name, address (including room, suite, or other unit number), and TIN in the spaces provided on the form.

Filer.—The name, address, and TIN of the filer on this form must be the same as those you enter in the upper left area of Form 1099, 1098, 5498, or W-2G. A filer includes a payer, a recipient of mortgage interest payments (including points), a broker, a barter exchange, a creditor, a person reporting real estate transactions, a trustee or issuer of an individual retirement arrangement (including an IRA or SEP), and a lender who acquires an interest in secured property or who has reason to know that the property has been abandoned.

Transmitting to the IRS.—Send the forms in a flat mailing (not folded). Group the forms by form number and transmit each group with a **separate** Form 1096. For example, if you must file both Forms 1098 and 1099-A, complete one Form 1096 to transmit your Forms 1098 and another Form 1096 to transmit your Forms 1099-A. You need not submit original and corrected returns separately.

Box 1 or 2.—Complete only if you are not using a preprinted IRS label. Individuals not in a trade or business must enter their social security number in box 2; sole proprietors and all others must enter their employer identification number in box 1. However, sole proprietors who do not have an employer identification number must enter their social security number in box 2.

Box 3.—Enter the number of forms you are transmitting with this Form 1096. Do not include blank or voided forms or the Form 1096 in your total. Enter the number of correctly completed forms, not the number of pages, being transmitted. For example, if you send one page of three-to-a-page Forms 5498 with a Form 1096 and you have correctly completed two Forms 5498 on that page, enter "2" in box 3 of Form 1096.

Box 4.—Enter the total Federal income tax withheld shown on the forms being transmitted with this Form 1096.

Box 5.—No entry is required if you are filing Form 1099-A or 1099-G. For all other forms, enter the total of the amounts from the specific boxes of the forms listed below:

Form W-2G	Box 1
Form 1098	Boxes 1 and 2
Form 1099-B	Boxes 2 and 3
Form 1099-C	Box 2
Form 1099-DIV	Boxes 1a, 5, and 6
Form 1099-INT	Boxes 1 and 3
Form 1099-MISC	Boxes 1, 2, 3, 5, 6, 7, 8, and 10
Form 1099-OID	Boxes 1 and 2
Form 1099-PATR	Boxes 1, 2, 3, and 5
Form 1099-R	Box 1
Form 1099-S	Box 2
Form 5498	Boxes 1 and 2

For more information and the Paperwork Reduction Act Notice, see the Instructions for Forms 1099, 1098, 5498, and W-2G.   Form **1096** (1994)

Cat. No. 14400O

Form 1 (top)

9595 ☐ VOID ☐ CORRECTED

PAYER'S name, street address, city, state, and ZIP code	**1** Rents $	OMB No. 1545-0115	**Miscellaneous Income**
	2 Royalties $	**1994**	
	3 Other income $		
PAYER'S Federal identification number / RECIPIENT'S identification number	**4** Federal income tax withheld $	**5** Fishing boat proceeds $	**Copy A** For **Internal Revenue Service Center**
RECIPIENT'S name	**6** Medical and health care payments $	**7** Nonemployee compensation $	File with Form 1096.
Street address (including apt. no.)	**8** Substitute payments in lieu of dividends or interest $	**9** Payer made direct sales of $5,000 or more of consumer products to a buyer (recipient) for resale ▶ ☐	For Paperwork Reduction Act Notice and instructions for completing this form,
City, state, and ZIP code	**10** Crop insurance proceeds $	**11** State income tax withheld $	see **Instructions for Forms 1099, 1098, 5498, and W-2G.**
Account number (optional)	2nd TIN Not. ☐ **12** State/Payer's state number		

Form **1099-MISC**   Cat. No. 14425J   Department of the Treasury - Internal Revenue Service

Do NOT Cut or Separate Forms on This Page

(Form repeated twice more identically.)

Form **2553**
(Rev. September 1993)

Department of the Treasury
Internal Revenue Service

Election by a Small Business Corporation

(Under section 1362 of the Internal Revenue Code)

▶ For Paperwork Reduction Act Notice, see page 1 of instructions.

▶ See separate instructions.

OMB No. 1545-0146

Expires 8-31-96

Notes: 1. *This election, to be an "S corporation," can be accepted only if all the tests are met under Who May Elect on page 1 of the instructions; all signatures in Parts I and III are originals (no photocopies); and the exact name and address of the corporation and other required form information are provided.*

2. *Do not file Form 1120S, U.S. Income Tax Return for an S Corporation, until you are notified that your election is accepted.*

Part I Election Information

Please Type or Print	Name of corporation (see instructions)	A Employer identification number (EIN)
	Number, street, and room or suite no. (If a P.O. box, see instructions.)	B Date incorporated
	City or town, state, and ZIP code	C State of incorporation

D Election is to be effective for tax year beginning (month, day, year) . . . . ▶ / /

E Name and title of officer or legal representative who the IRS may call for more information

F Telephone number of officer or legal representative

( )

G If the corporation changed its name or address after applying for the EIN shown in **A**, check this box . . . . ▶ ☐

H If this election takes effect for the first tax year the corporation exists, enter month, day, and year of the **earliest** of the following: (1) date the corporation first had shareholders, (2) date the corporation first had assets, or (3) date the corporation began doing business . . . . ▶ / /

I Selected tax year: Annual return will be filed for tax year ending (month and day) ▶ ....

If the tax year ends on any date other than December 31, except for an automatic 52-53-week tax year ending with reference to the month of December, you **must** complete Part II on the back. If the date you enter is the ending date of an automatic 52-53-week tax year, write "52-53-week year" to the right of the date. See Temporary Regulations section 1.441-2T(e)(3).

J Name and address of each shareholder, shareholder's spouse having a community property interest in the corporation's stock, and each tenant in common, joint tenant, and tenant by the entirety. (A husband and wife (and their estates) are counted as one shareholder in determining the number of shareholders without regard to the manner in which the stock is owned.)	K Shareholders' Consent Statement. Under penalties of perjury, we declare that we consent to the election of the above-named corporation to be an "S corporation" under section 1362(a) and that we have examined this consent statement, including accompanying schedules and statements, and to the best of our knowledge and belief, it is true, correct, and complete. (Shareholders sign and date below.)*		L Stock owned		M Social security number or employer identification number (see instructions)	N Share-holder's tax year ends (month and day)
	Signature	Date	Number of shares	Dates acquired		

*For this election to be valid, the consent of each shareholder, shareholder's spouse having a community property interest in the corporation's stock, and each tenant in common, joint tenant, and tenant by the entirety must either appear above or be attached to this form. (See instructions for Column K if a continuation sheet or a separate consent statement is needed.)

Under penalties of perjury, I declare that I have examined this election, including accompanying schedules and statements, and to the best of my knowledge and belief, it is true, correct, and complete.

Signature of officer ▶

Title ▶

Date ▶

See Parts II and III on back.

Cat. No. 18629R

Form **2553** (Rev. 9-93)

Form 2553 (Rev. 9-93)   Page **2**

Part II Selection of Fiscal Tax Year (All corporations using this part must complete item O and one of items P, Q, or R.)

O   Check the applicable box below to indicate whether the corporation is:
    1. ☐ A new corporation adopting the tax year entered in item I, Part I.
    2. ☐ An existing corporation retaining the tax year entered in item I, Part I.
    3. ☐ An existing corporation changing to the tax year entered in item I, Part I.

P   Complete item P if the corporation is using the expeditious approval provisions of Revenue Procedure 87-32, 1987-2 C.B. 396, to request: (1) a natural business year (as defined in section 4.01(1) of Rev. Proc. 87-32), or (2) a year that satisfies the ownership tax year test in section 4.01(2) of Rev. Proc. 87-32. Check the applicable box below to indicate the representation statement the corporation is making as required under section 4 of Rev. Proc. 87-32.

    1. Natural Business Year ▶ ☐ I represent that the corporation is retaining or changing to a tax year that coincides with its natural business year as defined in section 4.01(1) of Rev. Proc. 87-32 and as verified by its satisfaction of the requirements of section 4.02(1) of Rev. Proc. 87-32. In addition, if the corporation is changing to a natural business year as defined in section 4.01(1), I further represent that such tax year results in less deferral of income to the owners than the corporation's present tax year. I also represent that the corporation is not described in section 3.01(2) of Rev. Proc. 87-32. (See instructions for additional information that must be attached.)

    2. Ownership Tax Year ▶ ☐ I represent that shareholders holding more than half of the shares of the stock (as of the first day of the tax year to which the request relates) of the corporation have the same tax year or are concurrently changing to the tax year that the corporation adopts, retains, or changes to per item I, Part I. I also represent that the corporation is not described in section 3.01(2) of Rev. Proc. 87-32.

Note: *If you do not use item P and the corporation wants a fiscal tax year, complete either item Q or R below. Item Q is used to request a fiscal tax year based on a business purpose and to make a back-up section 444 election. Item R is used to make a regular section 444 election.*

Q   Business Purpose—To request a fiscal tax year based on a business purpose, you must check box Q1 and pay a user fee. See instructions for details. You may also check box Q2 and/or box Q3.

    1. Check here ▶ ☐ if the fiscal year entered in item I, Part I, is requested under the provisions of section 6.03 of Rev. Proc. 87-32. Attach to Form 2553 a statement showing the business purpose for the requested fiscal year. See instructions for additional information that must be attached.

    2. Check here ▶ ☐ to show that the corporation intends to make a back-up section 444 election in the event the corporation's business purpose request is not approved by the IRS. (See instructions for more information.)

    3. Check here ▶ ☐ to show that the corporation agrees to adopt or change to a tax year ending December 31 if necessary for the IRS to accept this election for S corporation status in the event: (1) the corporation's business purpose request is not approved and the corporation makes a back-up section 444 election, but is ultimately not qualified to make a section 444 election, or (2) the corporation's business purpose request is not approved and the corporation did not make a back-up section 444 election.

R   Section 444 Election—To make a section 444 election, you must check box R1 and you may also check box R2.

    1. Check here ▶ ☐ to show the corporation will make, if qualified, a section 444 election to have the fiscal tax year shown in item I, Part I. To make the election, you must complete **Form 8716**, Election To Have a Tax Year Other Than a Required Tax Year, and either attach it to Form 2553 or file it separately.

    2. Check here ▶ ☐ to show that the corporation agrees to adopt or change to a tax year ending December 31 if necessary for the IRS to accept this election for S corporation status in the event the corporation is ultimately not qualified to make a section 444 election.

Part III Qualified Subchapter S Trust (QSST) Election Under Section 1361(d)(2)**

Income beneficiary's name and address	Social security number
Trust's name and address	Employer identification number

Date on which stock of the corporation was transferred to the trust (month, day, year) . . . . ▶ _____ / _____ / _____

In order for the trust named above to be a QSST and thus a qualifying shareholder of the S corporation for which this Form 2553 is filed, I hereby make the election under section 1361(d)(2). Under penalties of perjury, I certify that the trust meets the definitional requirements of section 1361(d)(3) and that all other information provided in Part III is true, correct, and complete.

_____   _____
Signature of income beneficiary or signature and title of legal representative or other qualified person making the election   Date

**Use of Part III to make the QSST election may be made only if stock of the corporation has been transferred to the trust on or before the date on which the corporation makes its election to be an S corporation. The QSST election must be made and filed separately if stock of the corporation is transferred to the trust after the date on which the corporation makes the S election.

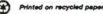 *Printed on recycled paper*   *U.S. Government Printing Office: 1993 — 301-628/80271

Simplified Small Business Accounting

a Control number	22222	Void ☐	For Official Use Only ► OMB No. 1545-0008	

b Employer's identification number		1 Wages, tips, other compensation	2 Federal income tax withheld
c Employer's name, address, and ZIP code		3 Social security wages	4 Social security tax withheld
		5 Medicare wages and tips	6 Medicare tax withheld
		7 Social security tips	8 Allocated tips
d Employee's social security number		9 Advance EIC payment	10 Dependent care benefits
e Employee's name (first, middle initial, last)		11 Nonqualified plans	12 Benefits included in box 1
		13 See Instrs. for box 13	14 Other

15 Statutory employee ☐	Deceased ☐	Pension plan ☐	Legal rep. ☐	942 emp. ☐	Subtotal ☐	Deferred compensation ☐

f Employee's address and ZIP code

16 State	Employer's state I.D. No.	17 State wages, tips, etc.	18 State income tax	19 Locality name	20 Local wages, tips, etc.	21 Local income tax

Cat. No. 10134D — Department of the Treasury—Internal Revenue Service

Form W-2 Wage and Tax Statement 1994

Copy A For Social Security Administration

For Paperwork Reduction Act Notice, see separate instructions.

Do NOT Cut or Separate Forms on This Page

---

a Control number	22222	Void ☐	For Official Use Only ► OMB No. 1545-0008	

b Employer's identification number		1 Wages, tips, other compensation	2 Federal income tax withheld
c Employer's name, address, and ZIP code		3 Social security wages	4 Social security tax withheld
		5 Medicare wages and tips	6 Medicare tax withheld
		7 Social security tips	8 Allocated tips
d Employee's social security number		9 Advance EIC payment	10 Dependent care benefits
e Employee's name (first, middle initial, last)		11 Nonqualified plans	12 Benefits included in box 1
		13 See Instrs. for box 13	14 Other

15 Statutory employee ☐	Deceased ☐	Pension plan ☐	Legal rep. ☐	942 emp. ☐	Subtotal ☐	Deferred compensation ☐

f Employee's address and ZIP code

16 State	Employer's state I.D. No.	17 State wages, tips, etc.	18 State income tax	19 Locality name	20 Local wages, tips, etc.	21 Local income tax

Cat. No. 10134D — Department of the Treasury—Internal Revenue Service

Form W-2 Wage and Tax Statement 1994

Copy A For Social Security Administration

For Paperwork Reduction Act Notice, see separate instructions.

DO NOT STAPLE

a Control number	33333	For Official Use Only ▶ OMB No. 1545-0008		

b **Kind of Payer** ▶	941 ☐ Military ☐ 943 ☐	1 Wages, tips, other compensation	2 Federal income tax withheld
	CT-1 ☐ Hshld. ☐ Medicare govt. emp. ☐	3 Social security wages	4 Social security tax withheld

c Total number of statements	d Establishment number	5 Medicare wages and tips	6 Medicare tax withheld
e Employer's identification number		7 Social security tips	8 Allocated tips
f Employer's name		9 Advance EIC payments	10 Dependent care benefits
		11 Nonqualified plans	12 Deferred compensation
		13 Adjusted total social security wages and tips	
		14 Adjusted total Medicare wages and tips	
g Employer's address and ZIP code			
h Other EIN used this year		15 Income tax withheld by third-party payer	
i Employer's state I.D. No.			

Under penalties of perjury, I declare that I have examined this return and accompanying documents, and, to the best of my knowledge and belief, they are true, correct, and complete.

Signature ▶   Title ▶   Date ▶

Telephone number ( )

Form **W-3** **Transmittal of Wage and Tax Statements** **1995**   Department of the Treasury
Internal Revenue Service

Paperwork Reduction Act Notice

We ask for the information on this form to carry out the Internal Revenue laws of the United States. You are required to give us the information. We need it to ensure that you are complying with these laws and to allow us to figure and collect the right amount of tax.

The time needed to complete and file this form will vary depending on individual circumstances. The estimated average time is 27 minutes. If you have comments concerning the accuracy of this time estimate or suggestions for making this form simpler, we would be happy to hear from you. You can write to the **Internal Revenue Service,** Attention: Tax Forms Committee, PC:FP, Washington, DC 20224. **Do NOT** send the form to this address. Instead, see **Where To File.**

Item To Note

Change to Kind of Payer Box.—The 942 box was retitled "Hshld." for household because **Form 942,** Employer's Quarterly Tax Return for Household Employees, is obsolete for wages paid after 1994. For more details, get **Pub. 926,** Employment Taxes for Household Employers.

Need Help?

Information Reporting Call Site.—The IRS operates a centralized call site to answer questions about reporting on

Forms W-3, W-2, 1099, and other information returns. If you have questions related to reporting on information returns, you may call (304) 263-8700 (not a toll-free number).

Bulletin Board Services.—Using a personal computer and a modem, you can get information from either of two electronic Bulletin Board Systems (BBS)—the SSA-BBS or the IRP-BBS (IRS). You can access the SSA-BBS by dialing (410) 965-1133 or the IRP-BBS (IRS) by dialing (304) 263-2749.

Information available includes magnetic media and paper filing information, some IRS and SSA forms and publications, correct social security number information, information on electronic filing, and general topics of interest about information reporting. You can also use the bulletin board systems to ask questions about magnetic media or electronic filing programs, and reporting on information returns.

Substitute Forms.—Employers filing privately printed Forms W-2 must file Forms W-3 that are the same width as Form W-2. The forms must meet the requirements in **Pub. 1141,** General Rules and Specifications for Private Printing of Substitute Forms W-2 and W-3.

Forms and Publications.—You can get any of the forms and publications mentioned in these instructions by calling 1-800-TAX-FORM (1-800-829-3676).

Cat. No. 10159Y

Form W-4 (1995)

Want More Money In Your Paycheck?
If you expect to be able to take the earned income credit for 1995 and a child lives with you, you may be able to have part of the credit added to your take-home pay. For details, get Form W-5 from your employer.

Purpose. Complete Form W-4 so that your employer can withhold the correct amount of Federal income tax from your pay.
Exemption From Withholding. Read line 7 of the certificate below to see if you can claim exempt status. *If exempt, complete line 7; but do not complete lines 5 and 6.* No Federal income tax will be withheld from your pay. Your exemption is good for 1 year only. It expires February 15, 1996.
Note: *You cannot claim exemption from withholding if (1) your income exceeds $650 and includes unearned income (e.g., interest*

and dividends) and (2) another person can claim you as a dependent on their tax return.
Basic Instructions. Employees who are not exempt should complete the Personal Allowances Worksheet. Additional worksheets are provided on page 2 for employees to adjust their withholding allowances based or itemized deductions, adjustments to income, or two-earner/two-job situations. Complete all worksheets that apply to your situation. The worksheets will help you figure the number of withholding allowances you are entitled to claim. However, you may claim fewer allowances than this.
Head of Household. Generally, you may claim head of household filing status on your tax return only if you are unmarried and pay more than 50% of the costs of keeping up a home for yourself and your dependent(s) or other qualifying individuals.
Nonwage Income. If you have a large amount of nonwage income, such as interest or dividends, you should consider making

estimated tax payments using Form 1040-ES. Otherwise, you may find that you owe additional tax at the end of the year.
Two Earners/Two Jobs. If you have a working spouse or more than one job, figure the total number of allowances you are entitled to claim on all jobs using worksheets from only one Form W-4. This total should be divided among all jobs. Your withholding will usually be most accurate when all allowances are claimed on the W-4 filed for the highest paying job and zero allowances are claimed for the others.
Check Your Withholding. After your W-4 takes effect, you can use Pub. 919, Is My Withholding Correct for 1995?, to see how the dollar amount you are having withheld compares to your estimated total annual tax. We recommend you get Pub. 919 especially if you used the Two Earner/Two Job Worksheet and your earnings exceed $150,000 (Single) or $200,000 (Married). Call 1-800-829-3676 to order Pub. 919. Check your telephone directory for the IRS assistance number for further help.

Personal Allowances Worksheet

A Enter "1" for **yourself** if no one else can claim you as a dependent . . . . **A** _____

B Enter "1" if: {
- You are single and have only one job; or
- You are married, have only one job, and your spouse does not work; or
- Your wages from a second job or your spouse's wages (or the total of both) are $1,000 or less.
} . . **B** _____

C Enter "1" for your **spouse.** But, you may choose to enter -0- if you are married and have either a working spouse or more than one job (this may help you avoid having too little tax withheld) . . . . **C** _____

D Enter number of **dependents** (other than your spouse or yourself) you will claim on your tax return . . . . **D** _____

E Enter "1" if you will file as **head of household** on your tax return (see conditions under **Head of Household** above) . **E** _____

F Enter "1" if you have at least $1,500 of **child or dependent care expenses** for which you plan to claim a credit . . **F** _____

G Add lines A through F and enter total here. **Note:** This amount may be different from the number of exemptions you claim on your return ▶ **G** _____

For accuracy, do all worksheets that apply. {
- If you plan to **itemize or claim adjustments to income** and want to reduce your withholding, see the Deductions and Adjustments Worksheet on page 2.
- If you are **single** and have **more than one job** and your combined earnings from all jobs exceed $30,000 OR if you are **married** and have a **working spouse or more than one job,** and the combined earnings from all jobs exceed $50,000, see the Two-Earner/Two-Job Worksheet on page 2 if you want to avoid having too little tax withheld.
- If **neither** of the above situations applies, **stop here** and enter the number from line G on line 5 of Form W-4 below.
}

-------------------- **Cut here and give the certificate to your employer. Keep the top portion for your records.** --------------------

Form **W-4** Department of the Treasury Internal Revenue Service	**Employee's Withholding Allowance Certificate** ▶ **For Privacy Act and Paperwork Reduction Act Notice, see reverse.**	OMB No. 1545-0010 **19 95**

1 Type or print your first name and middle initial	Last name	2 Your social security number

Home address (number and street or rural route)

3 ☐ Single ☐ Married ☐ Married, but withhold at higher Single rate.
Note: *If married, but legally separated, or spouse is a nonresident alien, check the Single box.*

City or town, state, and ZIP code

4 If your last name differs from that on your social security card, check here and call 1-800-772-1213 for a new card . . . . ▶ ☐

5 Total number of allowances you are claiming (from line G above or from the worksheets on page 2 if they apply) . **5** |____

6 Additional amount, if any, you want withheld from each paycheck . . . . **6** $ |____

7 I claim exemption from withholding for 1995 and I certify that I meet **BOTH** of the following conditions for exemption:
- Last year I had a right to a refund of **ALL** Federal income tax withheld because I had **NO** tax liability; **AND**
- This year I expect a refund of **ALL** Federal income tax withheld because I expect to have **NO** tax liability.
If you meet both conditions, enter "EXEMPT" here . . . . ▶ **7** |____

Under penalties of perjury, I certify that I am entitled to the number of withholding allowances claimed on this certificate or entitled to claim exempt status.

Employee's signature ▶ _____ Date ▶ _____ , 19 _____

8 Employer's name and address (Employer: Complete 8 and 10 only if sending to the IRS)	9 Office code (optional)	10 Employer identification number

Cat. No. 10220Q

240

TAX YEAR ➤
MONTH

EMPLOYER IDENTIFICATION NUMBER ➤

BANK NAME/
DATE STAMP

Name _____

Address _____
_____

City _____

State _____ ZIP _____

Telephone number ( ) _____

		1st Quarter
941	945	
990C	1120	2nd Quarter
943	990-T	3rd Quarter
720	990PF	4th Quarter
CT-1	1042	
940		35

FOR BANK USE IN MICR ENCODING

Federal Tax Deposit Coupon
Form 8109-B (Rev. 1-94)

. . . .

⬆ **SEPARATE ALONG THIS LINE AND SUBMIT TO DEPOSITARY WITH PAYMENT** ⬆

OMB NO. 1545-0257

IMPORTANT
Read instructions carefully before completing Form 8109-B, Federal Tax Deposit Coupon.

Note: *Except for the name, address, and telephone number, entries are processed by optical scanning equipment and must be made in pencil. Please* **use a soft lead** *(for example, a #2 pencil) so that the entries can be read more accurately by the optical scanning equipment. The name, address, and telephone number may be completed other than by hand. You* **CANNOT** *use photocopies of the coupons to make your deposits.* **DO NOT** *staple, tape or fold the coupons.*

Schedule A, Form 941 Filers (4th quarter 1993 ONLY).—If you are making a deposit for the 4th quarter 1993 during January 1994, darken the **945 box** under TYPE OF TAX and the **4th quarter box** under TAX PERIOD.

Paperwork Reduction Act Notice.—We ask for the information on this form to carry out the Internal Revenue laws of the United States. You are required to give us the information. We need it to ensure that you are complying with these laws and to allow us to figure and collect the right amount of tax.

The time needed to complete and file this form will vary depending on individual circumstances. The estimated average time is 3 min. If you have comments concerning the accuracy of this time estimate or suggestions for making this form more simple, we would be happy to hear from you. You can write to both the **Internal Revenue Service,** Attention: Reports Clearance Officer, PC:FP, Washington, DC 20224; and the **Office of Management and Budget,** Paperwork Reduction Project (1545-0257), Washington, DC 20503. **DO NOT** send this form to either of these offices. Instead, see the instructions on the back of this page.

Purpose of Form.—Use Form 8109-B deposit coupons to make tax deposits **only** in the following two situations:

1. You have not yet received your resupply of preprinted deposit coupons (Form 8109); or

2. You are a new entity and have already been assigned an employer identification number (EIN), but have not yet received your initial supply of preprinted deposit coupons (Form 8109).

Note: *If you do not receive your resupply of deposit coupons and a deposit is due or you do not receive your initial supply within 5–6 weeks of receipt of your EIN, please contact your local IRS office.*

If you have applied for an EIN, have not received it, and a deposit must be made, send your payment to your Internal Revenue Service Center. Make your check or money order payable to the Internal Revenue Service and show on it your name (as shown on **Form SS-4,** Application for Employer Identification Number), address, kind of tax, period covered, and date you applied for an EIN. Also attach an explanation to the deposit. Do **NOT** use Form 8109-B in this situation. Do **NOT** use Form 8109-B to deposit delinquent taxes assessed by the IRS. Pay those taxes directly to the IRS.

How To Complete the Form.—Enter your name exactly as shown on your return or other IRS correspondence, address, and EIN in the spaces provided. If you are required to file a Form 1120, 990-C, 990-PF (with net investment income), 990-T, or 2438, enter the month in which your tax year ends in the **TAX YEAR MONTH** boxes. For example, if your tax years ends in January, enter 01; if it ends in June, enter 06; if it ends in December, enter 12. Please make your entries for EIN and tax year month (if applicable) in the manner specified in *Amount of Deposit* below. Darken one box each in the *Type of Tax* and *Tax Period* columns as explained below.

Amount of Deposit.—Enter the amount of the deposit in the space provided. Enter the amount legibly, forming the characters as shown below:

Hand-print money amounts without using dollar signs, commas, a decimal point, or leading zeros. The commas and the decimal point are already shown in the entry area. For example, a deposit of $7,635.22 would be entered like this:

DOLLARS							CENTS	
				7	6	3	5	2 2

If the deposit is for whole dollars only, enter "00" in the **CENTS** boxes.

Types of Tax.—

Form 941 —Withheld Income From Wages and Other Compensation, Social Security, and Medicare Taxes (includes Form 941 series of returns)

Form 945 —Withheld Income Tax From Pension, Annuities, Gambling, and Backup Withholding.

Form 990-C —Farmers' Cooperative Association Income Tax.

Form 943 —Agricultural Withheld Income, Social Security, and Medicare Taxes (includes Form 943PR).

Form 720 —Excise Tax.

Form CT-1 —Railroad Retirement and Railroad Unemployment Repayment Taxes.

Form 940 —Federal Unemployment (FUTA) Tax (includes Form 940-EZ and Form 940PR).

Form 1120 —Corporate Income Tax (includes Form 1120 series of returns and Form 2438).

Form 990-T —Exempt Organization Business Income Tax.

Form 990-PF —Excise Tax on Private Foundation Net Investment Income.

Form 1042 —Withholding On Foreign Persons.

How To Determine the Proper Tax Period.—

Payroll Taxes and Withholding (Forms 941, 940, 943, 945, CT-1, and 1042. (See the separate Instructions for Form 1042. **Schedule A (Form 941) filers see information above.)).**

If your liability was incurred during:

• January 1 through March 31, darken the 1st quarter box

• April 1 through June 30, darken the 2nd quarter box

• July 1 through September 30, darken the 3rd quarter box

• October 1 through December 31, darken the 4th quarter box

Note: *If the liability was incurred during one quarter and deposited in another, darken the box for the quarter in which the tax liability was incurred. For example, if the liability was incurred in March and deposited in April, darken the 1st quarter box.*

(Continued on back of page.)

Department of the Treasury
Internal Revenue Service

Cat. No. 61042S

Form **8109-B** (Rev. 1-94)

Simplified Small Business Accounting

Form **8829**

Department of the Treasury
Internal Revenue Service (O)

Expenses for Business Use of Your Home

▶ File only with Schedule C (Form 1040). Use a separate Form 8829 for each
home you used for business during the year.

▶ See separate instructions.

OMB No. 1545-1266

1994

Attachment
Sequence No. **66**

Name(s) of proprietor(s)

Your social security number

Part I   Part of Your Home Used for Business

1	Area used regularly and exclusively for business, regularly for day care, or for inventory storage. See instructions	1	
2	Total area of home	2	
3	Divide line 1 by line 2. Enter the result as a percentage	3	%

● For day-care facilities not used exclusively for business, also complete lines 4–6.

● All others, skip lines 4–6 and enter the amount from line 3 on line 7.

4	Multiply days used for day care during year by hours used per day .	4	hr.
5	Total hours available for use during the year (365 days × 24 hours). See instructions	5	8,760 hr.
6	Divide line 4 by line 5. Enter the result as a decimal amount . . .	6	.
7	Business percentage. For day-care facilities not used exclusively for business, multiply line 6 by line 3 (enter the result as a percentage). All others, enter the amount from line 3 . . . . . ▶	7	%

Part II   Figure Your Allowable Deduction

		(a) Direct expenses	(b) Indirect expenses		
8	Enter the amount from Schedule C, line 29, **plus** any net gain or (loss) derived from the business use of your home and shown on Schedule D or Form 4797. If more than one place of business, see instructions			8	
	See instructions for columns (a) and (b) before completing lines 9–20.				
9	Casualty losses. See instructions	9			
10	Deductible mortgage interest. See instructions .	10			
11	Real estate taxes. See instructions	11			
12	Add lines 9, 10, and 11.	12			
13	Multiply line 12, column (b) by line 7 . . .		13		
14	Add line 12, column (a) and line 13			14	
15	Subtract line 14 from line 8. If zero or less, enter -0-			15	
16	Excess mortgage interest. See instructions . .	16			
17	Insurance	17			
18	Repairs and maintenance	18			
19	Utilities	19			
20	Other expenses. See instructions	20			
21	Add lines 16 through 20	21			
22	Multiply line 21, column (b) by line 7	22			
23	Carryover of operating expenses from 1993 Form 8829, line 41 . .	23			
24	Add line 21 in column (a), line 22, and line 23			24	
25	Allowable operating expenses. Enter the **smaller** of line 15 or line 24			25	
26	Limit on excess casualty losses and depreciation. Subtract line 25 from line 15			26	
27	Excess casualty losses. See instructions	27			
28	Depreciation of your home from Part III below	28			
29	Carryover of excess casualty losses and depreciation from 1993 Form 8829, line 42	29			
30	Add lines 27 through 29			30	
31	Allowable excess casualty losses and depreciation. Enter the **smaller** of line 26 or line 30 . .			31	
32	Add lines 14, 25, and 31			32	
33	Casualty loss portion, if any, from lines 14 and 31. Carry amount to **Form 4684**, Section B .			33	
34	Allowable expenses for business use of your home. Subtract line 33 from line 32. Enter here and on Schedule C, line 30. If your home was used for more than one business, see instructions ▶			34	

Part III   Depreciation of Your Home

35	Enter the **smaller** of your home's adjusted basis or its fair market value. See instructions . .	35	
36	Value of land included on line 35	36	
37	Basis of building. Subtract line 36 from line 35	37	
38	Business basis of building. Multiply line 37 by line 7	38	
39	Depreciation percentage. See instructions	39	%
40	Depreciation allowable. Multiply line 38 by line 39. Enter here and on line 28 above. See instructions	40	

Part IV   Carryover of Unallowed Expenses to 1995

41	Operating expenses. Subtract line 25 from line 24. If less than zero, enter -0-	41	
42	Excess casualty losses and depreciation. Subtract line 31 from line 30. If less than zero, enter -0- .	42	

For Paperwork Reduction Act Notice, see page 1 of separate instructions.   ✱ *Printed on recycled paper*   Cat. No. 13232M   Form **8829** (1994)

U.S. Government Printing Office: 1994 — 375-468

Glossary of Accounting Terms

Account: A separate record of an asset, liability, income, or expense of a business.

Accounting: The process for recording, summarizing, and interpreting business financial records.

Accounting method: The method of recording income and expenses for a business; can be either *accrual method* or *cash method*.

Accounting period: A specific time period covered by the financial statements of a business.

Accounting system: The specific system of record-keeping used to set up the accounting records of a business; see also *single-entry* or *double-entry*.

Accounts payable: Money owed by a business to another for goods or services purchased on credit. Money that the business intends to pay to another.

Accounts receivable: Money owed to the business by another for goods or services sold on credit. Money that the business expects to receive.

Accrual method: Accounting method in which all income and expenses are counted when earned or incurred regardless of when the actual cash is received or paid.

Accrued expenses: Expenses that have been incurred but have not yet been paid.

Accrued income: Income that has been earned but has not yet been received.

ACRS: Accelerated Cost Recovery System. Generally, a method of depreciation used for assets purchased between 1980 and 1987.

Aging: The method used to determine how long accounts receivable have been owed to a business.

Assets: Everything that a business owns, including amounts of money which are owed to the business.

Balance sheet: The business financial statement that depicts the financial status of the business on a specific date by summarizing the assets and liabilities of the business.

Balance sheet equation: Assets = liabilities + equity or Equity = Assets - liabilities.

Bookkeeping: The actual process of recording the figures in accounting records.

C corporation: A business entity owned by shareholders that is not an *S corporation*.

Capital: The *owner's equity* in a business. The ownership value of the business.

Capital expenses: An expense for the purchase of a fixed asset; an asset with a useful life of over 1 year. Generally, must be depreciated rather than deducted as a business expense.

Cash: All currency, coins, and checks that a business has on hand or in a bank account.

Cash method: Accounting method in which income and expenses are not counted until the actual cash is received or paid.

Chart of accounts: A listing of the types and numbers of the various accounts which a business uses for its accounting records.

Check register: A running record of checks written, deposits made, and other transactions for a bank account.

Corporation: A business entity owned by shareholders; may be a *C* or an *S type corporation*.

Cost of Goods Sold: The amount that a business has paid for the inventory that it has sold during a specific period. Calculated by adding beginning inventory and additions to inventory and then deducting the ending inventory value.

Credit: In double-entry accounting, an increase in liability or income accounts or a decrease in asset or expense accounts.

Current assets: Cash and any other assets which can be converted to cash or consumed by the business within 1 year.

Current liabilities: Debts of a business that must be paid within 1 year.

Current ratio: A method of determining the liquidity of a business. Calculated by dividing current assets by current liabilities.

Debit: In double-entry accounting, a decrease in liability or income accounts or an increase in asset or expense accounts.

Debt: The amount which a business owes to another. Also known as liability.

Debt ratio: A method of determining the indebtedness of a business. Calculated by dividing total liabilities by total assets.

Dividends: In a corporation, a proportionate share of the net profits of a business which the board of directors has determined should be paid out to shareholders, rather than held as *retained earnings*.

Double-entry accounting: An accounting system under which each transaction is recorded twice: as a credit and as a debit. A very difficult system of accounting to learn and understand.

Expenses: The costs to a business of producing its income.

Equity: Any debt which a business owes. It is *owner's equity* if owed to the business owners and *liabilities* if owed to others.

FICA: Federal Insurance Contributions Act. Taxes withheld from employees and paid by employers for Social Security and Medicare.

FIFO: First in, first out method of accounting for inventory. The inventory value is based on the cost of the latest items purchased.

Financial statements: Reports which summarize the finances of a business; generally a *profit and loss statement* and a *balance sheet*.

Fiscal year: A 12-month accounting period used by a business.

Fiscal year reporting: For income tax purposes, reporting business taxes for any 12-month period that does not end on December 31st of each year.

Fixed assets: Assets of a business which will not be sold or consumed within 1 year. Generally, fixed assets (other than land) must be depreciated.

FUTA: Federal Unemployment Tax Act. Federal business unemployment taxes.

General journal: In double entry accounting, used to record all of the transactions of a business in chronological order. Transactions are then posted (or transferred) to the appropriate accounts in the general ledger.

General ledger: In double entry accounting, the central listing of all accounts of a business.

Gross profit: Gross sales minus the cost of goods sold.

Gross sales: The total amount received for goods and services during an accounting period.

Gross wages: The total amount of an employee's compensation before the deduction of any taxes or benefits.

Income statement: Financial statement which shows the income and expenses for a business. Also referred to as *operating statement* or *profit and loss statement*.

Initial capital: The money or property which an owner or owners contribute to starting a business.

Intangible personal property: Generally, property not attached to land and which you can not hold or touch (for example: copyrights, business goodwill, etc.).

Inventory: Goods that are held by a business for sale to customers.

Invoice: A bill for the sale of goods or services which is sent to the buyer.

Ledgers: The accounting books for a business. Generally, refers to the entire set of accounts for a business.

LIFO: Last in, first out method of valuing inventory. Total value is based on the cost of the earliest items purchased.

Liabilities: The debts of a business.

Liquidity: The ability of a company to convert its assets to cash and meet its obligations with that cash.

Long-term assets: The assets of a business which will be held for over 1 year. Those assets of a business which are subject to depreciation (except for land).

Long-term liabilities: The debts of a business which will not be due for over 1 year.

MACRS: Modified accelerated cost recovery system. A method of depreciation for use with assets purchased after January 1, 1987.

Net income: The amount of money which a business has after deducting the cost of goods sold and the cost of all expenses. Also referred to as *net profit*.

Net loss: The amount by which a business has expenses and costs of goods sold greater than income.

Net profit: The amount by which a business has income greater than expenses and cost of goods sold. Also referred to as *net income*.

Net sales: The value of sales after deducting the cost of goods sold from gross sales.

Net wages: The amount of compensation which an employee actually will be paid after the deductions for taxes and benefits.

Net worth: The value of the owner's share in a business. The value of a business determined by deducting the debts of a business from the assets of a business. Also referred to as *owner's equity*.

Operating margin: Net sales divided by gross sales. The actual profit on goods sold, before deductions for expenses.

Operating statement: Financial statement which shows the income and expenses for a business. Also referred to as *income statement* or *profit and loss statement*.

Owner's equity: The value of an owner's share in a business. Also referred to as *capital*.

Partnership: An unincorporated business entity that is owed by 2 or more persons.

Payee: Person or business to whom a payment is made.

Payor: Person or business which makes a payment.

Personal property: All business property other than land and the buildings which are attached to the land.

Petty cash fund: A cash fund which is used to pay for minor expenses which can not be paid by check. Petty cash is not to be used for handling sales revenue. Considered part of cash on hand.

Petty cash register: The sheet for recording petty cash transactions.

Physical inventory: The actual process of counting and valuing the inventory on hand at the end of an accounting period.

Posting: In double entry accounting, the process of transferring data from journals to ledgers.

Plant assets: Long-term assets of a business. Those business assets which are subject to depreciation (other than land).

Pre-paid expenses: Expenses which are paid for before they are used (for example: insurance, rent, etc.).

Profit and loss statement: Financial statement which shows the income and expenses for a business. Also referred to as *income statement* or *operating statement*.

Retail price: The price for which a product is sold to the public.

Retained earnings: In a corporation, the portion of the annual profits of a business which are kept and reinvested in the business, rather than paid to shareholders in the form of *dividends*.

Real property: Land and any buildings or improvements which are attached to the land.

Reconciliation: The process of bringing a bank statement into agreement with the business check register.

Revenue: The income which a business brings in from the sale of goods or services, or through investments.

S-corporation: A type of business corporation in which all of the expenses and profits are passed through to its shareholders to be accounted for at tax time individually in the manner of partnerships.

Salary: Fixed weekly, or monthly, or annual compensation for an employee.

Sales: Money brought into a business from the sale of goods or services.

Salvage value: The value of an asset after it has been fully depreciated.

Single-entry accounting: A business record-keeping system which generally tracks only income and expense accounts. Used generally by small business; it is much easier to use and understand than *double-entry accounting*.

Shareholder's equity: In a corporation, the owner's equity of a business divided by the number of outstanding shares.

Sole proprietorship: An unincorporated business entity in which 1 person owns the entire company.

Supplies: Materials used in conducting the day-to-day affairs of a business (as opposed to raw materials used in manufacturing).

Tangible personal property: Property not attached to land that you can hold and touch (for example, machinery, furniture, equipment).

Taxes payable: Total of all taxes due but not yet paid.

Trial balance: In double-entry accounting, a listing of all the balances in the general ledger in order to show that debits and credits balance.

Wages: Hourly compensation paid to employees. As opposed to *salary*.

Wages payable: Total of all wages and salaries due to employees but not yet paid out.

Wholesale price: the cost to a business of goods purchased for later sale to the public.

Working capital: The money available for immediate business operations. Current assets minus current liabilities.

Index

Index

Index

Index

Nova Publishing Company

The Finest in Small Business and Consumer Legal Books

Incorporate Your Business: The National Corporation Kit (1st Edition) *[available 10/95]*

ISBN 0935755098	256 pp.	8.5" X 11"	$18.95
Forms on Disk (ASCII format)	IBM or MAC	3.5" or 5.25"	$12.95

Contains clear, straight-forward information to help you maximize your business profits by turning your business into a corporation. Includes all of the forms and instructions that you will need to incorporate in any state. Forms are also available on computer disk.

Debt Free: The National Bankruptcy Kit (1st Edition) *[available 11/95]*

ISBN 0935755187	256 pp.	8.5" X 11"	$17.95

Everything you will need to file for personal bankruptcy. Contains forms, questionnaires, worksheets, checklists and instructions--all in understandable plain English. Includes information to allow you to prevent creditors from harassing you, keep the maximum amount of your property, and obtain a Chapter 7 personal bankruptcy.

Simplified Small Business Accounting (1st Edition) *[available 11/95]*

ISBN 0935755152	256 pp.	8.5" X 11"	$17.95

Everything that a small business will need to set up their accounting and bookkeeping records. Contains all of the forms and instructions necessary. Ledgers, expense records, profit and loss statements, balance sheets, payroll records, inventory records, and many more--all in plain and understandable English.

The Complete Book of Small Business Legal Forms (1st Edition)

ISBN 0935755039	248 pp.	8.5" X 11"	$17.95
Forms on Disk (ASCII format)	IBM or MAC	3.5" or 5.25"	$12.95

A comprehensive business reference containing over 125 legal documents and instructions for use in small businesses. Includes contracts, leases, deeds, partnerships, collections documents, promissory notes, and many more. Forms are also available on computer disk.

The Complete Book of Personal Legal Forms (1st Edition)

ISBN 0935755101	248 pp.	8.5" X 11"	$16.95
Forms on Disk (ASCII format)	IBM or MAC	3.5" or 5.25"	$12.95

A complete family legal reference containing over 100 plain-language legal forms and clear instructions for their use. Includes contracts, leases, marital agreements, wills, trusts, bills of sale, powers of attorney, and many others. Forms are also available on computer disk.

Prepare Your Own Will: The National Will Kit (4th Edition)

ISBN 0935755128	256 pp.	8.5" X 11"	$15.95
Forms on Disk (ASCII format)	IBM or MAC	3.5" or 5.25"	$12.95

The most highly-recommended book available on preparing a will without a lawyer. Includes everything you will need to prepare your own will, living will, and medical power-of-attorney. Easy to use and understandable. Forms are also available on computer disk.

Divorce Yourself: The National No-Fault Divorce Kit (3rd Edition)

ISBN 0935755136	320 pp.	8.5" X 11"	$24.95
Forms on Disk (ASCII format)	IBM or MAC	3.5" or 5.25"	$12.95

The most critically-acclaimed divorce guide available. Contains all of the legal forms and instructions necessary to obtain a no-fault divorce in any state without a lawyer. Includes clear and understandable instructions. Forms are also available on computer disk.

♦ Ordering Information ♦

- **by Phone:** (800)462-6420 (MasterCard and Visa)
- **by FAX:** (301)459-2118 (MasterCard and Visa)
- **by Mail:** Nova Publishing Company
  1103 West College Street
  Carbondale IL 62901
  Phone: (800)748-1175

- **Library and book trade orders:**
National Book Network
4720 Boston Way
Lanham MD 20706
Phone: (800)462-6420 *or*
Baker and Taylor/Ingram/Quality/Unique

Please include shipping and handling of $3.50 for first book or disk and $.75 for each additional book or disk.
Forms on Disk must be ordered by mail from Nova Publishing Co. Please indicate IBM or MAC and disk size.
Forms on Disk are in ASCII format and may be used with any computer word-processing program.